Expert Systems and Intelligent CAI

The Educational Technology Anthology Series

Volume Two

Expert Systems and Intelligent Computer-Aided Instruction

EDUCATIONAL TECHNOLOGY PUBLICATIONS
ENGLEWOOD CLIFFS, NEW JERSEY 07632

Library of Congress Cataloging-in-Publication Data

Expert systems and intelligent computer-aided instruction.
    p.   cm. — (The Educational technology anthology series ; v.
2)
    Articles reprinted from Educational technology magazine.
    Includes bibliographical references and index.
    ISBN 0-87778-224-5
    1. Computer-assisted instruction—United States. 2. Expert
systems (Computer science)—United States. I. Educational
technology magazine. II. Series.
    LB1028.5.E95   1990   90-39124
    371.3'34—dc20   CIP

Printed in the United States of America.

Library of Congress Catalog Card Number:
90-39124.

International Standard Book Number:
0-87778-224-5.

First Printing: January, 1991.

Table of Contents

Part I: Expert Systems

Part II: Intelligent CAI

All of these articles are reprinted from *Educational Technology Magazine*, published by Educational Technology Publications, Englewood Cliffs, New Jersey 07632. This volume is one of a series of anthologies of articles from *Educational Technology*; for original dates of publication, see pages 197-198.

Expert Systems and Intelligent CAI

Part I
Expert Systems

Part I
Section One

Introduction to Expert Systems

Small Knowledge-Based Systems in Education and Training: Something New Under the Sun

Brent G. Wilson and Jack R. Welsh

Purpose of This Article

During the twenty or thirty years that computers have been used to teach, they have often tried to emulate human tutors (O'Shea and Self, 1983). The TICCIT computer-assisted instructional system (Merrill, Schneider, and Fletcher, 1980) implemented "intelligent" strategies through the use of learner control of well-defined instructional components, supported by a system "advisor" that guided learners through appropriate instructional paths. The idea was to program the computer to act "smart," like a human tutor might in the same situation. On the whole, however, educators' efforts at building adaptability and intelligence into teaching machines resulted in fairly simple, crude approximations of the complex, subtle behaviors exhibited by human tutors.

The field of artificial intelligence may provide some new approaches to making computers act smart (Barr and Feigenbaum, 1982). This article introduces artificial intelligence and its main subfields, including expert systems development. We review past efforts in developing large expert systems, and contrast those efforts with newly affordable, small-scale expert systems available for personal computers.

Reasons Why People Are Interested in AI

John McCarthy of Stanford University coined the term artificial intelligence (AI) in 1956 to describe an emerging field of research. Different researchers had different interests. Some AI researchers were interested in modeling human cognition with computers. They believed that by creating computer programs to mimic intelligent

Brent G. Wilson is Assistant Professor of Instructional Technology at Northern Illinois University, DeKalb, Illinois. Jack R. Welsh is a Senior Product Developer at Deltak Training Corporation.

human information processing, they would learn more about human cognition.

Other AI researchers were interested in the potential of symbolic rather than numeric computers. They felt, like Alan Turing, that a general purpose computing machine based on logical operators would have wide-ranging uses beyond numeric machines.

Part of the AI research tradition has been a lively dialogue about the nature of intelligence and whether it is possible to build an intelligent machine. Much of the current popular literature about AI reflects this research tradition. Popular reactions to AI, which are often not very thoughtful, are frequently based on discussions about man's essential nature or the nature of intelligence. In some cases, these popular reactions reflect some of the naive statements of AI researchers.

Most recently, AI has received a great deal of commercial attention. Many large companies are investing significant resources in AI. For instance, about half of the companies in the Fortune 500 are actively pursuing one area of AI, expert system development (Newquist, 1986).

Some of the companies investing in AI want to create commercial products to sell. More often, companies want to use AI to improve productivity. They believe that AI is a way for them to maintain or capture a strategic advantage within their industry and the marketplace. In other words, companies are investing in AI because they believe that there is substantial commercial value in using machines to emulate portions of human behavior that have not been captured by traditional numeric computing. This is in contrast to the reasons AI researchers have traditionally had for doing AI research.

Three Areas of AI Research

As you read various things about AI, you are likely to notice differences in viewpoint regarding what the field is about. Often these reflect the history of AI. They reflect the types of differences we have just examined. Because of different viewpoints, you are not likely to find a single definition of AI with which everyone will agree. A way of thinking about AI, however, is to divide the field into three broad areas:

1. **Robotics.** Some AI scientists are interested in developing smart robots that can analyze, perceive, and decide. Some of these scientists are especially interested in visual and tactile programs that will allow robots to deal with the ongoing changes that take place as they move around in an environment.

2. **Natural language processing.** English, French, Navajo, and Hindi are examples of natural languages as opposed to artificial languages like COBOL or FORTRAN. In Stanley Kubrick's movie, *2001: A Space Odyssey*, characters are able to converse with a computer named HAL much the same as they would with another person. Some AI researchers are interested in developing computer programs that understand natural language.

3. **Expert systems or knowledge-based systems.** Expert systems or knowledge-based systems are computer programs that, like a human expert, can advise, consult, diagnose, or solve problems in a narrow, technical domain. Typically, the program is given a problem. It queries the user for additional information. The program then gives a solution. Knowledge-based systems typically deal with diagnostic/prescriptive kinds of problems. They differ from traditional computer programming in several ways. For instance, knowledge-based systems:

   - deal with heuristics (i.e., rules of thumb) rather than algorithms (i.e., step by step procedures) in solving problems. Sometimes the information they use is incomplete or ambiguous;
   - can show the rules used to arrive at a conclusion; and
   - may include a measure of how confident the program is of its conclusion.

Currently, of the three areas, expert systems are receiving the most commercial and public attention. That is because expert systems are likely to have the most immediate commercial impact. Expert systems are projected by the consulting firm of Arthur D. Little to be a multibillion dollar business by 1990. However, many AI analysts believe that the long-term commercial impact of robotics and natural language processing will be even greater than that of expert systems.

Some Examples of Expert Systems

Let's examine two well-known expert systems, MYCIN and XCON, to get a more concrete idea of what expert systems are able to do.

MYCIN

MYCIN was developed at Stanford University in the mid-1970s. It was the first large expert sys-

tem to perform at the level of a human expert in solving "real-world" problems rather than trivial problems or games. Harmon and King (1985) give the following description of the types of problems MYCIN was designed to solve and how it works:

> MYCIN is a computer program designed to provide attending physicians with advice comparable to that which they would otherwise get from a consulting physician specializing in bactermia and meningitis infections . . . MYCIN reasons about data associated with a patient. It considers, for example, laboratory results of body fluid analyses, symptoms that the patient is displaying, and general characteristics of the patient such as age and sex. MYCIN obtains this information by interrogating the physician.
>
> A MYCIN consultation proceeds in two phases. First a diagnosis is made to identify the most likely infectious organisms. Then one or more drugs are prescribed that should control for all of the possible organisms. The antibiotics prescribed must rid the patient of the disease. They must also interact favorably with each other, and be appropriate for the specific patient. (p. 15)

Researchers have carefully compared MYCIN's performance with human experts. In one double blind study, MYCIN performed as well as or better than the best physicians on the Stanford Medical Faculty who were specialists in infectious diseases (Harmon and King, 1985, p. 20-21).

MYCIN is important for a couple of reasons. First, it demonstrated a system that dealt with a real-world problem at levels of performance as good or better than most very skilled human experts. MYCIN demonstrated the exciting potential of expert systems to emulate a portion of human behavior that was not amenable to traditional computing.

There is a second reason that MYCIN is noteworthy. The software has served as a shell in the development of other expert systems. In the case of MYCIN, the specific content and rules about bactermia and meningitis infections were removed while parts of the computer programs structure and code were retained. This was called EMYCIN or Essential MYCIN. Rules and content for another problem area were then added to this "shell" to create a different expert system.

Expert system shells are a powerful tool for building expert systems. If a new problem area generally conforms to the same type of problem that the shell was made for, they make the task of building an expert system easier. They also dramatically increase productivity. Many of the shells that are currently available are derived from MYCIN.

XCON

XCON represents the first large expert system that runs in a commercial environment on a production basis. It represents the move of expert systems from an academic to a business environment. Harmon and King (1985) give the following description of XCON:

> XCON is an operational expert system that routinely configures Digital Equipment Corporation's (DEC) VAX-11/780 computer systems. XCON's input is a customer's order and its output is a set of diagrams displaying the spatial relationships among the components on an order. These diagrams are used by the technicians who physically assemble the system. (p. 155)

Since XCON came into production in 1980, DEC has added a number of other expert systems. DEC feels that these expert systems play a strategic role important to DEC's competitive position.

We should note two things about XCON. First, notice that it is dealing with an entirely different content domain. MYCIN deals with medical diagnosis. XCON deals with configuring computer systems. Expert systems deal with many content areas. The commonality among expert systems is that most expert systems are best at:

- solving a limited class of problems. Diagnostic and prescriptive problems, in particular, are often amenable to expert systems;
- dealing with a fairly narrow, specialized domain of knowledge. The knowledge domain for both MYCIN and XCON is very specialized and relatively narrow. Currently, an expert system could not be built that deals with a very broad area such as strategic business planning.

There is a second reason that XCON is noteworthy. It suggests how expert system technology can be applied in a commercial environment. According to Dennis O'Conner, one of the original designers of XCON, DEC estimates that XCON saves it about $18 million per year.

While the dollar savings from XCON are substantial, the more important benefit to DEC is the strategic role that XCON plays in DEC's business. XCON does not just save DEC money or increase productivity, though it does both of those. XCON is important in giving DEC a strategic advantage in the marketplace.

Resources Required to Build a Large Expert System

What kinds of resources does it take to build the kind of expert systems we have been discussing? While building a large expert system, like MYCIN or XCON, is still difficult and complicated, the process for building them is now becoming fairly well established. So the resources required are less than some of the earlier pioneering efforts of five and ten years ago. Also, the chances that a project is going to result in a usable system have increased substantially.

Arthur D. Little, Inc., as noted above, is a consulting firm. As one of its services, it builds custom expert systems for business and industry. The information in Table 1 shows their experience in building large-scale custom expert systems. As you can see, the resources required can vary substantially.

In addition to the information shown, it is important to recognize the specialized skills represented in a typical project team. A project team will frequently have the following people:

- **Knowledge engineer.** The knowledge engineer is responsible for "unpacking" the content knowledge from the expert and representing that information to the computer.
- **Content or subject expert.** This is the person that is a master performer at solving the problems of interest. The expert provides the content upon which the system is modeled.
- **Specialized programmer.** Typically, specialized programming support is required in building a large expert system. Often the programming is done in either LISP or Prolog. even when using a shell, the tools are specialized enough to require special expertise.

In addition, development of a large expert system also often involves special hardware such as Symbolics, Apollo, or Sun computers. Often, systems are developed on special workstations and then either downloaded or rewritten to run on more conventional machinery and software.

The people building and deploying traditional expert systems do not think of themselves as solving training problems as such. While large expert systems are interesting, they are outside the mainstream of instructional problems. Given the substantial resources needed to build large expert systems, there are not likely to be many training problems that justify the substantial resources of large expert systems.

Summary of Important Points

Let's summarize a few of the key points in the information we just covered.

1. The technology of expert systems is now reliable enough that it is possible to build them on a commercial basis. A knowledgeable person can

Table 1

Resources Required to Build a Large Expert System

Stage	System Components	Duration	Level of Effort	Cost
Proof of Concept	Small, simple knowledge base; skeletal control logic; skeletal user interface; operable by developers; no documentation	4 to 6 months	1 to 2 man-years	$150,000 to $400,000
Demonstration	Medium-size knowledge base of moderate complexity; skeletal control logic; rough user interface; operable by trained experts; internal documentation	4 to 6 months	1 to 2 man-years	$150,000 to $400,000
Prototype	Multiple, large knowledge bases; complete, complex control logic; complete user interface; operable by trained users; design documentation	12 to 18 months	8 to 12 man-years	$1.2 to $2.4 million
TOTAL RESOURCE COMMITMENT:		20 to 30 months	10 to 16 man-years	$1.5 to $3.2 million

All information is from Davis (1986), based on figures from Arthur D. Little, Inc.'s experience in developing more than 30 large-scale, strategic knowledge-based systems, typically for Fortune 500 companies.

make a reasonable estimate about the time and resources required to build an expert system. Knowledgeable builders can also feel reasonably confident about which kinds of problems an expert system can solve and which are beyond the scope of the present technology. They can therefore give a plausible guess about what a finished system will be able to do early in a project.

2. The costs for building large expert systems are substantial. While there are problems that are worth investing the substantial resources to solve via an expert system, it is a comparatively restricted class of problems.

3. Training plays a negligible role in current expert systems. There have been few commercial expert systems built that focus on what would be considered as first and foremost a training problem. Given the resources required to

build a large expert system, this is understandable. There are few training problems that can justify the significant expenditure of resources required to build a large expert system.

Expert Systems Vs. Knowledge-Based Systems

So far we have primarily used the term 'expert system.' You may hear people also use the term 'knowledge-based system.' Often people use the two terms interchangeably.

If a distinction is made between the two terms, here is how they are usually distinguished. The term 'expert system' is used to refer to a system that has successfully captured the expertise of a world-class expert. In other words, the program solves problems that only a handful of human experts can solve. The program performs on a par with very skilled human experts. The term 'expert system' is also used to indicate the size of the project and the types of resources that a project requires.

The term 'knowledge-based system' is used to refer to a system that has successfully captured the knowledge of a specialist in some area. The program solves problems that do not require as much expertise to solve. These systems come closer to being an adviser or assistant rather than an expert. Often there are many skilled performers who can solve the problem. Also, the scope of the problem is limited. The term 'knowledge-based system' is also used sometimes to indicate that the project is smaller and requires fewer resources. Following the tradition in the field, we will continue to use both terms, often interchangeably. We will use 'knowledge-based systems', however, to refer especially to smaller-scale systems.

Something New Under Our Instructional Sun

A landmark event occurred in August of 1984. That was when two different software products for building knowledge-based systems on personal computer class machines were announced. For the first time, tools became available to build small knowledge-based systems on widely available hardware without special programming expertise in LISP or Prolog.

By July of 1985, there were over twenty such products commercially available. (See Appendix A for a list of some of the vendors and products currently available.) These products vary widely in price and quality. The prices range from just under $100 to about $12,000. In some cases they are carefully written software packages with impressive capabilities. In other cases, they are unpolished and have limited capabilities. The important point here is not the characteristics of any one package currently available. The important point is what those packages represent to the field of instruction.

They represent the opening of a door. It is now possible to find ways to use small knowledge-based systems to teach and support human performance. By analogy, the importance of Apple computers during the 1970s was not that they represented the final destination of a technology, but instead they represented the beginning of a vast technological change in society. That change has significant implications for society as a whole, which we are just beginning to glimpse. One small part of the overall implications had to do with education and training.

Similarly, the door is now opened on a type of computing, symbolic processing, that is likely to change the ways that we think of computers and what they are able to do. One exciting implication of this technology is the potential it has to address some educational problems in new ways. There is also the potential for solving some educational problems that we currently are not able to solve.

We expect that people will find a number of ways to use the technology for instruction. One way to use knowledge-based system technology is to build them into tutorial shells. IMSATT is a newly-marketed product that includes an expert system shell as a component of an authoring system. Although the price is a little steep, $7500 for software and hardware, an IMSATT system offers an intelligent, interactive-video tutoring system. Intelligent computer-assisted instruction is finally out of the AI research labs!

We expect the most used application of knowledge-based systems to be in support of job performance—as job aids, essentially. Intelligent job aids can be built into a product, such as a statistical analysis program like SAS or SPSS. The job aid could advise users on appropriate uses of different statistical tests. Some firms are incorporating expert systems into traditional office software. There are many potential uses.

Knowledge-based systems can also be built to stand alone as a performance aid. A special educator might make use of a knowledge-based system to assist in correctly diagnosing learning difficulties according to state regulations.

Resources Required to Build
Intelligent Job Aids

Earlier we examined the types of resources required to build large expert systems. What kinds of resources are required to build a small knowledge-based system? Given the comparative newness of this technology, no one yet has a significant base of experience building intelligent job aids.

However, based on limited information, let's give some preliminary guesses. The strongest base of experience may well be using the Personal Consultant system developed by Texas Instruments (TI). However, Personal Consultant is being used to build small knowledge-based systems, not intelligent job aids per se.

According to Mark Linesch, a knowledge engineer for TI, knowledge-based systems typically take up to a year for a full-scale project, and cost up to $100,000 for development. On the low end, small-scale projects can be completed in two to three months with correspondingly lower costs.

Level Five Research, Inc., the company that developed and markets a product called Insight, also develops knowledge-based systems and provides consulting services. Karl Seiler, of Level Five Research, estimates costs to be similar to those made by TI. Projects may take up to a year for full-scale systems (e.g., 500-1000 rules), but as short as one to two months for problems of smaller scope. Learning to use Insight II was estimated to take about two weeks for novices. Seiler described an in-house system developed to recommend appropriate billing procedures for customers. The system was completed in two weeks by experienced users of Insight.

The initial start-up costs include:

1. Procurement of appropriate hardware (e.g., personal computer) and software (e.g., knowledge-based system shell). Most organizations can utilize existing personal computer systems for job-aid applications. Knowledge-based system shells typically cost $500 to $5,000.
2. Train instructional designers or other personnel to function as knowledge engineers in extracting and structuring the content for the knowledge-based system. We see a parallel between the traditional instructional designer role and the "knowledge engineer" role. In both cases, the person must draw expertise out of a subject expert in a methodical, structured way so as to represent it accurately and efficiently. In both cases, the process is iterative. We believe, in fact, that an experienced instructional designer may be a good choice to serve as a "knowledge engineer" for small knowledge-based system projects.
3. Train instructional designers to use a knowledge-based system shell. Instructional designers who play a knowledge engineering role must learn to use a knowledge-based system shell such as Insight II or EXSYS.

The important point is that substantially fewer resources are required to build a small knowledge-based system than a large system. This suggests that the technology can immediately be cost-justified for many more problems. In other words, there are more problems that can be approached with expert systems technology today than prior to August 1984. Given the general trend in computing, it is likely that the biggest obstacle to the development and use of this technology is having people with the skills and background to use it effectively.

Conclusion

The advent of small knowledge-based systems has been so sudden that we have not yet begun to understand or effectively use this technology. Traditional AI researchers often consider small expert system shells as trivial or "toy-like." However, for many small, tightly defined problems, these shells have enormous importance.

Small expert systems shells can have important implications for education and training. One of the most immediate and direct uses of small knowledge-based systems is as intelligent job aids (Harmon, 1986; Welsh and Wilson, in press). We are excited that there are many inexpensive and powerful shells currently available. We are even more excited that what is currently available is only the shadow of things to come within the next two to four years. □

References

Davis, J.R. Custom-Developed Expert Systems Offer Strategic but Costly Alternative. *Computerworld*, January 13, 1986, 52-53.

Barr, A., and Feigenbaum, E.A. *Handbook of Artificial Intelligence, Volume 2.* Stanford, CA: Heuristech Press, 1982.

Harmon, P. Expert Systems, Job Aids, and the Future of Instructional Technology. *Performance and Instruction*, 1986, *26*(2), 26-28.

Harmon, P., and King, D. *Expert Systems: Artificial Intelligence in Business.* New York: John Wiley and Sons, 1985.

Merrill, M.D., Schneider, E.W., and Fletcher, K.A. *TICCIT.* Englewood Cliffs, NJ: Educational Technology Publications, 1980.

Newquist, H.P. Expert Systems: The Promise of a Smart Machine. *Computerworld*, January 13, 1986, 43-57.

O'Shea, T., and Self, J. *Learning and Teaching with Computers: Artificial Intelligence in Education.* Englewood Cliffs, NJ: Prentice-Hall, 1983.

Welsh, J.R., and Wilson, B.G. *Expert System Shells: Tools to Aid Human Performance.* In press, 1986.

Appendix A

List of Expert System Vendors and Products

Expert System Product	Vendor
Expert Ease Expert Edge	Human Edge 2445 Faber Place Palo Alto, CA 94303
ICL Adviser ICL Reveal	ICL Wenlock Way West Gorton, Manchester M12 5DR, England
Rulemaster	Radian Corporation 8501 Mo-Pac Blvd. P.O. Box 9948 Austin, TX 78766

(Continued)

Expert System Product	Vendor	Expert System Product	Vendor
Ex-Tran7	Intelligent Terminals George House 36 North Hanover Street Glasgow G12AD Scotland	KES	Software A and E 1500 Wilson Boulevard Suite 800 Arlington, Virginia 22209
Reveal	Tymshare UK Kew Bridge House Kew Bridge Road Brentford, Middlesex TW8 0EJ, England	ExperOPS5	Expertelligence 559 San Ysidro Road Santa Barbara, CA 93018
Sage Envisage	Systems Designers Scientific Software Technology Centre Pembroke House Pembroke Broadway Camberley, Surrey England	Advisor	Ultimate Media Inc. 275 Magnolia Avenue Larkspur, CA 94939
Apes	Logic Programming Associates 10 Burntwood Close London SW1 England	KEE	Intellicorp Knowledge Systems Division 707 Laurel Street Menlo Park, CA 94025
ES/P Advisor	Expert Systems International 1700 Walnut Street Suite 1024 Philadelphia, PA 19103	Timm	General Research Corpora- tion Software Sales and Marketing 7655 Old Springhouse Road McLean, VA 22101
Inference Art	Inference Corporation 5300 W. Century Blvd. Los Angeles, CA 90045	Insight 2	Level 5 Research Inc. 4980 South A-1-A Melbourne Beach, FL 32951
Savoir Micro Expert	ISI 11 Oakdene Road Redhill, Surrey RH1 6BT England	Nexpert	Neuron Data 444 High St. Palo Alto, CA 94301
Xi	Expertech Expertech House 172 Bath Road Slough, Berks SL1 3XE England	EXSYS	Jeffrey Perron & Associates 3685 17th St. San Francisco, CA 94114
S.1 M.1	Teknowledge 525 University Avenue Palo Alto, CA 94301	GURU	Micro Data Base Systems Inc. P.O. Box 248 Lafayette, IN 47902
Knowledge Craft	Carnegie Group, Inc. Commerce Court at Station Square Pittsburgh, PA 15219	IMSATT	IMSATT Corporation 500 N. Washington Suite 101 Falls Church, VA 22046
MP-LRO	CRIL 12 bis rue Jean Jaure 92807 Puteaux, France		

Expert Systems Authoring Tools for the Microcomputer: Two Examples

Joseph M. Ferrara, James D. Parry, and Margaret M. Lubke

Artificial intelligence (AI) is one of the most exciting areas within the field of computer science. Much of the current interest in AI has been a result of the practical success of computer-based expert systems (Buchanan and Shortliffe, 1984; Clancey and Shortliffe, 1984; Feigenbaum and McCorduck, 1983; Weiss and Kulikowski, 1984; Winston and Pendergast, 1984). Expert systems are computer programs which provide users with advice. During a consultation with an expert system, the user answers computer-generated questions. Those answers are used to test a series of knowledge-based rules. When enough information is provided to allow the system's advice-related rules to succeed, a potential solution to the user's problem is provided by the system (Weiss and Kulikowski, 1984).

Although expert systems have been successful in a variety of fields, two key factors have delayed their use in education (Hofmeister and Ferrara, in press). One factor has been a lack of equipment. Most computers owned by public schools do not provide an ideal expert system authoring environment. Expert systems have typically been developed using mainframe computers or dedicated LISP machines like the XEROX 1108 or the Symbolics 3600. Few public schools have access to that type of hardware.

Programming problems have also limited the use of expert systems in education. Until recently, expert systems were usually written in LISP and PROLOG. These languages are flexible and lend themselves to the logical rule representation required by expert systems. They are not, however, easy to learn or to use. The development of a usable expert system often has required years of work by a team of skilled programmers and

The authors work at Utah State University's Development Center for Handicapped Persons in Logan, Utah. **Joseph M. Ferrara** is a Research Associate; **James D. Parry** and **Margaret M. Lubke** are Research Assistants.

content-area experts (Sleeman and Brown, 1982). Public education has lacked the resources which the development of expert systems has demanded.

Improvements in microcomputer hardware coupled with the development of microcomputer-based expert system authoring tools have made the use of AI programs within public schools appear more feasible today (Hofmeister and Ferrara, in press). AI authoring tools allow non-LISP programmers to build expert systems. These authoring tools may provide users with a unique language or approach to program generation. In addition, debugging aids, designed to assist the programmer, may be part of the authoring tool.

Microcomputer-based expert system authoring tools can be used effectively to train novice knowledge engineers. In addition, these tools can be used to produce small scale, practical, expert systems which may be useful in solving a variety of educational problems (Hofmeister and Ferrara, 1984a; Hofmeister and Ferrara, 1984b; Parry and Ferrara, in press).

Expert-Ease (Export Software International Ltd.), *M.1* (TEKNOWLEDGE, Inc.), and *EXPERT-2* (Miller Microcomputer Services) are authoring tools designed for use with microcomputers. What follows is a discussion of two of these authoring tools: *Expert-Ease* and *M.1*. This discussion is not a formal review but rather an informal reflection based on the experiences of the Special Education AI project staff at Utah State University.

The goal of the Special Education AI project at Utah State University is to test the feasibility of using expert systems to solve immediate problems in special education. Prototype programs in the areas of diagnosis, classification, program evaluation, classroom management, and videodisc control are currently in various stages of development and testing.

As a result of our project we have had an opportunity to use *Expert-Ease* and *M.1*. Readers should keep in mind that the comments which follow are not those of AI experts, but rather reflect our subjective judgments after several months of work with these two authoring tools.

Computer Hardware

M.1 and *Expert-Ease* are made for IBM-PC and IBM-PC XT microcomputers. Both *M.1* and *Expert-Ease* can be used with either a monochrome or color monitor. *M.1*, however, is designed to take advantage of a color display, while *Expert-Ease* is not. *M.1* operates under PC-DOS, and we have found little or no problem running *M.1* on PC-compatible machines. *Expert-Ease*, on the other hand, uses UCSD and has caused problems for us on several IBM-compatible machines. Both systems are quicker and easier to use with a hard disk machine (more about this later).

Learning to Use the Tools

Expert-Ease is simple to learn and use. One project staff person lightheartedly contends that it takes about 40 minutes to learn to use *Expert-Ease* and that within five hours you are about as proficient as you are likely to get. While this is clearly an exaggeration, it isn't far from reality. We believe that a person with limited computer experience can learn the system in less than one day. Everything one needs to know about *Expert-Ease* is contained in the manual which accompanies the program. The manual provides information on program installation, a careful tutorial giving step-by-step instruction in system use, and additional information on knowledge organization and advanced (larger and more complex) applications.

M.1 takes longer to learn than *Expert-Ease*. A four-day workshop, designed to teach students to use *M.1*, is provided by TEKNOWLEDGE. In addition, *M.1* novices should plan on additional practice before they use *M.1* for serious expert system development. This is not to say that *M.1* is horribly difficult. Even staff members with limited computer experience were able to become competent *M.1* users within a reasonable amount of time.

During training, TEKNOWLEDGE provides three volumes of well-organized materials: (a) Sample Knowledge Systems; (b) Training Materials (illustrated lecture notes); and (c) Reference Manual and User's Guide. The formal workshop instruction, combined with the *M.1* program materials, was viewed by the project staff as effective training.

In addition to learning the syntax of *M.1* and *Expert-Ease*, a novice user of either system would benefit from training in knowledge representation (Hayes-Roth, Waterman, and Lenat, 1983). We believe that knowledge representation skills facilitate the design and production of improved expert systems. In our judgment, these skills are not covered adequately by either the *M.1* or *Expert-Ease* training packages.

Creating a Program

Users developing programs with *Expert-Ease* employ a four-step process: (1) identify possible answers; (2) identify critical attributes for use in discriminating between differing examples; (3) write questions which are designed to help the system assign values to critical attributes; and (4) enter examples of problems. *Expert-Ease* then induces a logic matrix which determines and controls the presentation of appropriate questions to the user. The user's responses to those questions lead through the logic matrix to the "expert" conclusions. Explanations for the conclusions reached by the system can be identified by reviewing the logic matrix generated by *Expert-Ease*. In short, once appropriate outcomes, attributes, questions, and examples have been entered, the system does the work.

A single *Expert-Ease* program can handle a problem with up to 30 critical attributes and 300 examples. Larger problems can be addressed by chaining together several expert systems and having each system deal with a component of the larger problem. When this is done, however, the system must load each sub-program. Without a hard-disk system, this can be a long and noisy operation.

Our staff found creating *M.1* programs to be more complex. In *M.1* the programmer must identify a system goal and then develop a set of rules which will allow the system to question potential users, make inferences based on user responses, and arrive at conclusions which achieve the system's goal. *M.1* is much more flexible and feature-laden than *Expert-Ease*. As a result, debugging a large *M.1* system is a complex job.

To make this job easier, *M.1* provides programmer-friendly facilities; these include: (a) a series of error messages which identify syntax problems; (b) a command which displays a system's intermediate conclusions; (c) a command which allows the programmer to print out a history of the system's use of rules throughout each consultation; and (d) a command which provides an on-screen collection of useful information throughout the consultation.

Use of a hard-disk system makes authoring *M.1* programs faster. *M.1* programs are not usually written while an authoring tool is running. Instead, a text editor (we use *WordStar*) is used to actually write the program. The program is then submitted to *M.1* for analysis and debugging. When using a floppy disk system, the process of moving large files from *WordStar* to *M.1* and back is time consuming. The PC-XT's hard-disk speeds this process.

Consulting an Expert System

During a consultation with an *Expert-Ease* program, questions are displayed on the screen in the sequence dictated by the logic tree and the user's answers to the program's questions. When the system has collected enough information to reach a conclusion, advice is printed for the user. When *Expert-Ease* is unable to arrive at a conclusion, the user is alerted and the program can quickly be changed to accommodate the new case.

Since the user may question the program in a number of ways, a consultation with an *M.1* program can be more complex than an *Expert-Ease* consultation. For example, an *M.1* program can provide the user with information about the content-related rules which have caused specific questions to be asked. Furthermore, an *M.1* user can halt a consultation and have the system display its intermediate conclusions. In addition, the *M.1* "trace" command can be used to print a list of the rules used throughout a consultation.

Expert Systems in Education

In the United States, only a few AI programs have been designed for use in schools. Furthermore, the educational market is still limited by hardware costs. PC-XTs are not commonly found in public school classrooms.

Additional information on microcomputer-based expert systems may be obtained from:

- TEKNOWLEDGE Inc. (for *M.1*)
  525 University Ave.
  Palo Alto, CA 94301-1982
  Tel. (415) 327-6600
- Jeffrey Perrone and Assoc., Inc. (for *Expert-Ease*)
  3685 17th Street
  San Francisco, CA 94114
  Tel. (415) 431-9562
- Miller Microcomputer Services (for *EXPERT-2*)
  61 Lake Shore Road
  Natick, MA 01760
  Tel. (617) 653-6136

We believe that current problems limiting the use of microcomputer-based expert systems in schools are not insurmountable and that within the next few years expert systems will play an important role in American education. □

References

Buchanan, B.G., and Shortliffe, E.H. (Eds.) *Rule-Based Expert Systems: The MYCIN Experiments of the Stanford Heuristic Programming Project.* Reading, MA: Addison-Wesley, 1984.

Clancey, W.J., and Shortliffe, E.H. (Eds.) *Readings in Medical Artificial Intelligence: The First Decade.* Reading, MA: Addison-Wesley, 1984.

Feigenbaum, E.A., and McCorduck, P. *The Fifth Generation.* Reading, MA: Addison-Wesley, 1983.

Hayes-Roth, F., Waterman, D.A., and Lenat, D.B. (Eds.) *Building Expert Systems.* Reading, MA: Addison-Wesley, 1983.

Hofmeister, A.M., and Ferrara, J.M. Expert Systems and Special Education. *Exceptional Children*, in press.

Hofmeister, A.M., and Ferrara, J.M. (1984a). *Artificial Intelligence Applications in Special Education: How Feasible?* Grant Award to Utah State University No. 023 CH 40219.) Washington, DC: Special Education Programs, Department of Education, 1984a.

Hofmeister, A.M., and Ferrara, J.M. *A Study of Selected Microcomputer-Based Artificial Intelligence Systems in Special Education.* (Grant Award to Utah State University No. 023 HH 40051.) Washington, DC: Special Education Programs, Department of Education, 1984b.

Parry, J.D., and Ferrara, J.M. The Potential of Computer-Based Expert Systems for Special Educators in Rural Settings. *Small School Forum*, in press.

Sleeman, D., and Brown, J.S. (Eds.). *Intelligent Tutoring Systems.* London: Academic Press, 1982.

Weiss, S.M., and Kulikowski, C.A. *A Practical Guide to Designing Expert Systems.* Totowa, NJ: Rowman and Allanheld, 1984.

Winston, P.A., and Pendergast, K.A. (Eds.) *The AI Business: Commercial Uses of Artificial Intelligence.* Cambridge, MA: MIT Press, 1984.

This article was prepared with the assistance of funds from Special Education Programs, Department of Education Grant G008400650; Project Officer: Jane Hauser. Principal Investigator: Alan Hofmeister.

Expert Systems in Education and Training: Automated Job Aids or Sophisticated Instructional Media?

Alexander J. Romiszowski

Where Are We? Fact and Fiction of Expert Systems

Every month, the educational and training journals publish an ever growing stream of articles on the topic of Artificial Intelligence and particularly Expert Systems. Why the sudden interest in a relatively slowly developing field of research, which has "been around" so to speak for some thirty years and has been more noted for its failure to deliver promised results on time than for real progress in terms of successful practical applications? Some twenty years ago, we were "on the verge" of automatic language translation by computer. Today, despite significant progress in natural language interpretation and programming, the goal of a practical automated interpreter remains out of reach. Despite much progress in industrial robotics (little more than rather sophisticated numerically programmed machinery) we are a long way from constructing the type of general purpose robot exemplified by Hal in "2001: A Space Odyssey," or indeed any of the "intelligent" automated butlers that we see so often in television programs set "just a little into the future." Finally, we are yet a long way indeed from constructing the all-purpose reasoning machine that could pass the Turing test of intelligence (machine and human decision-making being indistinguishable).

It is in this latter field, however, that some limited progress of a significant and practical nature has recently been achieved: in the development and economic application of Expert Systems that emulate human expertise in small, tightly defined and highly structured domains of complex problem-solving.

Alexander J. Romiszowski is Professor, Instructional Design, Development, and Evaluation, Syracuse University, Syracuse, New York.

Of the three main areas of Artificial Intelligence (AI) research, referred to above, namely Natural Language Processing, Robotics, and Expert Systems, the third is the area in which, suddenly, there seems to be real promise of commercially viable large-scale application. Perhaps for this reason, more than any other, Expert Systems have caught the attention of educators, especially the "high-tech" fringe. Perhaps for this reason, also, reactionary voices have been raised, questioning the educational utility, economic viability, or indeed relevance to education, of Expert Systems.

On the one hand, AI enthusiasts point to the very rapid growth of interest and development effort in the field among business. Newquist (1986) claims that about half the Fortune 500 companies are already investing in the development of expert systems. Their use in education is but a question of time. Wilson and Welsh (1986) refer to knowledge-based expert systems as "something new under the (education and training) sun," emphasizing the very rapid growth in the methodology for developing such systems and the proliferation of software already available at economic prices for use on personal computers, that may enable any educator to become involved. But they do not really clarify WHY an educator should wish to get involved.

On the other hand, performance technologists such as Harmon (1986) and Kearsley (1986a), see expert systems, especially the small and relatively simple knowledge-based "advisors," as just "a new medium for developing complex job-aids." This would seem to limit their application to the non-training aspects of real-life performance problem-solving in industry and, in education, to the role of labor-saving devices, like slide-rules, pocket calculators, word processors, and spreadsheets. But, as expert systems are job aids to assist with the solution of "complex" problems, which require the use of a modicum of "intelligence," is it in fact a "good thing" to supply students with a job aid? Will it stop students from thinking for themselves? Should expert systems be banned from education?

Yet other authors point out that at this time, the technology is only capable of dealing with very tightly defined problem-solving tasks and, although some of the very big (and very expensive) expert systems (such as MYCIN) do emulate world-class expertise in a difficult problem area (Harmon and King, 1985), the smaller systems, incorporating knowledge bases of some 20, 50, or 100 rules, are no more than glorified algorithms that can be (and indeed were) developed by non-computer techniques, such as decision-tables (Pipe, 1986).

All these viewpoints represent rather extreme positions, all contain a modicum of truth, but none really pinpoint the true potential, or indeed the true limitations, of knowledge-based expert systems for education. Knowledge-based expert systems, even those developed on relatively cheap and low-power software (for example, Texas Instruments' PERSONAL CONSULTANT, 1985) can handle 200 or more interdependent rules, even "fuzzy" probabilistic relations, with differing levels of confidence and can supply alternative solutions with different resultant levels of probability. Even simple algorithmic job-aids can lead to effective learning, and expert systems offer much more potential for productive learning. On the other hand, they are not a panacea for all learning problems—what is?

Where Have We Come From?
The Evolution of the Job Aid

Expert systems, in their intended practical applications, are indeed, job aids (or to use the more correct term, job PERFORMANCE aids). They are ".... software programs that HELP YOU SOLVE complex reasoning tasks that normally require an expert..." (Texas Instruments, 1985). The expert system will help a novice or relatively inexperienced problem solver to match the skill of acknowledged experts in the domain in question. The very large expert systems that emulate world-class expertise in a domain that is so complex that few humans ever qualify as "experts" may contain many hundreds, even thousands of separate, but interrelated rules (and therefore take thousands of manweeks and millions of dollars to develop—see Wilson and Welsh, 1986). The more modest systems, however, may emulate only reasonable levels of expertise in a domain where many humans actually reach proficiency, but where many more need to take decisions and may need advice. The first category may replace a very rare and expensive human expert. The second category rarely replace, but rather ASSIST the user in the search for an optimum solution to a complex problem.

Let us look at the history of job-performance aids for decision-making tasks, to see where these "expert advisors" fit in. The impetus to the use of decision-making job-performance-aids came in the mid-1960s, from the work of early performance technologists, such as Gilbert (1967), Harless (1968), and the work of US-based consultancy organizations such as Geary Rummler's Praxis Corporation. On the other side of the Atlantic, in England, the Cambridge Consultants group was developing the "art" of flowcharting into a powerful technology for the systematic design, development, and use of algorithms, logical trees, and decision tables as job aids that reduced the training requirement (Lewis et al., 1967: Lewis and Wolfenden 1969; Lewis 1970; Wheatley and Unwin 1972). It was only natural that these two developments should be fused and popularized. Thus, in 1970, the book Analyzing Performance Problems (Mager and Pipe, 1970) was published. This explained, with typical Mager-style clarity and with bags of practical examples, the principles of analysis and solution of job-performance problems (including the use of algorithms as job aids) and provided the reader with a job aid in the form of an algorithm (see Figure 1).

Now, unlike most of the applications of this technique developed by Lewis and his collaborators, which were "true" algorithms, the flowchart in Figure 1 is a "quasi-algorithm." A true algorithm is "a procedure that, if followed correctly, all users solve all the problems in a domain correctly and in the same way" (Landa, 1976).

Examples of true algorithms are procedures for the division of two numbers, for the calculation of an annual income tax return (given a set of earnings and claims data), and so on. On the other hand, the procedures for analyzing a complex problem in order to decide how to solve it (what to divide by what), or to decide how to enter and represent a given taxpayer's earnings and claims, are seldom truly algorithmic. There is usually some degree of value judgment, weighing of viable alternatives, or decision-making on the basis of incomplete data involved. For example, in Figure 1, the second question lozenge—"skill deficiency?"—demands a complex analytical process of observing performers and perhaps interviewing them, as well as an appropriately formed concept of "skill" on the part of the observer/interviewer. No wonder that in the same case study simulation, trainee performance technologists often disagree as to whether the correct answer is YES or NO. Even experienced performance technologists disagree sometimes. The "skill deficiency" decision point, as indeed most of the others in Figure 1, involves a complex of subordinate "if-then" decisions that the "expert" performance analyst learns to apply through experience. The job aid in Figure 1 is useful, but only insofar as it reminds the analyst to ASK all the relevant questions in an efficient SEQUENCE. It does little to help him or her ANSWER the questions—for this it was necessary to write the whole book of rules and illustrate with adequate examples and, in practice, then follow up with more practical examples in simulated case study situations.

A further example of a "quasi-algorithm" is

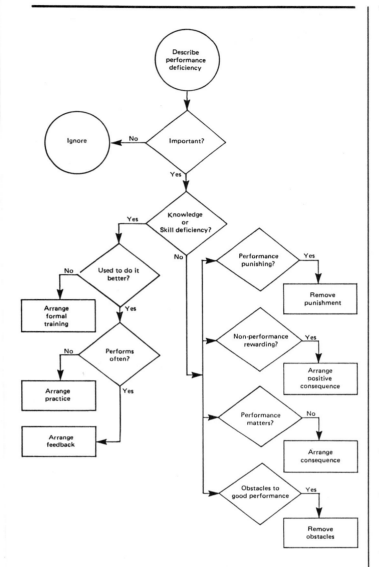

Figure 1. Example of a "Quasi-Algorithm" to assist the task of performance problem analysis and solution.

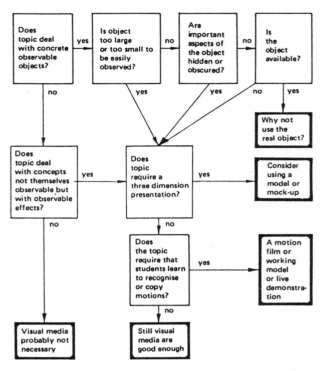

Figure 2. Example of part of a "Quasi-Algorithm" to assist the task of media selection (Romiszowski, 1968, 1974).

presented in Figure 2. This is part of a set of flowcharts developed by the author (Romiszowski, 1968, 1974) to act as instructors' job aids for the selection of instructional media. Experience in using these with many groups of instructors led to the observation that although the use of job-aid flowcharts significantly improved lesson planning decisions, SOME instructors were SOMETIMES misled by the very form of the flowcharts in that the YES/NO decision format was taken to always imply a categorical one-way route through the decision process. But due to the quasi-algorithmic nature of the task, one may

need to follow several paths at once (Romiszowski, 1970). In Figure 2, for example, a topic may deal with BOTH concrete observable objects AND abstract concepts (an airplane's wing); and in Figure 1, an analyst following the flowchart may correctly diagnose a deficiency in the skills of a given group of performers and may set about the development and implementation of a costly training program, only to find later on that there are a series of factors in the job environment—inbuilt punishments and obstacles—that are beyond his power to influence and that totally undermine even the most efficient training effort (e.g., the civil service career structure and its negative influence on job motivation).

During the 1970s, therefore, there was a trend away from the use of algorithmic job aids, except in the case of true algorithmic procedures. Job aids for quasi-algorithmic, part-heuristic decision-making procedures tended towards the use of IF-THEN tables and WHIF (WHen and/or IF) charts (Horabin, 1971; Horn, 1974) and Cognitive Schemata (Romiszowski, 1980, 1981). IF-THEN and WHIF charts are a step towards the listing of the

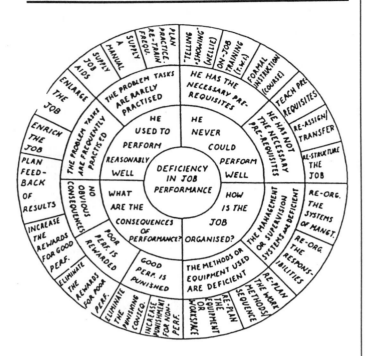

Figure 3. An Analysis schema for performance problems: Questions to ask, answers to compare and solution—components to select (Romiszowski, 1980, 1981).

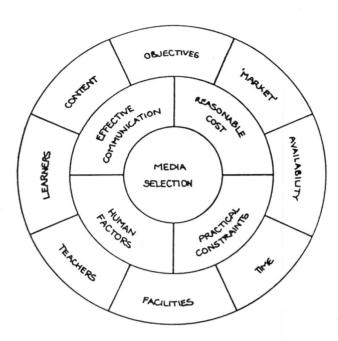

Figure 4. Factors affecting the selection of media for instruction: a conceptual schema of factors to consider and their interrelation (Romiszowski, 1981).

separate but often interrelated rules that underlly complex decisions—a step towards the development of knowledge bases for expert systems.

Cognitive schemata were an attempt to represent the structure and interrelatedness of a set of factors that should, together, be taken into consideration in complex decision-making. Figures 3 and 4 are two such cognitive schemata developed by the author for the same areas of decision-making represented by the flowcharts in Figures 1 and 2. The circular nature was intended to emphasize the integrated nature of the decision-making process. As job aids, they succeeded in overcoming the "blinkered" one-route decision-making which algorithmic flowcharts tend to promote, but apart from that they are no real advance—they also only act as memory aids to the factors that should be considered, but do not aid much with HOW to decide.

An exhaustive set of IF-THEN rules set out in a chart are more helpful in this respect. But, again, if the number of interrelated rules is large, and the decision-maker is not experienced, there is a limit to the number of separate rules that a human being can keep in short-term memory and consider in relation to each other—probably related to Miller's (1967) "magic number 7 . . . plus or minus 2." Once more, we cannot seem to get away from

the need to build up expertise through practical experience and training.

It is in this area of quasi-algorithmic, but partly heuristic decision-making that expert systems should have ONE of their principal impacts on education and training. The type of decision-making tasks described in the two examples above, although not as precisely defined as some, are amenable to the development of REASONABLY expert systems, capable of diagnosis and decisions equivalent to most successful instructional designers, or performance technologists. There are precedents for this belief. Kearsley (1986b) has developed two working knowledge-based systems, which assist the trainer to take cost-benefit analysis decisions in relation to training programs and assess the suitability of a given course or topic for computer-based instruction. Under military contract, Singer and Perez (1986) have successfully developed a first version of an expert system for the design of training devices for military training applications, an area of application which involves an annual budget of over seven billion dollars a year. The present author is currently working to develop experimental systems in the two skill areas exemplified above—performance problem solution and media selection.

COMPUTER AS: USER:	TUTOR	TOOL	TUTEE
STUDENT	Intelligent computer-assisted instruction (ICAI) ——— Intelligent data-base search assistant. (EMBEDDED TRAINING)	Commercially produced expert systems used to solve problems. (JOB AID) ——— Student learns by repeated use.	Use of LISP or PROLOG in schools. ——— Students construct expert systems for the domain under study.
TEACHER/INSTRUCTION DESIGNER/ AUTHOR	Intelligent EMBEDDED training in school applications software. ——— Intelligent teacher-training systems.	Stand-alone expert systems on I.D. decision making, planning, controlling, etc. ——— Intelligent authoring systems for CAI.	Teacher/SME constructs expert systems on specific domains to use in modes 1 and 2.

Figure 5. The "Field" of A.I. applications in education and training (Romiszowski, 1986).

Where Are We Going?
The Educational Benefits of Expert Systems

Readers with an interest in formal education, rather than training, may be excused for wondering if this article was written for them. Hopefully, in this section, they will see that it is of relevance to the loftier aims of a general education—and how!

Elsewhere (Romiszowski, 1986; 1987, in press) I have used Taylor's (1980) schema of computers in education, "Tutor, Tool, Tutee," as an organizing framework for the analysis of potential AI applications in education. The overall schema is reproduced in Figure 5. We shall not examine all the entries in all the cells in full detail, as this would be repeating earlier works. Instead, we shall single out the applications of expert systems that seem, in this author's opinion, to offer the greatest potential for educational benefits at not too excessive cost.

The reader will note that Taylor's three categories of "role" that the computer may adopt, have in my schema been crossed with two categories of user—our students (whether they be young children in school, university students, or trainees in business) and "ourselves" (whether we be teachers, instructors, instructional designers or authors/developers of instructional materials).

Expert Systems/AI as "TUTORS"

In the left-most column of our schema, we have "Intelligent Tutoring Systems" or "Intelligent Computer-Assisted Instruction" (ICAI). These are custom-designed, special-purpose, tutorial packages such as those described by Sleeman and Brown (1982), Carbonell (1970), Pask (1984), and Park and Seidel (1986), the last authors making an interesting comparison between the roots, the methodologies, and the results of "conventional" CAI and the new, "intelligent" ICAI.

Intelligent tutoring systems are more complex in basic structure than expert systems, being in a sense a combination of subject matter expert, student-results-analysis-and-interpretation expert, as well as expert tutor. Being extra complex and extra specialized, they are extra costly to develop. This alone might rule them out as practical solutions to formal educational problems. Coupled to this, however, is the almost total absence in the literature of any evidence that this high cost results in any benefit. Of the 15 or so intelligent tutorial systems which according to the literature seem to have reached the stage of full development, only about five have been used regularly on anything like a large scale and of these, not one seems to have been systematically evaluated.

Let us leave the TUTOR mode, therefore, and concentrate our analysis on the TOOL and TUTEE columns of the schema. Here we seem to get a very different picture of educational promise and cost-benefit ratio.

Expert Systems as "TOOLS"

In the TOOL category, we have, at the top, use by students of existing knowledge bases and expert systems as, firstly, job aids to assist in the solution of relevant categories of problems. For example, an economics course might incorporate an expert "stockbroker" system, an engineering course will use an existing "bridge designer" system, a high school class may tune into an existing "weather forecasting" system as part of a geography unit and an elementary group may use an expert advisor on "productive writing." All these, except perhaps the last, may be commercial expert systems, developed for real-time use: their application in education is a spin-off benefit, at reasonable cost once the systems are in widespread use.

The main spin-off benefit, however, is from the learning processes that may be associated with the use of these job aids. When using a job aid frequently enough, the user inevitably learns much, if not all of the procedure involved. In the case of algorithmic procedures, this learning is mere memorization. In the case of general-purpose algorithms, which have some grounding in theory (arithmetical procedures, for example, as opposed to one-purpose algorithms like the procedure to operate a particular photocopier) it is desirable to get away from mere memorization by getting the learners to derive their own algorithms from "first principles" (Landa, 1976). But in the case of learning from expert systems, the situation is much more interesting from a learning theory viewpoint. In the first place, most respectable expert system software shells provide the means to include explanatory messages. The user may, whenever asked to furnish data, inquire WHY that particular information is required for the problem. And when the expert system presents a decision or solution, the user may ask HOW that decision was reached, where upon the system retraces the logic of its decision-making process. Thus, the user not only gets a solution, but a full explanation. And all this is restricted to a series of SPECIFIC EXAMPLES of problems. Unlike the case of using an algorithm as a job aid (the user receives a set of

rules and a sequence and applies them to examples—RUL-EG), using an expert system as a job aid involves working on a series of specific examples of problem solving and, perhaps discovering in time, not only the individual rules that the system uses to solve the problems, but the interrelationships that exist between them.

In the hands of a skillful teacher, an appropriate expert system, used initially as a problem-solving job aid, may become a medium for the discovery learning by the student of the original experts' cognitive structures that are built into the system's knowledge base. Far from being the threat to the student's independent thinking processes, hinted at in our opening paragraphs, expert systems in the classroom may be used to promote deep analytical and productive thinking, through a process of guided discovery.

In the lower part of the TOOL category, we have the use of expert systems as, principally, instructional design and development tools, by teachers and designers. We have already analyzed some existing and proposed stand-alone expert systems for individual tasks like cost-benefit analysis, media selection, or simulator design. The armed forces are, as a whole, convinced that such tools are essential to maintain both the quantity and the quality of instructional design decisions in military training. Any progress registered here will, no doubt, seep through to educational decision-making in time. The other significant movement in this field is the development of embedded expert system tools within CAI authoring systems (Merrill, 1985; Merrill and Wood, 1984; McAleese, 1986). This development is seen by educators as essential to ensure quality in computer-based courseware design. It may be that intelligent tutoring systems are a thing of the distant future, but intelligent authoring systems may indeed be instrumental in saving our "conventional" CAI systems from extinction due to self-destructive mediocrity (Romiszowski, 1986).

Expert Systems as "TUTEES"

Turning now to the TUTEE category, we encounter another potential development and one about which I am personally very excited. This is the use of simple expert system "shells" to enable students in school to develop their own expert systems on topics that they are studying. This combines a whole series of pedagogically attractive aspects in a practical and motivational new type of exercise:

- Learning by doing and in the process creating new knowledge, or at least new structure for the knowledge found in books and other sources, as well as working job-aids that may be useful later.

- Learning by discovery, in the domain of higher-order problem-solving and the creation of cognitive strategies and theories.
- Applying a logic of the structure of knowledge to segments of one's own store of knowledge in order to create a computerized knowledge-base and thus learning to reflect on and recognize the rest of one's personal knowledge-base.

An interesting application of this approach is reported by Lippert and Trollip (1986), using a specially constructed, simplified expert system shell with 12- to 15-year-old students on a variety of domains of problem-solving.

Other researchers have been working along similar lines with older age-groups. Starfield *et al.* (1983) have been using the approach for some time with engineering students.

The use of expert system software in this way is, in its intent, very similar to the use of LOGO in schools (Papert, 1980). Apart from the direct learning that takes place, associated to the CONTENT which is being processed (geometry in turtle LOGO and almost any well structured set of principles in expert system development), the students learn "powerful ideas" of general applicability; in the latter case, associated with general approaches to problem formulation and problem solving.

Finally, there may be the one other important development, analogous to students constructing expert systems to structure their knowledge-base on a specific subject domain. This is the possible use of expert system software, in the TUTEE mode, by teachers, instructional designers and, especially, the authors of books and other educational materials.

To illustrate this point and to conclude this section, I quote from the final paragraphs of the paper of Singer and Perez (1986), when describing their project to design an expert system for the design of training devices:

> With the use of a knowledge engineering tool such as KES, we have SUCCESSFULLY structured what is known about the characteristics and instructional features of training devices. As researchers in training and training devices, we have ACQUIRED SOME KNOWLEDGE about the design of training devices. We believe that this process CAN BE APPLIED TO OTHER FUZZILY BOUNDED AND NON WELL-DEFINED KNOWLEDGE DOMAINS as well. The process has FORCED US TO STRUCTURE THE KNOWLEDGE AVAILABLE from field experiments and technical reports of validation studies. THAT STRUCTURING HAS SHOWN US WHERE ANSWERS ARE NEEDED AND WHAT VARIABLES ARE INVOLVED IN OBTAINING THE ANSWERS.

***

Will We Get There? When?

To take the last question first, many of the potential benefits of using expert systems in education and training are attainable *now*. Commercial knowledge bases and expert systems are beginning to appear and will do so at an ever-increasing rate. Initially, they will be hard to come by, due to the cost of their development and the commercial value of the embedded expertise to the developer and client. But some public-domain and subscription service systems are already in development, and these will serve to start the ball rolling in the TOOLS department. Tools for teachers and instructional designers are also in the pipeline, but their ready availability may be somewhat delayed by the normal budget restrictions that exist in education.

The TUTEE applications depend on the availability of simple, easy-to-use knowledge-base building software. Some of the commercially available packages may be suitable for use by university students, but even in these cases the learning time involved in mastering the software may be excessive. Research projects like the ones described earlier have in the main found it necessary to develop special, much simplified software, especially when young school children are to be the budding "knowledge engineers." These simplified shells will no doubt soon become generally available, and should open the way for many other teachers to follow. Given a suitable, easy-to-learn shell, the rest depends only on the imagination of the teacher to choose suitable knowledge-base building projects and on his or her instructional skills to ensure that the students get the most out of the experience.

Returning now to the first question—will educators reap the potential benefits we have outlined?—I would hesitate to make a guess. Apart from the flavor of futurology in this article, and the plethora of perhaps shaky hypotheses derived from a few as yet unfinished studies, the other great unknown is the general posture that the teaching profession will adopt to AI's inroads into the traditional preserves of the teacher. At the 1986 ADCIS International Conference, Peter Dean of IBM addressed a number of the underlying, but in his opinion perhaps mistaken, assumptions made by the users and the practitioners of computer-based education. Among these were:

- Teachers will never be replaced by computers (in his view, they will be partly replaced and, thus, their role will change drastically).

- The best use of computers in education is as TOOLS—word processing, spreadsheets, and so on (in his view, this is not the best use, but is presented to teachers as such, since it is the least threatening use and is thus a way of "getting a foot in the door").

If teachers as a body were to perceive the tools-use of expert systems (and the tutee approach as well) as "getting a foot in the door," so as to eventually introduce some more role-threatening forms of "intelligent tutoring systems," then maybe progress will be much slower than here predicted. But maybe they will perceive the potential educational benefits and see themselves in full control as managers of the resources at their disposal. In that case, we may expect some interesting innovations in the classroom. □

References

Carbonell, J.R. AI in CAI: An Artificial Intelligence Approach to Computer Assisted Instruction. *IEEE Transactions on Man-Machine Systems*, November 1970.

Dean, P.M. CBI: Some Widely Held Assumptions. The Dean Lecture, presented at the 28th International Conference of the Association for the Development of Computer-based Instructional Systems (ADCIS), Washington, DC, November 1986.

Dear, B.L. Artificial Intelligence Techniques: Applications for Courseware Development. *Educational Technology*, July 1986, *26*(7), 7-15.

Gilbert, T.F. Praxeonomy: A Systematic Approach to Identifying Training Needs. *Management of Personnel Quarterly*, 1967, *6*(3).

Harless, J. An Ounce of Analysis (Is Worth a Pound of Objectives). Newnan, GA: Harless Performance Guild, 1968.

Harmon, P. Expert Systems, Job Aids, and the Future of Instructional Technology. *Performance and Instruction Journal*, March 1986.

Harmon, P., and King, D. *Expert Systems: Artificial Intelligence in Business*. New York: John Wiley and Sons, 1985.

Horabin, I.S. *Towards Greater Employee Productivity*. Summit Point, WV: 1971.

Horn, R.E. *Course Notes for Information Mapping Work-*Instructional Systems (ADCIS), Washington, DC, November, 1986a.

Kearsley, G. CBT Analyst—DISKETTE and Costs/Benefits—DISKETTE. (Expert Systems). LaJolla, CA: Park Row Software, 1986b.
Instructional Systems (ADCIS), Washington, DC, November 1986a.

Kearsley, G. CBT Analyst—DISKETTE and Costs/Benefits—DISKETTE. (Expert Systems). LaJolla, CA: Park Row Software, 1986b.

Landa, L.N. *Instructional Regulation and Control: Cybernetics, Algorithmization, and Heuristics in Education*. Englewood Cliffs: Educational Technology Publications, 1976.

Lewis, B.N. *Decision Logic Tables for Algorithms and Logical Trees*. London: HMSO, 1970.

Lewis, B.N., Horabin, I.S., and Gane, C.P. *Flow Charts, Logical Trees and Algorithms for Rules and Regulations*. London: HMSO, 1967.

Lewis, B.N., and Wolfenden, P.J. *Algorithms and Logical Trees: A Self-Instructional Course*. Cambridge, UK: Algorithms Press, 1969.

Lippert, R., and Trollip, S. Building Knowledge Bases for Expert Systems. Paper presented at the 28th International Conference of ADCIS, the Association for the Development of Computer-based Instructional Systems, Washington, DC, November 1986.

Mager, R.F., and Pipe, P. *Analyzing Performance Problems*. Belmont, CA: Fearon, 1970.

Miller, G.A. The Magic Number 7—Plus or Minus 2. In C.A. Miller, *The Psychology of Communication*. London: Penguin, 1967.

McAleese, R. The Representation of Knowledge in Authoring Environments. In N. Rushby and A. Howe (Eds.), *Aspects of Educational Technology—XIX: Educational, Training, and Information Technologies—Economics and Other Realities*. London: Kogan Page, 1986.

Merrill, M.D. Where Is the Authoring in Authoring Systems? *Journal of Computer-Based Instruction*, 1985, *15*(2).

Merrill, M.D., and Wood, L.E. Computer Guided Instructional Design. *Journal of Computer Based Instruction*, Spring 1984, *11*(2).

Newquist, H.P. Expert Systems: The Promise of a Smart Machine. *Computerworld*, January 1986.

Papert, S. *Mindstorms: Children, Computers, and Powerful Ideas*. New York: Basic Books, 1980.

Park, O., and Seidel, R.J. ICAI: Intelligent Applications of AI. Paper presented at the 28th International Conference of ADCIS, the Association for the Development of Computer-based Instructional Systems, Washington, DC, November 1986.

Pask, G. Review of Conversation Theory and a Protologic (or protolanguage)—Lp. *ERIC/ECTJ Annual Review Paper. Educational Communications and Technology Journal (ECTJ)*, January 1984, *32*(1).

Pipe, P. Decision Tables: The Poor Person's Answer to Expert Systems. *Performance and Instruction Journal;* March 1986.

Romiszowski, A.J. *Selection and Use of Teaching Aids*. London: Kogan Page, 1968.

Romiszowski, A.J. Classifications, Algorithms, and Check Lists as Aids to the Selection of Instructional Methods and Media. In A. Bajpai and J. Leedham (Eds.), *Aspects of Educational Technology. Volume IV*. London, Pitman, 1970.

Romiszowski, A.J. *Selection and Use of Instructional Media: A Systems Approach*. London: Kogan Page, 1974.

Romiszowski, A.J. Problem Solving in Instructional Design: A Heuristic Approach. In A. Howe (Ed.), *International Yearbook of Educational and Instructional Technol-*

ogy—1980/81. London: Kogan Page, 1980.

Romiszowski, A.J. *Designing Instructional Systems: Decision-Making in Course Planning and Curriculum Design.* London: Kogan Page, 1981.

Romiszowski, A.J. Artificial Intelligence and Expert Systems in Education: Progress, Promise, and Problems. Paper presented to EDTECH '86, the International Conference of the Australian Society for Educational Technology, Perth, Western Australia, December 1986.

Romiszowski, A.J. Artificial Intelligence and Expert Systems in Education: Potential Promise or Threat to Teachers? *Educational Media International*, 1987, in press.

Singer, M.J., and Perez, R.S. A Demonstration of an Expert System for Training Device Design. *Journal of Computer-Based Instruction.* Spring 1986, *13*(2).

Sleeman, D.H., and Brown, J.S. *Intelligent Tutoring Systems.* New York: Academic Press, 1982.

Starfield, A.M., Butala, K.L., England, M.M., and Smith, K.A. Mastering Engineering Concepts by Building an Expert System. *Engineering Education*, November 1983.

Taylor, R.P. (Ed.). *The Computer in the School: Tutor, Tool, Tutee.* New York: Teachers College Press, 1980.

Texas Instruments, Inc. *Personal Consultant: Expert System Development Tools.* User's Guide (manual) and Software (for PC), 1985.

Wheatley, D.M., and Unwin, A.W. *The Algorithm Writer's Guide.* London: Longman, 1972.

Wilson, B.G., and Welsh, J.R. Small Knowledge-Based Systems in Education and Training: Something New Under the Sun. *Educational Technology*, November 1986, *26*(11), 7-13.

Applications of Expert Systems in Education: A Technology for Decision-Makers

Stephen W. Ragan and Thomas D. McFarland

Susan Marshall was in her first year as an English teacher in grades 9-12 at Central High School, a secondary school of about 500 students. It was October. Susan was in trouble, and she knew it.

She had been hired to teach approximately 125 students in three sophomore and two junior level classes. Central High School has both "regular" and college-bound level English classes. Being new on the staff, Susan received the privilege of teaching the "regular" classes.

First hour each morning is not unlike most of Susan's classes. Every morning John, Mary, Stewart, and Frank were late to class. John was frequently absent. Steve had turned in two of the last eighteen assignments; Margaret three. Although Susan didn't know it, Jim, Francis, Tom, and Karen were off-task approximately 75 percent of the time. The average on-task time for the class was about 55 percent. Marilyn and Tony vied for honors as the class clown. They loved the attention that chronic disruption brought them. At the time about half of the class was failing or achieving "D's."

Central High had no uniform tardy policy. The teachers "preferred to handle lateness in their own individual ways." The administration could be described as moderately supportive. In the previous two months Susan had seen her principal five times in teacher's meetings and twice in the faculty lounge, but never in her classroom.

Is this a salvagable situation? Are these students a "bad group?" Is Susan not a "natural" teacher? What can be done to turn this situation around?

Unfortunately, this is not a new or unusual situation for first-year teachers. Some teachers swim. Some sink. Most survive, but with help could certainly do more than "make it to the end

of the year." What Susan (and teachers like her) need is some advice, some consultation over a period of weeks or months.

Also, unfortunately, most high schools do not employ consultants for regular classroom teachers. Nonetheless, what Susan needs is a consultant to advise her about documenting on- and off-task behavior; to provide advice in dealing with disruptive and tardy students; and to suggest ways of achieving more productivity from students who seemingly refuse to turn in assignments.

In addition, the school could probably use some advice regarding the value of schoolwide policies in some areas of student life. And, finally, the district could probably benefit from advice related to student grouping, grading, retention, and other issues where there appears to be a clearly defined body of knowledge regarding what works and what doesn't.

Purpose

The purpose of this article is to suggest what could be done with current technology to help Susan, and Central High School, with several relatively difficult problems. The technology is that of expert system development.

An expert system is a computer program that combines knowledge in the form of rules and an "inference engine" that uses the rules to draw conclusions and make recommendations about a problem presented to the system. The data are drawn either from the rules and facts in the knowledge base or from answers to questions that the computer is programmed to ask the user about the case problem.

Need

The need for the creation of these systems in education is clear. Teachers make many critical decisions in the lives of their students each day. Such decisions as when to reinforce or punish, how to teach specific tasks effectively, and how to remediate are often made without the consultation of others. Teachers are asked to be accountable and systematic often without assistance or guidance during the decision-making process.

Likewise, schools as institutions must render decisions even more far-reaching, such as when to retain a child in grade, or when to classify a student as "handicapped" or "learning disabled." Frequently, teachers and other educators must act with incomplete information about the student. Decisions are often made without a knowledge of best practices or research findings.

Recent research has focused on teacher planning and interactive decision-making (Clark and Peterson, 1986). Research findings are beginning to

Stephen W. Ragan and Thomas D. McFarland are with the Special Education Department at Lewis-Clark State College, Lewiston, Idaho.

clarify the planning process which effective teachers utilize. Studies of interactive decision-making are beginning to identify information, rules, and procedures that teachers think about when making classroom choices. Although this research has been limited, it provides a direction for future studies. If "intelligent" computers can be programmed to assist teachers with recordkeeping and decision-making using the knowledge from research and "best practices," then teaching and learning can be improved.

This type of computer assistance is presently being utilized in other professions. Applications appear to be feasible in education. Will the design of human-machine cognitive systems lead to a clarification of the planning and decision-making process and to expert systems which will support effective decision-making? The answers to that question range from optimistic (Harmon and King, 1985) to cautious (Dreyfus and Dreyfus, 1986). If effective, expert systems must provide the information and knowledge support that educators need both during the planning process and during interactive teaching.

There are at least four major areas of expert system application that hold promise for educators. They are:

(1) knowledge clarification,
(2) computer consultants,
(3) decision support systems, and
(4) content modules for intelligent tutoring systems.

How can these four areas be applied to Susan Marshall's situation and the situation at Central High School? That will be the focus of the remainder of this article.

Knowledge Clarification and the Knowledge Engineering Process

In Susan Marshall's case, the simple procedure of clarifying the problems, listing alternative solutions, and monitoring student progress toward the goals given a likely solution might well have solved several of her problems. Knowledge engineering is such a process. Building an expert system consists of developing the rules, inference procedures, and strategies for problem solving that are then analyzed and built into the computer system. Knowledge engineers responsible for building systems present specific cases to the "problem solver" and clarify each step in the decision-making process.

Hayes-Roth, Waterman, and Lenat (1983) have offered Table 1 as a description of the developmental process involved in building and validating an expert system. This process is not unlike many research and development or instructional design models in education. The process, therefore,

Table 1

Stages in the Evolution of an Expert System*

Identification: Determining problem characteristics.

Conceptualization: Finding concepts to represent knowledge.

Formalization: Designing structures to organize knowledge.

Implementation: Formulating rules that embody knowledge.

Testing: Validating rules that embody knowledge.

*From Hayes-Roth, Waterman, and Lenat (1983).

whether it results in a validated, usable consultant program or not, is a valuable enterprise for the developers. Waterman (1986), for example, has stated that knowledge clarification through the knowledge engineering process is a useful activity which makes heuristic knowledge ("rules of thumb") used by experts explicit and accessible.

Hofmeister and Lubke (in press) have indicated that rule-based expert system development tools have recently become available for use with microcomputers. These tools will allow individuals with limited amounts of training to build expert systems. Thus, the clarification process can also be used with novices (perhaps with expert guidance) to identify what they know and do not know during case analysis.

The authors of this article have used the procedures of knowledge engineering with teacher education students utilizing classroom management cases of individuals and groups who failed to remain on-task. These teacher education students were able to make more effective case decisions and identify needed information following the knowledge clarification activities.

Susan Marshall might have benefitted from a similar exercise, particularly in the areas of off-task, disruptive, and tardy behavior. The exercise might also have been valuable in the area of assignments not being turned in for evaluation. The process might also have led the Central High staff, given a school-wide activity, to more appropriate conclusions regarding policies and practices where tardy behavior and student grouping is concerned.

Computer Consultants

As previously indicated, one of the things Susan Marshall and Central High could have used was access to an expert consultant. More than just taking the staff through the process, which is valuable if the staff has some knowledge about the problem areas, the consultant offers general and/or specific recommendations along with a prediction about the probability for success with a given solution. A microcomputer can do that.

The expert system guides decision-making by engaging the user in a dialogue which parallels the session a person might have with a human consultant who has specific expertise in the area of decision-making. The computer consultant asks questions that clarify the problem and requests the facts and information needed by the expert system to suggest one or more solutions. Many expert systems have the capability to explain why the consultant program has asked a question, showing the rules used in the search for a solution, and assigning confidence factors to each solution.

Prototype expert systems have been developed at Utah State University to serve as classification and compliance consultants in special education. These rule-based expert systems guide teachers, administrators, and parents in compliance with federal and state rules and regulations during placement meetings for learning disabled students (Ferrara *et al.*, this issue). They provide the capabilities of advising the user, explaining "why" the consultant program has asked a question, and tracing the logic of the decision through the rules in the program.

The authors of this article are in the process of developing prototype expert systems for behavior consultation and materials evaluation and selection. When validated these systems will aid teachers in making day-to-day behavior decisions and annual or longer range decisions regarding which materials may be most effective for a given classroom situation.

One or more expert systems could have assisted Susan and her colleagues in any of the problem areas identified at the beginning of this article. From deciding on a strategy for increasing assignment completion to developing a policy regarding grouping students for instruction, sufficient information is available to provide a higher level of success, given consultation, than without such consultation.

Decision Support Systems

A third application that Susan and her colleagues could make of computers is the application of data to their problems. Data related to specific skills that the students in her classes have mastered, and

have yet to master, would have allowed her to focus on the skills most in need of development. Those data are often not available to classroom teachers. Susan was no exception.

Database management systems (DBMS) are computer programs that allow the user to create, modify, delete, and retrieve information. Although both humans and computers can be effective at information processing, computers have an advantage in the amount of information they can hold and in the length of time which they can remember it. Expert system modules can provide additional support and guidance in the form of knowledge regarding decision-making options. Database management systems with expert system modules will provide teachers with both the information and knowledge required to make effective decisions. These decision support systems do not *make* decisions, but instead serve the role of a consultant that provides appropriate information and suggestions of alternative choices.

A prototype expert/database management system is being developed in reading. When completed, the reading diagnosis and prescription system being developed at universities in Canada will maintain student records, identify reading needs, and recommend reading instruction materials (Colbourn and McLeod, 1983). These programs will provide data to support the classroom teacher in making planning decisions.

Content Modules for Intelligent Tutoring Systems

Finally, Susan and her colleagues could benefit by using intelligent Tutoring Systems (ITS). ITS is an area of future AI application with the potential of significantly impacting education. Research in ITS has been limited to only a few areas because of the high costs of development. ITS programs have been developed in mathematics, medicine, science, electronics, and problem solving.

An expert system may be developed and evaluated prior to its use as a content or knowledge system module in an ITS program. If that content is established as a separate entity or module, the expert system provides a clear source of information such as rules, objects, attributes, examples, or values which will guide instructional design analysis. Expert systems, then, may serve as the content for instructional design analysis in an intelligent tutoring system (ITS). A modular approach to ITS development has several advantages over the traditional approach that integrates content and instruction. Each module can be developed and evaluated separately from other modules. For example the content can be developed as a separate expert system module. Roberts and Park (1983) suggest that separate modules will provide opportunities for research on areas such as student characteristics (the student module), teaching effectiveness (the instruction module), and the clarity of the knowledge base (the expert system module).

Future of Experts Systems in Education

The computer is currently a useful tool for teachers in the classroom. In the future, "intelligent" computers will be of even greater assistance. Expert systems have demonstrated expertise in narrow areas of knowledge such as medical diagnosis and chemical analysis. Knowledge engineering is emerging as a profession which will assist with the development of expert/knowledge-based programs for decision-making in all professions.

As previously noted, the future of expert systems is viewed optimistically by Harmon and King (1985) and, at best, cautiously by Dreyfus and Dreyfus (1986). The authors of this article are basically optimistic about the application of expert systems in education.

The recent development of expert system shells for microcomputers other than the IBM PC (e.g., the Apple Macintosh 512K) increases the probability of adaptation for public schools, if for no other reason than that the schools have more Apple products in place. While the school district business manager probably uses an IBM system, the curriculum director, building principals, and other administrators probably do not.

Also, the development of megabyte storage for the Apple IIe increases the probability that the use of expert systems by classroom teachers is feasible. For, while some administrators and only a few teachers have access to the Macintosh 512K, most teachers are using the Apple IIe and probably will be for some time to come. The remaining link to be made will be the development of expert systems to run on the Apple IIe. When (not if) that happens, the average teacher, like Susan Marshall, will have an expert consultant in her classroom to help her decide on alternative courses of action. Those alternative courses of action will be defined in terms of any area or areas that are important, require multiple sources of data, and require adherence to rules, facts and "rules of thumb." A few areas of potential interest in education are:

(1) diagnosis and labelling of exceptional learners;
(2) consultation related to due process procedures;
(3) assessment of skill strengths and weaknesses;
(4) recommendation of behavioral intervention;
(5) material evaluation and selection advice;
(6) recommendations to increase instructional effectiveness;
(7) staff evaluation for employment and retention;
(8) deciding whether to retain a student in grade; and
(9) counseling students into programs of study.

It should be recognized in support of this optimistic portrayal that the first five of the above areas *already* have representative prototypes either under development or in the field test stages. Thus, some optimism appears warranted.

Also, a survey of popular literature and computer magazines indicates an increasing interest in expert systems. Expert systems have demonstrated effectiveness in areas such as medicine, law, military affairs, science, and agriculture (Waterman, 1986). There is no conceivable technical reason, certainly not a lack of need, nor is there a lack of expertise that would prevent expert systems from becoming an important tool for educators. □

References

Bonczek, R.H., Holsapple, D.W., and Whinston, A.B. *Microdatabase Management: Practical Techniques for Application Development*. Orlando, Florida: Academic Press, 1984.

Buchanan, B.G., and Shortliffe, E.H. *Rule-Based Expert Systems: The MYCIN Experiments of the Stanford Heuristic Programming Project*. Reading, MA: Addison-Wesley, 1984.

Clark, C.M., and Peterson, P.L. Teacher's Thought Processes. In Wittrock, M.C. (Ed.), *Handbook of Research on Teaching*, 3rd Ed. New York: Macmillan, 1986.

Colbourn, M., and McLeod, J. Computer Guided Educational Diagnosis: A Prototype Expert System. *Journal of Special Education Technology*, 1983, 6(1), 30-9.

Dreyfus, H.L., and Dreyfus, J.E. *Mind Over Machine*. New York: The Free Press, 1986.

Ferrara, J.M. *et al*. Using an Expert System for Complex Conceptual Training, *Educational Technology* (this issue).

Ferrara, J.M., Parry, J.D., and Lubke, M.M. CLASS. LD: An Expert System for Student Classification. Technical Paper. Logan, UT: Utah State University. (ERIC Document Reproduction Service No. ED 263 734), 1985.

Harmon, P., and King, D. *Expert Systems: Artificial Intelligence in Business*. New York: John Wiley and Sons, 1985.

Hayes-Roth, F., Waterman, D.A., and Lenat, D.B. *Building Expert Systems*. Reading, MA: Addison-Wesley, 1983.

Hofmeister, A.M., and Lubke, M. Expert Systems: Implications for Diagnosis and Treatment of Learning Disabilities. *Journal of Learning Disabilities*. (in press).

Roberts, F.C., and Park, O. Intelligent Computer-Assisted Instruction: An Explanation and Overview. *Educational Technology*, December 1983, 23(12), 7-12.

Waterman, D.A. *A Guide to Expert Systems*. Reading, MA: Addison-Wesley, 1986.

Part I
Section Two

A Variety of Applications in Education and Training

Expert Systems for Educational Decision-Making

Jacqueline A. Haynes, Virginia H. Pilato, and David B. Malouf

For education, expert system technology finally is "coming of age." Until the last few years, expert systems required computing hardware and computer science expertise that were both expensive and difficult for educators to obtain. Recently, however, microcomputer-based, affordable authoring tools for expert systems have become available, enabling subject matter experts, such as educators, to develop expert systems for use in their own domains. These advancements have encouraged the development of educational expert systems that have great potential benefit for a variety of educational applications. In this article, several recently developed educational expert systems will be described. They exemplify only a few of the potential uses for this technological advance.

This discussion is limited to systems that meet three important criteria for expert systems:

- the system's recommendations are comparable to those offered by a human expert in that domain;
- the systems have separable components for representing knowledge and for reasoning with that knowledge; and
- the reasoning process is *traceable*; i.e., the system has the ability to explain its reasoning process to a user (Waterman, 1986).

Systems that do not meet these criteria are not being considered, since lack of these features would seriously limit their uses.

Four basic categories of expert system use will be described in this article:

(1) expert systems for planning;
(2) expert systems for decision support;
(3) expert systems for teacher training; and
(4) expert systems as research tools.

Each use will be explained and instantiated with an existing educational expert system.

Jacqueline A. Haynes, Virginia H. Pilato, and David B. Malouf are with the Institute for the Study of Exceptional Children and Youth, Department of Special Education, University of Maryland, College Park, Maryland.

Expert Systems for Planning

Examples

An expert system has great potential as a tool for educational planning. Given information about the current status of a student, or a program and a desired goal, an expert system could infer intermediate steps that should be achieved sequentially, and the amount of time or money required to reach the goal, or it could define strategies for achieving the goal. For example, a knowledge base consisting of production rules concerning desirable ratios of teachers to students under various conditions (grade, subject, physical size of a classroom, years of teacher experience, contractual obligations, etc.) and current information such as enrollment figures, number and experience of teachers currently on staff, etc., could be used to plan staffing of school buildings within large school systems, as well as to plan for hiring or staff reductions.

CAPER (Computer-Assisted Planning for Educational Resources) is an expert system that is intended to serve a planning function. It is being developed at the Institute for the Study of Exceptional Children and Youth at the University of Maryland. CAPER is an attempt to address the problem of over-referral for special education services in schools that have a large number of students identified as "at risk" by their teachers. The goal is to develop an expert system that will help in planning sound instructional programs for individual students during the referral, diagnosis, and instructional planning processes. The system will recommend the best instructional program for a student prior to his/her placement in special education. Using information about effective classroom interventions for students who are experiencing specific problems, the expert system will recommend feasible instructional options within the regular class setting. In addition, it will guide formal diagnostic procedures and consideration of special placements. Currently naturalistic research is being conducted to determine what processes would help to alleviate problems of over-referral and inappropriate recommendations for special education placement, and what classroom interventions would be most useful to include in the system.

Two other educational expert systems which would be useful for planning were developed by the Artificial Intelligence Research and Development Unit, Developmental Center for Handicapped Persons, Utah State University. "Mandate Consultant" (Parry, 1985) reviews the IEP (Individualized Educational Program) development procedures. As a planning tool, it can be used to help plan IEP development, ensuring that all legal requirements are met so that hearings to resolve parent-school system disputes are needed less frequently. "Behavior Consultant" (Ferrara, Serna, and Baer, 1986) is an expert system designed to recommend interventions for behavior-disordered students. Like CAPER, it can be used to plan individual student programs.

Potential Problems

A restriction on using expert systems for educational planning (and for other domains as well) is that good results will strongly depend on good data. For example, if a teacher who is using "Behavior Consultant" does not accurately describe the student's behavior, or if the collected data is incorrect, the interventions recommended by the system will probably be ineffective. Part of the expert knowledge of a human behavior consultant is in recognizing and questioning data that looks faulty. While it may be theoretically possible to emulate within an expert system the human ability to question data, that capability is not currently part of the system (or other similar systems). Likewise, it will be impossible for the CAPER system to help plan instructional interventions that will be effective if the data describing a student's current status is incomplete or inaccurate.

Decision Support

Examples

A second use for expert systems in education—and the most common one in general—is for decision support, or as a "second opinion" for decision-making. Many medical expert systems, such as MYCIN (Davis, Buchanan, and Shortliffe, 1975) have been developed for this purpose. Examples of educational expert systems that are designed for use in decision support are CAPER, CLASS. LD, and "Mandate Consultant," though some serve other purposes as well. One use of the CAPER expert system will be to offer recommendations for diagnostic procedures leading to appropriate instructional placements for students. Because of the expert knowledge embodied in the system, these recommendations will include only those tests and procedures that are valid for a student's age, language/cultural background, etc. These recommendations might add a new point of view to the deliberations of the instructional planning team, or may simply reinforce (or refute) their opinion. CAPER will also be helpful in a decision-support role for interpreting test data, since it is designed to yield technically valid interpretations of the test scores. In this capacity, CAPER would help to provide decision support that is not biased by race or ethnicity, is not forgetful of technical limitations of tests, and is not inaccurate in reporting data, as humans can sometimes be.

While CAPER is still in the development stage, so that its benefits can only be hypothesized, "Mandate Consultant" and CLASS. LD are completed systems that have been validated. "Mandate Consultant" can provide a reliable second opinion (Parry, 1986) in determining whether correct procedures have been followed in the development of a student's IEP. This information can be helpful to those in state and local agencies who are reviewing case histories, to officials preparing for hearings, or to parents who may question the correctness of educational procedures followed with their child's case. Likewise, CLASS. LD can provide a reliable second opinion regarding the appropriateness of a learning disabilities classification for a given student. Both of these expert systems have been subjected to extensive validation measures comparing their performance to that of human experts. Both systems have performed as well as the best of the experts, and better than many of them (Parry, 1986).

Potential Problems

Using expert systems as a "second opinion" is certainly less problematic than using them as a primary decision tool, but use in the second opinion capacity is still not without its problems. One problem is that it is not at all clear *whose* "expert" knowledge should be built into such a system; i.e., there is no consensus on who the "experts" are.

Who are the Experts? In education, expertise is divided among several sources including researchers, public officials, administrators and supervisors, and classroom teachers. While each of these sources of expertise can be important, they often present differing points of view on an issue. The result of considering all points could easily be unintelligible when the viewpoints do not come together neatly, or when they yield conflicting recommendations. In deciding whose expertise to build into an expert system, one should consider whose point of view would be most useful for the system's application.

For example, CLASS. LD (Hofmeister, 1984) uses knowledge derived from state and federal regulation to reach its decisions and recommendations. Similarly, "Mandate Consultant" (Parry, 1985) uses legal, regulatory information to review procedures for the development of IEPs. In these cases, clearly the best source of expertise to build into the knowledge base is the regulation itself, since that information is, by definition, the most authoritative source.

The answer to the question of whose expertise to include in the CAPER knowledge base, however, is much less clear. Who can provide the best expertise on the appropriate instructional program for a given student—researchers, university consultants, school principals, school district specialists, or talented classroom teachers? While many disciplines have acknowledged authoritative sources for their expertise, the only consensus among educators is that practitioners, researchers, and policy-makers know different things and need to share their expertise more. For this reason, the CAPER knowledge base is being designed to include information from specific sources for specific topics. Rather than combining sources of expertise for a single topic, the approach being used is to select one source of knowledge for each topic that can best be used in the decision-making process. Figure 1 indicates the source of information for the specified topics included in CAPER.

How much can you trust the experts? Another potential problem with using expert systems for decision support is deciding how much the recommendations of such a system can be trusted; i.e., how sure can the user be that the system's "reasoning" is correct? Two features of expert systems help with this dilemma. First, until its accuracy is tested, validated, scrutinized, and subjected to extensive evaluation, any system should be used only as a *second opinion*, and not as a primary decision-maker. Until both the technology for building expert systems and the specific system are more fully tested, expert systems should supplement, not replace, human decisions.

The second feature of expert systems addressing the issue of accurate reasoning is the requirement that an expert system's reasoning process be "traceable," allowing users to compare the inferences that the system makes with their own inferences. In this way, during a consultation, the intermediate results can always be checked. If there is error due to faulty data, the user can correct it. If faulty reasoning is detected, the knowledge-base author can make changes. The human user will always bear the ultimate responsibility for intelligent decision-making, for using the specific feature of the expert system efficiently, and for cautious use of expert systems in field applications.

Expert Systems for Teacher Training

A third educational use for expert systems is in training. Expert systems have potential as training tools in at least three ways. First, an expert system can recommend training for teachers. Second, they can teach information and processes to teacher

Figure 1

Sources of Expertise in CAPER

TOPIC	SOURCE
Effective interventions for a given student problem	Research literature
Feasibility of interventions	Naturalistic research
Availability of instructional options	Naturalistic research District personnel
Student data	Teacher input
Required procedures for assessment	District policy
Formal tests for obtaining specified data	Research literature State and local policy
Valid interpretations for formal test data	Technical manual for tests
Informal diagnostic procedures	Informal consultants' recommendations
Interpretation of informal diagnosis	Informal consultants' recommendations

trainees. Third, they can serve a training function simply by being used by novices who learn from the process of interacting with the expert knowledge embodied in the system. An example of each of these training roles will now be discussed.

Recommending training. SNAP (Smart Needs Assessment Program) is a large, complex expert system that recommends training experiences for regular education teachers who teach mainstreamed handicapped students. The goal in designing SNAP was to produce a system that would create individualized training programs for teachers that would take into account the amount of prior training they have had, their attitudes toward mainstreaming and teaching handicapped students, their own goals for professional training, their knowledge about effective teaching methods and procedures, and their overall skill in implementing instruction in the classroom. Each of these areas and the source of information for them are listed in Figure 2. SNAP uses information from each area to determine, for an individual teacher, a set of training needs. These needs are, in turn, used to select appropriate training options from an exten-

Figure 2

Information Sources for SNAP

Teacher Characteristic	Computer Program	Description
Attitude toward mainstreaming and teaching handicapped students	SOC	A modification of the Stages of Concern to deal specifically with mainstreaming
Goals for training	GOALS	Teachers select a variable-size set of goals for their training
Classroom Effectiveness • Direct Instruction Ratio	DIRprob	Teachers collect self-observation data and the program evaluates their direct instruction ratio
• Questioning Skill	QUESprob	Teachers analyze their patterns of questioning, and the program evaluates its effectiveness
• Academic Learning Time	ALTprob	Teachers collect self-observation data, and the program evaluates the amount of academic learning time available in their classroom
Experience, training, age, etc.	PERSDATA	A collection of demographic information

sive database of modular training components. The components address a single training need or a group of needs. The selection of training options is also influenced by other factors, such as cost, location, situational requirements (such as whether videotape equipment is required or whether access to the handicapped population is required for an observation), and other factors that would affect the appropriateness of a training option for a particular teacher's training needs.

The educational value of SNAP is its ability to train teachers in what they need to know. The usual approach to training teachers for mainstreaming has been a "shotgun" approach; a general course (perhaps "Introduction to Special Education" or "Introduction to Mainstreaming") covering numerous topics and providing very general information to a group of teachers presumed to be homogeneous in their training needs. Like homogeneous classroom instruction for youngsters, this approach is clearly lacking in its ability to meet individual needs. SNAP, then, has the potential of addressing this need by providing an individualized approach to training teachers for mainstreaming and—if it is found effective—to

providing inservice training in other areas. The individual components of SNAP have already undergone field testing as they were being developed. The total system is currently undergoing extensive validation and evaluation, and the preliminary results look quite encouraging.

Teaching information and processes. Expert systems can also be designed specifically for teaching a specified group of individuals a body of information, skills, and/or processes. Expert systems which serve this pedagogical function have usually been preceded by the "second opinion" type of expert system, which was then modified for use as a training tool. MYCIN (Davis, Buchanan, and Shortliffe, 1975), for example, is a medical system for diagnosing bacterial diseases from the characteristics of bacterial cultures and patient symptoms. Subsequently, NEOMYCIN (Clancy and Letsinger, 1981) was developed as a modification of the MYCIN system for teaching students to diagnose bacterial diseases. Several expert systems developed at Utah State University have followed this two-step procedure of development from decision-support to training. For example, using CLASS. LD as the initial expert system, Ferrara and Prater (1985) modified the system to teach non-special education teachers to classify correctly students as learning disabled or not. Prater and Ferrara (1986) cite two approaches to the development of "training" expert systems. One approach is simply to teach the rules incorporated into the knowledge base so that novices will now have access to the same knowledge as the experts. The second is to use sample consultations of examples and non-examples to train teachers to make this discrimination in a conceptual learning approach. These approaches are being developed with "Mandate Consultant" and "Behavior Consultant" as well.

Novice use of expert procedures. Another way of using expert systems for training purposes is through the process of having novices run consultations with the system. By modelling the behavior of experts in seeking information, forming hypotheses, and providing recommendations, the expert system allows the novice user to deal with that expertise in a way that the novice can then emulate. Initial evaluation data from field tests of SNAP indicate that teachers believe they have learned a considerable amount of information about teacher effectiveness just by collecting and reporting the data requested by the expert system. With CAPER, it is also anticipated that by using the system's guidance through the referral, diagnosis, and planning processes for educationally at-risk students, decision-making team members will become more skilled in the process themselves.

Expert Systems as Research Tools

A fourth function for expert systems in education is for research. During the development of SNAP, the value of expert systems as a research tool emerged as an important contribution of the technology. As a research tool, expert system development can be used to examine the processes and information used by expert educators to solve particular problems. Second, in assembling the relevant knowledge and expertise needed to solve an educational problem, the system authors can discover instances of missing knowledge, inconsistent knowledge, and undocumented knowledge. Examples from the development of SNAP will help to explain these potential research benefits from the design of expert systems.

In developing SNAP, it was first necessary to determine what kind of reasoning processes human experts in staff development would use to plan individualized inservice training programs for teachers. By examining these processes, we learned that the most common inference method used in expert systems—production rules—was inappropriate for a major part of the SNAP system. We determined that production rule reasoning (described elsewhere in this issue) would be appropriate for determining training needs, but not for selecting training options. It then became necessary to "try out" other inference mechanisms available in authoring tools. This process led to our consideration of abductive reasoning, minimal covering and irredundant covering, developed to model diagnostic reasoning in medicine (Reggia *et al.*, 1985), for our problem. Engaging in this process of examining the appropriateness of inference methods has led to further research on the type of reasoning processes that are actually used by educators to make decisions, and the influence of that type of reasoning on decision-making (Haynes and Lubell, 1986a; 1986b).

The second advantage that expert system technology can provide to educational research is to demonstrate to researchers and users the limitations of currently existing knowledge in an area of their discipline. For example, an important component of SNAP is the production rule knowledge base that is used for evaluating observational data to determine an individual teacher's skill in the classroom. The large body of research on teacher effectiveness which was used to create the knowledge base was analyzed systematically and the results were then formed into production rules. By engaging in this process, we found some important limitations to this research including:

- lack of research dealing with students and classrooms at certain grade levels;
- over-generalized conclusions reached from significant but weak correlations;
- lack of rigorous outcome measures on many studies measuring non-achievement outcomes;
- over-reliance on highly inferential procedures for measuring factors such as students' engaged time;
- unjustified substitution of Academic Learning Time for achievement in studies interpreted as measuring achievement as an outcome measure; and
- many unresolved contradictions in findings regarding the relative merits of direct instruction vs. other instructional methods.

As a research tool, then, expert systems can be extremely helpful in guiding researchers to formalize and organize a large body of knowledge, and in understanding the reasoning processes used by experts to make educational decisions.

Cautions to Would-be Expert System Builders and Users

The experiences in building educational expert systems so far have been promising, but a few limits to this enthusiasm are in order.

1. Currently, expert system tools rely heavily on production rules and deductive inference. While considerable portions of educational expertise may be accurately represented in this format, we have found that much of it is not. It would therefore be extremely important that knowledge base authors recognize the influence of a given reasoning process on the outcome of an educational decision, and that either they select tools that can model that process or limit their applications to those areas that can accurately be represented by existing expert system authoring tools.

2. The expertise built into expert systems should reflect the *best* source of knowledge on a topic, and not simply the most easily obtained source of knowledge. Where multiple sources are available, they should all be evaluated and used appropriately.

3. Where expert systems are used for training, thorough evaluation of the system should take place *prior to* adaptation for training purposes so that trainees learn expert information and procedures, rather than novice-level skills.

4. Expert system technology in education is new. Its potential is great, but its performance record is not yet established. Until a successful record is established, expert systems use should be limited to decision support, or second-opinion status. ☐

References

Clancy, W.J., and Letsinger, R. NEOMYCIN: Reconfiguring a Rule-Based Expert System for Application to Teaching. *Proceedings of the Seventh International Joint Conference on Artificial Intelligence.* Vancouver, B.C., Canada: University of British Columbia, 1981.

Davis, R., Buchanan, B., and Shortliffe, E. *Production Rules as a Representation for a Knowledge-Base Consultant Program.* Report STAN-CS-75-519 MEMO AIM-226). Palo Alto, CA: Stanford University, 1975.

Ferrara, J.M., Serna, R.W., and Baer, R.D. *Behavior Consultant: An Expert System for the Diagnosis of Social/Emotional Behavioral Problems* (Computer Program). Logan, UT: Utah State University, 1986.

Haynes, J.A., and Lubell, J. Abductive and Deductive Inference in an Expert System for Needs Assessment in Teacher Training for Special Education. Paper presented at the Association for Behavior Analysis, Milwaukee, WI, 1986a.

Haynes, J.A., and Lubell, J. Artificial Intelligence and Inference Methods to Plan for Teacher Training Programs. *Technical Report # 202.* College Park, MD: University of Maryland, Institute for the Study of Exceptional Children and Youth, 1986b.

Hofmeister, A.M. *CLASS. LD: An Expert System for Classifying Learning Disabilities* (Computer Program). Logan, UT: Utah State University, 1984.

Parry, J.D. The Development and Validation of an Expert System for Reviewing a Special Education Practice. Paper presented at the Association for Behavior Analysis. Milwaukee, WI, 1986.

Prater, M., and Ferrara, J.M. Training Applications of Expert Systems. Paper presented at the Association for Behavior Analysis, Milwaukee, WI, 1986.

Reggia, J.A., Nau, D.S., and Wang, P.Y. A Theory of Abductive Inference in Diagnostic Expert Systems. *Technical Report TR-1338,* University of Maryland, Department of Computer Science, 1985.

Waterman, D.A. *A Guide to Expert Systems.* Reading, MA: Addison-Wesley Publishing Company, 1986.

This research was sponsored by Grants G008302314 and G008530156 from the United States Department of Education. However, the contents of this report do not necessarily reflect the policy of the Department of Education, and no official endorsement should be inferred.

Using an Expert System for Complex Conceptual Training

Joseph M. Ferrara, Mary Anne Prater, and Richard Baer

Suppose your two-year-old son, Tommy, has suddenly become infatuated with the word "blue." Every time you point to something and ask, "What color is this?" Tommy says, "blue." You're tired of him calling everything blue, so you decide to teach him that some things are blue and other things are not blue. Intuitively, you point to Tommy's blue shirt and say, "Tommy's shirt is blue." Next, pointing to Daddy's shirt you say, "Daddy's shirt is not blue, it's green." You are beginning the process of teaching Tommy the basic concept, "blue."

Basic Concepts

Basic concepts, like blue, comprise a good portion of any language. They are ideas or discriminations that cannot be easily described using words. Thus, one must employ both examples and nonexamples to teach them (Englemann and Carnine, 1982). To illustrate, consider that Tommy's parent, as described above, used Tommy's shirt as an example of something that was blue and his own shirt as an example of something that was not blue, a nonexample. By continually presenting Tommy with examples and nonexamples of blue, Tommy eventually will learn to discriminate between blue and other colors. When he has this skill, it can be said that Tommy has learned the concept of blue.

In recent years, educators and computer scientists have joined in efforts to develop computer programs that can assist in teaching basic concepts. Most of these programs generate examples and nonexamples of the basic concept they are designed to teach.

Complex Concepts

Basic concepts vary along only one dimension, for example, color—something is or is not blue; temperature—something is or is not cold; or shape—something is or is not round. In contrast,

Joseph M. Ferrara, Mary Anne Prater, and Richard Baer are with the Artificial Intelligence Research and Development Unit, Utah State University, Logan, Utah.

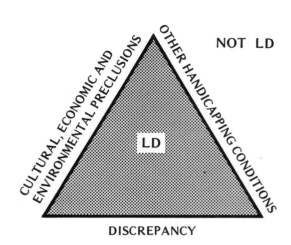

Figure 1

Concept of "Learning Disabilities"

complex concepts are (a) multifaceted, they vary along two or more dimensions, and (b) dynamic, the way they vary along each dimension is defined by a number of variables. Furthermore, several of the concept's dimensions may interact. Thus, a change in one dimension could have an impact on our judgment regarding another dimension.

The concept, "learning disabled student," provides an example of a complex concept. Before students can be classified as learning disabled, they must meet a variety of criteria. In Utah, these criteria define three discrete dimensions:

1. A discrepancy between students' expected academic performances and their actual academic performances must exist.
2. The students' learning problems must not be the result of some other handicapping condition (i.e., mental retardation, behavior disorder).
3. The students' learning problems must not be the results of cultural, economic, or environmental factors.

Thus, as is illustrated in Figure 1, the complex concept, "learning disabled student," is multifaceted.

The complex concept, "learning disabled student," is also dynamic. To illustrate, consider that in the State of Utah, the discrepancy between expected and actual academic performance is determined by administering an intelligence test and one or more achievement tests. A discrepancy formula is then used to calculate scores which describe the degree to which the students' academic performances fall below their expected performances. If students' discrepancy scores are greater than 40, they are eligible for a learning disabilities (LD) classification. This criterion defines one of the dimensions of the complex concept, "learning disabled student." However, this criterion may be influenced by a number of variables. For example, suppose a student who comes from a home where only Spanish is spoken has a discrepancy score of 45. If tests standardized only on Anglo students were administered to this student, our confidence in the discrepancy score is altered. We are less than 100 percent confident that the discrepancy is truly 45, because scores on tests not standardized on Spanish-speaking students were used in the calculation. The actual degree to which this fact decreases our confidence is unknown and requires a best estimate or professional judgment. That is, a degree of uncertainty has been introduced. Additionally, the information that the student comes from a Spanish-speaking home raises another issue. The learning problems of a Spanish-speaking student may be due to cultural factors.

The example above illustrates the dynamic nature of complex concepts. The fact that the student comes from a Spanish-speaking home alters the confidence we can have in two of the three dimensions that define "learning disabled students." This is illustrated in Figure 2.

When the best professionals identify learning disabled students, they consider the student's characteristics in all three dimensions that define this complex concept. They understand that the confidence with which one can conclude a student is learning disabled varies with specific circumstances. The student's age, IQ, and cultural background, as well as the quality of information provided by tests and other sources, are a few of the specific circumstances which modify judgments regarding learning disabled students. Skilled professionals understand that the criteria for a learning disabilities classification are dynamic rather than absolute.

Since the dynamic characteristics of complex concepts are not always obvious, they are often difficult to teach and learn. Research suggests that there are serious problems associated with learning disabilities classification decision-making (Hofmeister, 1983; Sabatino, 1983; Thurlow and Ysseldyke, 1979; Ysseldyke, 1983). It appears that many of those charged with the responsibility of qualifying students as learning disabled have failed to learn to accurately do so. This failure may be related to the difficulty associated with teaching complex concepts.

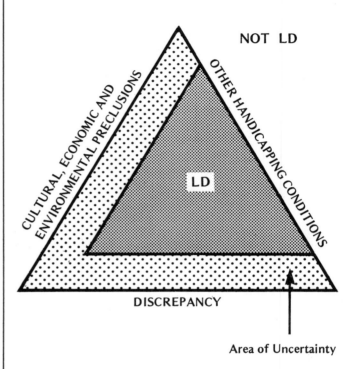

Figure 2

LD with Two Uncertain Dimensions

CLASS. LD2: An Expert System

In response to the need for better systems for classifying LD students Ferrara and Hofmeister (1984) developed an expert system, CLASS. LD2. Expert systems are computer programs which are designed to ask the user about a problem and to provide the same advice one might receive from an expert consultant (Harmon and King, 1984; Weiss and Kulikowski, 1984). CLASS. LD2 is designed to provide the user with a second opinion regarding the probability that a student can be classified as LD. The CLASS. LD2 knowledge base contains information and decision rules obtained from experts in the area of LD classification, federal law, state regulations, and current literature describing best practices in the area of student assessment (Ferrara, Parry, and Lubke, 1985).

The knowledge base of an effective expert system must be designed to explicitly define each dimension and dynamic characteristic of the complex concept or concepts associated with its knowledge area. CLASS. LD2's rules define the complex concept "learning disabled student" (Martindale, Ferrara, and Campbell, 1986).

LD.Trainer

LD.Trainer (Prater and Althouse, 1986), a computer-assisted instruction (CAI) program, was developed to teach preservice and inservice educators to make appropriate learning disabilities classification decisions. The program was designed to utilize the rules of CLASS. LD2 in a simple and cost-effective instructional format. Individuals who complete training with this system should be able to accurately discriminate between students who should and should not be classified as learning disabled in the State of Utah.

LD.Trainer consists of a series of 13 lessons, each of which presents a portion of the complex concept, "learning disabled student." The lessons are designed to teach trainees to determine whether a student meets the criteria for a learning disabilities classification.

In developing the lessons for LD.Trainer a modified version of the concept instruction model suggested by Merrill and Tennyson (1977) was employed. Each lesson was divided into two parts, instruction and practice.

During instruction, trainees are first given a definition which describes one or more important attributes distinguishing an LD student. Definitions are followed by matched examples and nonexamples of the attributes. Next trainees read a brief case study describing an LD student. Data from the case study are then fed into the computer, and trainees examine the system's conclusions regarding whether the student can qualify as LD. Following this, they read an explanation of how the system arrived at its conclusions. The explanations detail how certain attributes (i.e., those listed in the definition), were used to arrive at the conclusion. Trainees then read a second case study, a nonexample, and enter a second set of data. This time the value of the attributes of interest are changed and the trainees are provided an opportunity to view how changes in these attributes affect the system's conclusions. This process is repeated with different case studies focusing on the same attribute.

During the practice portion of each lesson trainees again read a brief case study. After doing so, they make decisions regarding whether the student is LD and write their decisions and justifications for them in the printed material provided. Trainees then enter the data from the case study into the computer and compare their written conclusions with the system's. The printed materials provide justification for the system's conclusions by focusing on the same attributes as were presented during the instructional part of the lesson. This process is repeated with a second case study.

Research

As part of a week-long inservice program, 21 practicing teachers and administrators participated in one of two training conditions. Eleven completed LD.Trainer materials and ten were given representative special education student files and ran consultations with the expert system, CLASS. LD2.

On pre-posttests trainees were given 12 case studies on which they were asked to identify the student as qualifying or not qualifying as learning disabled. Preliminary results indicate that the trainees in both groups improved their performance following participation in the training activities. However, trainees in the LD.Trainer group scored significantly ($p < .01$) higher than the CLASS.LD2 group.

Conclusions

Preliminary research comparing CLASS.LD2 and LD. Trainer suggests that both systems are effective in teaching the complex concept, "learning disabled student." Trainees who ran data from files on learning disabled students through the CLASS.LD2 expert system improved in their ability to accurately identify students who could and could not be classified as learning disabled. However, trainees who systematically completed the LD.Trainer materials showed even greater improvement in their ability to accurately identify learning disabled students.

The preliminary success of the LD.Trainer program demonstrates the potential of modified expert systems as tools for teaching complex concepts. LD.Trainer systematically varies each attribute which affects the three dimensions of the complex concept, "learning disabled student," and allows trainees to observe how changes in the attributes change the conclusions drawn. The essence of the system is that relative to each attribute, trainees are presented with examples and nonexamples of the complex concept "learning disabled student." This is essentially the procedure used in teaching simple concepts such as colors. However, LD.Trainer systematically applies the procedure to each attribute in each dimension of the complex concept, and provides trainees with an opportunity to learn how the attributes and dimensions interact.

LD.Trainer is one of the first CAI programs that has attempted to teach a complex concept. It has demonstrated that effective instructional programs can be developed by combining expert system technology with what is known about effective concept instruction. In so doing it opens the door for the development of other programs that could efficiently and cost-effectively teach other complex concepts. ☐

References

Engelmann, S., and Carnine, D. *Theory of Instruction: Principles and Applications.* New York: Irvington Publishers, 1982.

Ferrara, J.M., and Hofmeister, A.M. *CLASS. LD2: An Expert System for Classifying Learning Disabilities* [Computer program]. Logan: Utah State University, 1984.

Ferrara, J.M., Parry, J.D., and Lubke, M.M. CLASS. LD2: An Expert System for Student Classification. Technical Paper. Logan: Utah State University (ERIC Document Reproduction Service No. ED 263 734), 1985.

Harmon, P., and King, D. *Expert Systems: Artificial Intelligence in Business.* New York: John Wiley and Sons, 1984.

Hofmeister, A.M. *Comments on Part B, Section 618: Evaluation and Part E, Research and Education of the Handicapped, Public Law 94-142.* Testimony before the Senate Committee on Labor and Human Resources, Subcommittee on the Handicapped, *Congressional Record.* Washington, D.C.: Government Printing Office, 1983.

Martindale, E.S., Ferrara, J.M., and Campbell, B.W. Accuracy of CLASS. LD2: An Expert System for Classifying Learning Disabled Students. *Computers in Human Behavior,* in press, 1986.

Merrill, M.D., and Tennyson, R. *Teaching Concepts: An Instructional Design Guide.* Englewood Cliffs: Educational Technology Publications, 1977.

Prater, M., and Althouse, B. *LD.TRAINER* [Computer program]. Logan: Utah State University, 1986.

Sabatino, D.A. The House that Jack Built. *Annual Review of Learning Disabilities,* 1983, 1:23-24.

Thurlow, M., and Ysseldyke, J.W. Current Assessment and Decision-Making Practices in Model Programs for Learning Disabled Students. *Learning Disability Quarterly,* 1979, 2:15-24.

Weiss, S.M., and Kulikowski, C.A. *A Practical Guide to Designing Expert Systems.* Totowa, NJ: Rowman and Allanheld, 1984.

Ysseldyke, J.E. Current Practices in Making Psychoeducational Decisions About Learning Disabled Students. *Annual Review of Learning Disabilities,* 1983, 31-38.

A Comparison of Input and Output for a Knowledge Based System for Educational Diagnosis

Paul Juell and John Wasson

Expert systems (knowledge based systems), a branch of artificial intelligence, provide a way to codify knowledge relevant to a particular domain into a computer format in such a way that a user may utilize the information in the absence of the human expert who originally provided the information for the knowledge base.

The application of expert systems to psychoeducational diagnosis is needed and important (Abunawass, 1986; Hofmeister and Ferrara, 1986; Hofmeister and Lubke, 1986; Jones, 1984; Wilson and Welsh, 1986), although the area is just beginning to be developed.

This article describes a knowledge based system for educational diagnosis in the area of diagnosing learning problems in mathematics and compares the form diagnostic rules take when formulated by a subject matter expert with the form required for inclusion in an expert system shell. This information should be of interest to a person who wants to set up an expert system in the area of educational diagnosis. It should also be of interest if one wishes to compare the formulation of an educational diagnosis with the formulation necessary for inclusion in a computer based expert system.

One of the problems in the easy construction of knowledge based systems is the efficient translation of the information provided by the expert source in its original form to a form that can be utilized by the computer system. The original form of the knowledge may be provided in text (books and articles) or may be formulated by a human expert. This article will present both of these types of information for a described domain—the diagnosis of learning problems in ele-

Paul Juell is Assistant Professor of Computer Science at North Dakota State University, Fargo, North Dakota. John Wasson is Professor of Special Education and a member of the Education Department Faculty at Moorhead State University, Moorhead, Minnesota.

Area	Subtest
Content	A. Numeration B. Fractions C. Geometry and Symbols
Operations	D. Addition E. Subtraction F. Multiplication G. Division H. Mental Computation I. Numerical Reasoning
Applications	J. Word Problems K. Missing Elements L. Money M. Measurement N. Time

Table 1: Subtests of the KeyMath Diagnostic Arithmetic Test by Area.

mentary mathematics—by providing the source data used in interpreting the results of a diagnostic arithmetic test, the KeyMath Diagnostic Arithmetic Test (Connolly, Nachtman, and Pritchett, 1976) and the form the data must be in to be used by an expert system shell, MicroExpert Version 1.0 (Thompson and Thompson, 1985). Micro-Expert provides a vehicle which is relatively easy to use. The product provides consistency in diagnosis, it should yield the same results each time the system is used with a similar case, and it never ignores special circumstances no matter how infrequently they occur.

The KeyMath Diagnostic Arithmetic Test

The KeyMath Diagnostic Arithmetic Test is a standardized test widely used to assess problems in learning arithmetic among school children. The instrument consists of fourteen subtests measuring arithmetic skills in three broad areas: content, operations, and applications, see Table 1.

The results of this test could be interpreted by referring to a pupil's profile of relative standings on the fourteen subtests, but this interpretation would provide very little useful information as to where to start remediation and what specifically to do with a child encountering difficulty in learning arithmetic. A more profitable approach to the interpretation of this instrument follows.

The following procedures can be used to interpret the results of a KeyMath Diagnostic Arith-

Addition and subtraction facts
Column addition and subtracting without regrouping
Column addition with regrouping
Subtraction with regrouping
Multiplication and division facts
Multiplication and division by a one-digit number with-
    out regrouping
Multiplication by a one-digit multiplier with regrouping
Division by a one-digit divisor with regrouping
Multiplication by a two-digit or greater multiplier
Division by a two-digit or greater divisor

*Table 2. Hierarchy of arithmetic computational skills with
whole numbers.*

metic Test, and these procedures have been used by the second author to train educational diagnosticians. This method does not use the results of all the the subtests of KeyMath. Only eight of the fourteen subtests are used. In order to apply this strategy, it is necessary to know responses to all of the items on the addition, subtraction, multiplication, and division subtests and to know the total number of items correct on the word problems, money, measurement, and time subtests.

Interpretive Strategy for the KeyMath Diagnostic Arithmetic Test

Assume the KeyMath test has been administered to a pupil by an adequately trained test administrator. Assume further that motivational factors were such that the pupil put forth his or her best effort on the test and that the answers were correctly recorded by the examiner.

The first step is to place the student at the right stage in the hierarchy of arithmetical computational skills with whole numbers. These ten skills are listed in Table 2.

It is possible to classify the pupil's responses to the individual items that make up the addition, subtraction, multiplication, and division subtests in such a way as to indicate at which developmental stage of whole number operations the child falls down. For this analysis, items in the addition subtest will be referred to by "A" and the item number. Thus "A-7" refers to item number seven in the addition subtest. In a similar manner "S" refers to the subtraction subtest, "M" to the multiplication subtest, and "D" to the division subtest.

Rules for interpreting the results of the Key-Math Diagnostic Arithmetic Test:

1. If the pupil makes more than one error among the items A-1, A-2, A-3, A-4, A-5, A-7, S-1, S-2, S-3, S-4, S-5, and S-7, the level at which to commence instruction is addition and subtraction facts.
2. If the pupil makes any errors among the items A-6 and S-6, the level at which to commence instruction is column addition and subtraction without regrouping.
3. If the pupil makes any errors among the items A-8, A-9, and A-10, the level at which to commence instruction is column addition with regrouping.
4. If the pupil makes any errors among the items S-8, S-9, and S-10, the level at which to commence instruction is subtraction with regrouping.
5. If the pupil makes more than one error among the items M-1, M-2, M-3, M-4, M-5, D-1, D-2, D-3, and D-4, the level at which to commence instruction is multiplication and division facts.
6. If the pupil makes an error on item D-6, the level at which to commence instruction is multiplication and division by a one-digit number without regrouping.
7. If the pupil makes any errors among the items M-6 and M-7, the level at which to commence instruction is multiplication by a one-digit multiplier with regrouping.
8. If the pupil makes an error on item D-6, the level at which to commence instruction is division by a one-digit divisor with regrouping.
9. If the pupil makes an error on item M-8, the level at which to commence instruction is multiplication by a two-digit or greater multiplier.
10. If the pupil makes an error on item D-7, the level at which to commence instruction is division by a two-digit or greater divisor.

The above rules are checked sequentially starting with rule number 1 until the level at which to commence instruction is identified. Once the level at which the pupil's knowledge of arithmetic facts and procedures has been determined, it is necessary to establish the relative emphasis to be placed on word problems, money problems, measurement problems, or problems involving time. This determination is made by considering the level of performance on the four mentioned subtests in comparison to the identified level of skill in the ten stage hierarchy. This determination, to include or not to include problems in each of the four areas, can be made by referring to Table 3.

For a given level of skill development in whole number computational strategy, if the pupil's score on one of the four subtests is lower than the value shown in Table 3, then the pupil would need to emphasize that area in his or her remedial program. For example, say that the identified area at which to provide remediation is addition and subtraction facts for a pupil who receives the following subtest scores: word problems - 9, money - 8, measurement - 17, and time - 10.

These results would be interpreted as follows: Initial remediation should start with addition and subtraction facts. Word problems do not have to be emphasized (a score of 9 is not less than 9). Money problems should be emphasized (a score of 8 is less than 9). Measurement problems do not have to be emphasized (a score of 17 is not less than 16). Problems involving time should be emphasized (a score of 10 is less than 13).

This then is the way in which a specific diagnosis is made utilizing the pupil's pattern of scores on various subtests of the KeyMath. Later in this article we will consider how this interpretation would look if it were coded in such a way as to be utilized by a computer based expert system. For this purpose we will use the MicroExpert system (Thompson and Thompson, 1985).

The MicroExpert, Version 1.0
Consultation System

MicroExpert (Thompson and Thompson, 1985) is an expert system shell which requires little knowledge about computer programming to use. Rather than being written in Lisp or Prolog, two widely used computer languages for expert systems, it is written in UCSD Pascal. Pascal is a widely used computer programming language, and UCSD Pascal is written for use on a microcomputer such as the Apple Computer.

MicroExpert has an editor which allows the expert to prepare input to the program in an efficient manner. The raw data for the program is prepared in the form of rules, prompts, and translation.

An example of a rule is
    If KeyMath admin is yes
    and mult div facts is yes
    and sub with is no
    and add with is no
    and add sub without is no
    and add sub facts is no
    then area is five
An example of a prompt is
    prompt mult 1-dig with
    Is the number correct for items M-6 and M-7 less than 2?
Like most well designed expert system shells, MicroExpert allows the user to query the system about its rationale when running a program or in MicroExpert terms—"conducting a consultation."
Rules for interpreting the results of the KeyMath Diagnostic Arithmetic Test in a form usable by the MicroExpert system:

The 12 rules required by MicroExpert to identify the area of diagnostic significance for a particular child are as follows:

Rule 1
If KeyMath admin is no
then area is admin KeyMath.

Rule 2
If KeyMath admin is yes
and add sub facts is yes
then area is one.

Rule 3
If KeyMath admin is yes
and add sub without is yes
and add sub facts is no
then area is two.

Rule 4
If KeyMath admin is yes
and add with is yes
and add sub without is no
and add sub facts is no
then area is three.

Rule 5
If KeyMath admin is yes
and sub with is yes
and add with is no
and add sub without is no
and add sub facts is no
then area is four.

Rule 6
If KeyMath admin is yes
and mult div facts is yes
and sub with is no
and add with is no
and add sub without is no
and add sub facts is no
then area is five.

Rule 7
If KeyMath admin is yes
and mult div without is yes
and mult div facts is no
and sub with is no
and add with is no
and add sub without is no
and add sub facts is no
then area is six.

Rule 8
If KeyMath admin is yes
and mult 1-dig with is yes
and mult div without is no
and mult div facts is no
and sub with is no
and add with is no
and add sub without is no
and add sub facts is no
then area is seven.

Area	Word Problems	Money	Measurement	Time
Addition and subtraction facts	5	4	6	6
Column addition and subtraction without regrouping	5	5	8	8
Column addition with regrouping	7	7	12	11
Subtraction with regrouping	8	7	13	12
Multiplication and division facts	9	9	16	13
Multiplication and division by a one-digit number without regrouping	10	9	18	14
Multiplication by a one-digit multiplier with regrouping	10	9	18	14
Division by a one-digit divisor with regrouping	10	10	19	15
Multiplication by a two-digit or greater multiplier	10	10	20	15
Division by a two-digit or greater divisor	11	11	21	16

Table 3. Cutoff points for each of four KeyMath Diagnostic Arithmetic Subtests based on level of skill development.

Rule 9
If KeyMath admin is yes
and div 1-dig with is yes
and mult 1-dig with is no
and mult div without is no
and mult div facts is no
and sub with is no
and sub without is no
and add sub facts is no
then area is eight.

Rule 10
If KeyMath admin is yes
and mult 2-dig is yes
and div 1-dig with is no
and mult 1-dig with is no
and mult div without is no
and mult div facts is no
and sub with is no
and sub without is no
and add sub facts is no
then area is nine.

Rule 11
If KeyMath admin is yes
and div 2-dig is yes
and mult 2-dig is no
and div 1-dig with is no
and mult 1-dig with is no
and mult div without is no
and mult div facts is no

Expert Systems and Intelligent CAI

and add with is no
and sub without is no
and add sub facts is no
then area is ten.

Rule 12
If KeyMath admin is yes
and div 2-dig is no
and mult 2-dig is no
and div 1-dig with is no
and mult 1-dig with is no
and mult div without is no
and mult div facts is no
and add with is no
and sub without is no
and add sub facts is no
then area is no deficiency.

In addition to the above 12 rules the systems also has 20 rules each in the areas of word problems, money, measurement, and time.

Summary and Conclusions

This article shows how an expert system shell can be used to provide assistance in an area of educational diagnosis. It also shows the translation that is necessary to go from the operational rules used by the expert diagnostician to the rule base required by the expert system to be used in the absence of the expert. Preparation of this system requires an explicit formulation of rules used in educational diagnosis, and thus the rules might be more specific than if they were only used in practice rather than being formulated for inclusion in an expert system. This area of artificial intelligence is an important one and should be developed further to aid the educational practitioner in the specific assessment of school based learning problems. ☐

References

Abunawass, A.M. *SEDS: Special Education Diagnostic Expert System.* Unpublished master's thesis, North Dakota State University, Fargo, North Dakota, 1986.

Hofmeister, A.M., and Ferrara, J.M. Expert Systems and Special Education. *Exceptional Children*, 1986, *53*, 235-239.

Hofmeister, A.M., and Lubke, M.M. Expert Systems: Implications for the Diagnosis and Treatment of Learning Disabilities. *Learning Disability Quarterly*, 1986, *9*, 133-137.

Jones, M. Expert Systems: Their Potential Roles Within Special Education. *Peabody Journal of Education*, 1984, *62*, 52-66.

Thompson, W., and Thompson, B. *MicroExpert, Version 1.0.* New York: McGraw-Hill, 1985.

Wilson, B.G., and Welsh, J.R. Small Knowledge-Based Systems in Education and Training: Something New Under the Sun. *Educational Technology*, 1986, *26*(11), 7-13.

Expert Systems in the Classroom

Ronald D. Owston and Herbert Wideman

Over the last several years, expert systems have had a significant impact on business and industry. They are being used in such diverse fields as investment management, insurance underwriting, mineral exploration, and industrial design. Edward Feigenbaum reported that within IBM alone more than 100 different expert system applications have been developed ("AAAI Conference," 1988). Business and industry analysts typically credit expert systems with increases in productivity, distributing specialized expertise throughout the organization, systematizing decision-making, and making operations more cost-effective (Fiegenbaum, McCorduck, and Nii, 1988).

The impact of expert systems on the field of education, however, has been minimal. Most work to date has concentrated on developing prototype expert systems that either underlie intelligent computer-based instruction or diagnose student learning problems. One of the main reasons for the lag in applying expert systems to education lies in the high cost of developing knowledge bases in AI languages such as LISP and Prolog. But costs are now coming down. Within the last few years some 50 MS DOS and Macintosh expert system shells have become available. These shells allow users without AI programming expertise to construct knowledge bases using English-like rules much more rapidly than would be possible with AI languages. As a result expert systems can now be considered a feasible technology for use in schools.

The range of potential applications of expert systems as teacher instructional and management tools and as student learning tools is extremely diverse. For teachers, expert system advisors have the potential of improving productivity and aiding in consistent decision-making in such areas as classroom management, instructional planning and design, student diagnosis, and timetabling. They can

---

Ronald D. Owston is Director, Centre for the Study of Computers in Education, York University, North York, Ontario, Canada. **Herbert Wideman** is Research Associate at the Centre.

also be used to capture and share the expertise of master teachers within a school. These teachers have often accumulated considerable breadth and depth of knowledge and have developed rules of thumb for solving educational problems. Expert systems can provide a means letting others benefit from their expertise and of ensuring that it is not lost if they transfer or retire.

Another application of expert systems lies in teacher training and professional development. Teachers can learn how experts solve problems through interacting with knowledge bases of the kind mentioned above. While the knowledge bases may not be specifically designed as instructional tools, users can ask why the system is posing a particular question or how the system arrived at a given solution, and thereby gain insights into how experts obtain problem solutions.

For students, expert systems can be used to create learning environments in which knowledge can be explored and manipulated at will. Intelligent tutoring systems are one way in which this can be done. Ideally, these systems know how to teach, what they are teaching, and to whom they are teaching and, thus, can provide a rich interactive learning environment (Yazdani, 1988). Another application of expert systems as a student learning tool lies in having students create their own knowledge bases using expert system shells (Trollip and Lippert, 1987). When expert systems are used in this way, students must make explicit the classification schemes, multivariate reasoning, means-end analysis, and production rules employed on a given content domain to reach conclusions (Wideman and Owston, 1988). The process of making explicit cognitive strategies such as these has been shown to enhance metacognitive functioning and promote increased problem-solving performance (Brown et al., 1983). Moreover, students can develop knowledge bases in most curriculum areas and can do so without learning a programming language.

In this article, we describe two projects that we have undertaken. One involves the development of an expert system advisor for teacher use, the other looks at how children can develop their own expert systems.

The Teacher Advisory System

Our first project was directed at creating an expert system advisor to manage a school microcomputer network. We wanted to first build a prototype system and study the problems associated with the prototyping, and then develop a working system for routine classroom use.

The project was carried out in a large high school in Toronto. The school had a network of

Figure 1

Network Advisor

Figure 1

Network Advisor

knew what steps should be taken. One branch of the tree diagram for the system developed during the project is illustrated in Figure 1. This branch provides a solution to the problem of a student, with a valid ID and password, being able to log on at one workstation but not another.

We relied on the teacher/manager as domain expert to provide us with a description of the problem area and the heuristics used to solve network log-on difficulties. We then coded the knowledge base using the KES expert system shell on an MS DOS machine. One of the first problems we encountered in the development of the advisor was deciding on the format in which the teacher/manager would give us the domain facts and rules. Initially, we asked him to freely draw a tree diagram that would represent the knowledge domain. This did not prove satisfactory because it did not provide him enough structure to guide his work. The result was that branches were left incomplete and actions were sometimes omitted. To give him more structure we provided him with a copy of *Harvard Graphics,* a graphics presentation software package that has an easy-to-use, menu-driven component for creating tree diagrams. This solution generally proved workable as it imposed more rigor in the drawing and resulted in neat, readable diagrams. A drawback of the package is that only several branches or levels of the tree structure can be displayed at any one time so that an overview of the entire knowledge base could not be obtained. We are still searching for a more satisfactory representation procedure, but so far we have been unable to find one.

We faced another dilemma in designing the system: whether to structure the knowledge base so that the end user is presented with a series of binary questions (e.g., "Can the student log on at another terminal? Yes-No"), or whether to structure it so that multiple choice questions are presented (e.g. "Student can log on at (a) another terminal in class, (b) another terminal in school, (c) no other terminal?"). The former format is easier for users to answer, and requires that the user collect only that information specifically needed to diagnose the problem, yet it is not as efficient a way for the system to arrive at a diagnosis. The latter format, while more demanding and, perhaps, intimidating to the user, requires less coding and processing time. We ultimately chose to use the binary format because the knowledge base was not particularly large and thus efficiency was not a serious concern, and because we sought to make the advisor as user friendly as possible.

During the knowledge base design we encountered diagnoses that would have been too complex for teachers to implement. We handled this situa-

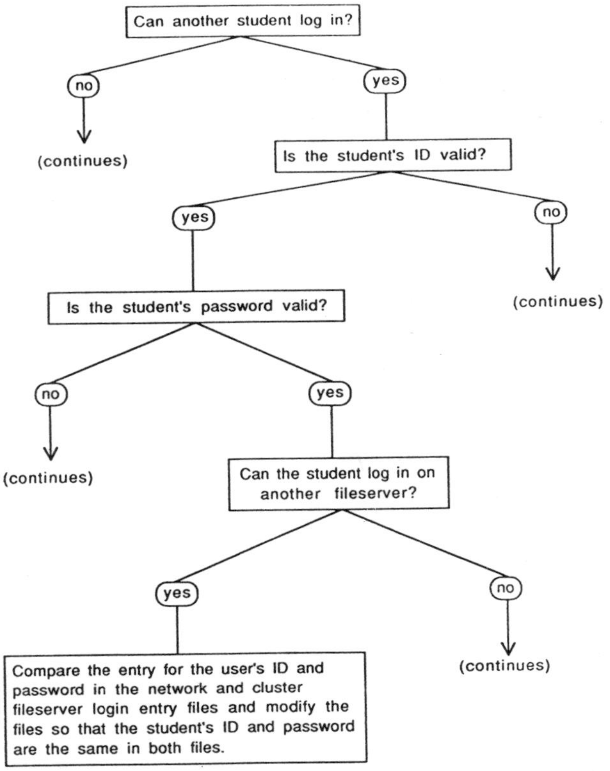

160 Unisys ICON educational microcomputers connected to a cluster of eight fileservers, the largest network of ICON computers then in use. These machines are distributed throughout the school in labs, as well as at individual sites for special purposes. Because of the uniqueness of the network, a large portion of one teacher's time was devoted to network maintenance and helping other teachers solve network-related problems. Many of the inquiries the teacher/manager received were routine in nature and therefore were considered good candidates for inclusion in an expert system advisor. The first area we chose for incorporating into an advisor consisted of a set of problems related to students being unable to log onto the network. This was thought to be a good problem area to begin with because (1) it was one of the most frequently encountered network difficulties, (2) it was a bounded problem area, one in which solutions to almost all log-on difficulties were known, and (3) classroom teachers could correct most of the problems themselves once they

tion by giving the user the message "See the network manager." An attempt was made to minimize the number of times this diagnosis appeared so that teachers would not view the advisor as unhelpful, not bother to use it, and go directly to the manager when they encountered log on problems.

While the network advisor is still undergoing development, early indications are that the system is usable and will likely result in increased productivity for teachers by helping them to rapidly diagnose some of the most common network problems and relieve the network manager of some routine work. The advisor will then be field tested to further assess its utility.

The Children's Expert System

The second project that we carried out involved the development and use of expert systems by children. (See Wideman and Owston, 1988, for a detailed description of the project.) Given that expert system shells allow users to structure their own expert systems by means of menu-driven interfaces and English-like rules, we were interested in testing the feasibility of using expert systems with younger students and examining some of the processes and outcomes related to student development of expert systems. Our study took place in a grade seven class of a senior elementary school outside of Toronto. Students accessed the IBM Expert System Environment on York University's mainframe computer via modems and two microcomputers in their resource centre.

Together with the science teacher (who had limited experience with computers and no background in expert systems), we planned a 17-hour unit of work on expert systems that integrated into a part of their science curriculum which focused on the classification of living organisms. First, the teacher introduced the unit with a discussion of classificatory systems in general, and demonstrated how a simple prototype expert system could be used for classification. We then took the students through the construction of a simple expert system designed to classify two-dimensional objects. The class was next divided into ten groups of three, and each group entered this simple knowledge base into the computer and debugged it. We concluded this introductory phase of the unit by having the student groups develop another simple expert system based on an example of a scheme for classifying common sports.

The main task of the unit, which was to develop an expert system to classify living organisms such as birds, fish, plants, and mammals at the class, order, and species level, was begun next. Each group was given a different assignment and a set of research materials from which they could extract the necessary classificatory keys and information. Before the students started we modeled a similar assignment by showing them how to use the reference materials, how to develop the classificatory keys, how to delineate the necessary parameters and rules, and the way to draw the tree diagram. As students worked on their assignments, the researchers and the teacher helped groups as needed by mediating their discussions, asking questions, and offering hints.

During and after each class period we wrote detailed notes on the classroom interactions and activities that occurred when the students were working both on and off the computer. In addition, throughout the project we conducted informal interviews with the teacher and with individual students or groups of students. Our aim was to develop a "thick description" of students' experiences and work processes as they engaged in their expert system projects, and from these data to develop working hypotheses using qualitative data analytic techniques.

By the end of the time allotted for the unit, all but one of the groups was able to complete their expert system. An example of a tree diagram developed by one group for classifying angiosperm plants by the type of fruit they produce is given in Figure 2. On the whole we found that the development of simple rule-based expert systems can provide a valuable educational experience at an age earlier than one might expect. Students were able to interact with the expert system shell with considerable ease after a short period of familiarization. Furthermore, we found that the project required students to develop a deep understanding of the interrelatedness of taxonomic strata and keys and of the procedures for rule-based classification. Our observations suggested that the project activities did, indeed, promote students' acquisition, practice, and extension of their cognitive and metacognitive skills.

We concluded from this study that student development of expert systems could likely be undertaken in any subject domain provided certain constraints are kept in mind. These include providing adequate time for planning and implementing the unit of work, introducing the unit gradually with many concrete examples and hands on activities, providing adequate assistance to students as they are working, and structuring the unit to allow group work.

Conclusions

Both of our projects suggest that expert systems do have a valuable role to play in the classroom, particularly when they are created using shell programs. Teachers can benefit from knowledge bases

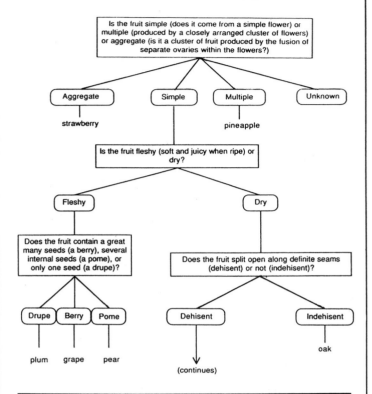

Figure 2
Fruit Classification Tree Diagram

by receiving direct advice on instructional concerns, by seeing how experts deal with these concerns, and by being able to capture the expertise of master teachers. Students can develop cognitive and metacognitive skills through creating expert systems in a variety of curriculum areas without having to learn a programming language. ☐

References

AAAI Conference Report. *Expert Systems,* 1988, *5*(4.), 340.

Brown, A. L., Bransford, J. D., Ferrara, R. A., and Campione, J. C. Learning, Remembering, and Understanding. In Flavell, J. H. and Markham, E. M. (Eds.), *Handbook of Child Psychology: Vol 1 Cognitive Development.* New York: Wiley, 1983, 77-166.

Feigenbaum, E., McCorduck, P., and Nii, H. P. *The Rise of the Expert Company.* New York: Times Books, 1988.

Trollip, S. R., and Lippert, R. C. Constructing Knowledge Bases: A Promising Instructional Tool. *Journal of Computer Based Instruction,* 1987, *14* (2), 44-48.

Wideman, H. H., and Owston, R. D. Student Development of an Expert System: A Case Study. *Journal of Computer Based Instruction,* 1988, *15* (3), 88-94.

Yazdani, M. Expert Tutoring Systems. *Expert Systems,* 1988, *5* (4), 270-271.

Developing a Low-Cost Expert System in a Liberal Arts Environment

Antonio M. Lopez, Jr.

Professor Edward Feigenbaum of Stanford University is quoted (Harmon and King, 1985) as defining an expert system as "a computer program that uses knowledge and inference procedures to solve problems that are difficult enough to require significant human expertise for their solution." The computer programs described by Professor Feigenbaum can be written in any computer language (procedural or applicative) or without a computer language. Pascal, Ada, C, and Modula-2 are examples of procedural languages used to build expert systems. The usual applicative languages used are LISP and PROLOG. On the market today, there are many available expert systems building tools (Harmon et al. 1985) that eliminate the programming aspect by having the "builder" answer a variety of questions asked by the software product. These packages, called expert system shells, provide a quick way of developing an expert system prototype. Such shells are limited in their scope.

Expert Systems and AI

Expert systems is a field of research rooted in Artificial Intelligence (AI) and thus is very young. However, the low-cost production of powerful 32-bit microprocessors has made developing an expert system on a desktop microcomputer possible, even if one develops the system from scratch using PROLOG. It is the combination of these powerful microprocessors and the commercially available expert system shells that have caused the subject to receive notoriety in the last two years. There has been too much hype and exaggeration about expert systems; too much has been promised at the desktop level and very little delivered (Liebowitz, 1987, Myers, 1986). This article details a realistic process of developing a low-cost expert system in a liberal arts environment.

In general, the development of an expert system is a challenging and all-consuming enterprise, hitherto left to special laboratories at Stanford, Carnegie-Mellon, MIT, and others (Bobrow et al., 1986). The process of learning about expert systems by developing one in a liberal arts environment is no longer cost-prohibitive nor time-impossible. However, the investigation of such a process on a small hardware and software budget and in a liberal arts setting does make the approach predestined.

The minimal hardware requirement can be met with a 32-bit microcomputer having one megabyte of main memory and 20 megabytes of secondary memory (total cost: $2,300). The minimal software requirement can be met with a small PROLOG interpreter, an applicative programming language (total cost: $100). Given this hardware and software, the "low road" (Brown, 1984) of expert system development is preordained. The low road of development in turn suggests "exploratory programming"—a style of program development in which there is incremental, parallel development of program specifications and implementation (Sheil, 1984). Even with these set parameters, the key to the successful development of an expert system lies in the appropriate selection of a problem to be solved (Prerau, 1985).

Academic inquiry into a problem domain does not operate in the same way that a commercial, for-profit, industrial endeavor would (Romiszowski, 1987). Industry, for example, might stress the value of solving the problem, the availability of a true expert, or the use of non-AI techniques, since AI is still in its infancy. Academic concerns, on the other hand, might be the knowledge gained by such an inquiry, the task difficulty (because students are going to be involved), and the availability of sufficient case studies to supplement the lack of a real expert on campus.

Liberal Arts Focus

Knowledge gained is probably the strongest liberal arts concern in the development of an expert system. What does the researcher want to learn? What does the researcher want students to learn? It is somewhat ironic that the answer to these questions revolves around the AI topic of knowledge acquisition. "Knowledge acquisition is the process of extracting, structuring, and organizing knowledge from several sources, usually human experts, so it can be used in a program" (Waterman, 1986). Computer science students bring to the development effort programming skills and an intimate knowledge of the computer hardware.

Antonio M. Lopez, Jr. is Chairman, Mathematical Sciences, Loyola University, New Orleans, Louisiana. This article was supported in part by a Loyola University Faculty Grant.

A campus expert brings experience and education that has been gained in a particular problem domain. The researcher wants to learn how to do knowledge acquisition and thus learn how to be a knowledge engineer. The students must learn that it is not the programming skills that they have nor the insightful knowledge of a campus expert that is the important ingredient in the development of an expert system, but instead the ability of all to effectively communicate. "All parties must be capable of thinking rationally and communicating well" (Fellers, 1987). This statement affords a bonus! Very often computer science students fail to see the value of a liberal arts education. Consequently, from a liberal arts point of view, an appropriately selected problem can effectively demonstrate the value of a broad education and being well-informed.

Since several students will be involved in the development process, the question of how long the development task will take becomes critical. Undergraduate academia seems to create time barriers of a quarter or a semester. Consequently, a project such as the development of an expert system cannot take much more time than that before there is a "changing of the guard." Given above-average students, time-on-task depends on the task difficulty. Task difficulty depends upon the type of expert system to be developed. Expert system applications have been classified into ten different types (Hayes-Roth et al., 1983); however, the type best suited for a semester of low road development in PROLOG is a diagnostic system. This is especially true if the student programmers selected for the project have had experience programming portions of such games as CLUEDO (Emond and Paulissen, 1986) and MASTER MIND (Sterling and Shapiro, 1986). "Diagnostic systems infer malfunctions from observables; this is to say, they relate observed behavioral irregularities to underlying causes" (Hayes-Roth et al., 1986). A couple of techniques can be used to produce such a system, yet task difficulty strongly suggests using a table of associations between behaviors and diagnosis. This technique supports the case study methodology that will have to be implemented because of the lack of a real expert on campus.

In the strictest definition of the word, an expert is "an individual who is widely recognized as being able to solve a particular type of problem that most other people cannot solve nearly as efficiently or effectively" (Harmon and King, 1985). The question of a true resident expert on campus that has the time and inclination to work on the development of an expert system is tenuous at best. Regardless of the presence of a true expert, the development of any expert system normally requires case analysis (Rolandi, 1986). However, without the involvement of a "widely recognized" expert in the field who can solve the problems "that most other people cannot," a case-oriented development methodology is absolutely necessary. Campus experts can be used to elaborate on or give more insight into what is stated in a particular case study. General domain knowledge is assumed in the detailing of a case study. Knowledge engineers and programmers do not have a great deal of this background knowledge; however, the campus expert would.

A successfully used problem domain that falls within the stated parameters of development is a diagnostic system for alcohol abuse—an important issue on many campuses today. Alcoholism is the subject of current research in clinical psychology. For the computer science students accustomed to an ON/OFF world, the discipline of psychology offers a significant educational broadening. Yet, the desired diagnostic table approach can still be achieved, to some extent, by using *The Diagnostic and Statistical Manual* (DSMIII). Furthermore, DSMIII supports the case study approach. Finally, the probability of finding a campus expert for the problem domain of alcohol abuse is very high.

Expert System Development

Technically, the development of an expert system can be divided into three main software modules: (1) The user interface, (2) the inference engine, and (3) the knowledge base. The user interface handles the communication between the user and the software product. It accepts the statement of the problem from the user and seeks to narrow and/or clarify the domain of the problem by asking the user specific questions. Upon request from the user, it also justifies the problem solving process that is being undertaken by the inference engine. The inference engine is a complicated piece of software that is really the essence of the expert system. It is the critical intermediary between the user interface and the knowledge base. As its name implies, it provides inference, but it also provides control. In a "fully-developed or ideal" expert system (Hayes-Roth et al., 1983), the inference engine would have three software subsystems and a separate storage area called a blackboard. These subsystems are called the interpreter, the scheduler, and the consistency enforcer. Each makes use of a specific and identifiable area of the blackboard. The interpreter creates and updates the plan area. This area holds the current plan of attack that the system is using to solve the problem. The scheduler sets and maintains the agenda area. This area records the potential actions awaiting execution.

The scheduler is probably the most complex component of the inference engine since it controls the "reasoning process." There are several reasoning schemes that can be implemented, but there is no one reasoning scheme that is "best" for all problems. The consistency enforcer establishes and adjusts the solution area. This area has the candidate hypothesis and the conclusions that the system has drawn so far. The knowledge base comprises the knowledge that is specific to the problem domain. It contains simple facts, rules that describe relations, and possibly heuristic ideas. The level of sophistication of all of these components can vary greatly.

Keeping everything as simple as possible when developing an expert system in a liberal arts environment under a one-semester time constraint is probably a very good idea. Complications will take place naturally as one prototype leads into another and more sophisticated components are added. User interfaces can be menu driven with specific questions being answered with a Y for yes, an N for no, a ? for don't know, and why for an explanation. The knowledge representation scheme should be allowed to develop on its own. The initial thought of passing "growing" lists as parameters in PROLOG predicates will eventually lead to (1) stack overflow because of backtracking techniques and (2) some fundamental realizations regarding knowledge representation. Let this happen. It is an excellent learning experience. The approach to the complexity of the inference engine is difficult to resolve. One approach might stress the scheduler while another the interpreter. It is doubtful that one would build a consistency enforcer first. If the problem domain is sufficiently narrow, such as with a diagnostic system on alcohol abuse, scheduling techniques are not as critical as interpretation. Attacking the interpreter first falls within the time constraint and task difficulty levels for a development project. However, it must be stressed that this observation is made because of the problem domain selected for the project. It is unlikely that within a semester much more than one subsystem of the inference engine can be developed.

The Human Aspect

Associated with each of the software modules are one or more human developers. Besides a campus expert and a knowledge engineer, there must be a programming team. At a minimum this team should consist of a project manager (senior programmer) and two programmers. Interaction between the programming team, the knowledge engineer, and a campus expert is multifaceted. The campus expert and one of the programmers must combine talents and skills to develop the user interface. Similarly, the campus expert and the other programmer must structure and organize rules and facts into a knowledge base. Both activities are accomplished under the scrutiny of both the knowledge engineer and the project manager. They often serve as the intermediaries between the expert and the programmers. The development of the inference engine involves all parties. Both programmers must develop their respective modules so that the inference engine can request information and expect its delivery in a predefined manner. The expert and the knowledge engineer are responsible for developing the rule-based system; that is, the codifying of the problem-solving know-how of the expert (Hayes-Roth, 1985).

Everyone involved must realize the cyclic nature of developing an expert system (Bell, 1987). The cycle is collecting expertise, understanding how and when it is used, implementing this expertise in a program, and planning for the next cycle. By definition, the project manager is responsible for keeping the project on schedule, but the project manager must also document the development of the system at the end of each cycle. Given a prototype with each cycle, documentation and evaluation are very important in the development of an expert system. Some software engineering concepts can be very helpful with both the documenting and the evaluating. Initially, there should be a project plan which will specify a tentative development schedule with expected milestones. A Software Requirements Specification Document can help crystalize the user interface's menues and lead to the eventual development of a User's Manual. The cyclic nature of the development clearly supports frequent "sign-off" by the expert after each review. At the end of a semester of work, a Project Legacy is an invaluable document. Student programmers leave the project, and new student programmers enter the project, they ask why certain designs were used in the development of the expert system—the Project Legacy. The documentation of problems encountered with designs during any cycle are recorded, alternatives are stated, and corrective actions are selected by eliminating alternatives. New programmers can use the Project Legacy to avoid "reinventing the wheel."

The development of an expert system on a small hardware and software budget can be achieved in a liberal arts setting. The selection of the development approach is predicated on the hardware and software available for the project. Aside from the normal AI considerations for a narrow problem domain, the selection of a problem domain is also critical because of the time constraints and task difficulty. This is the key to the project's success. The availability of numerous case studies must be the foundation on which the knowledge acquisition is based. Campus experts must be used to supplement the approach of case analysis. This is because the campus expert most likely is not an expert in the strictest definition, and the amount of time that a campus expert can spend on the project is limited. Student programmers must bring to the development task programming skills (e.g., PROLOG programming experience, if necessary) and an intimate knowledge of the hardware on which the expert system is being developed. The knowledge engineer must orchestrate the project without playing the role of expert or programmer. The expert system must be allowed to develop as the human developers themselves grow with experience. □

References

Bell, J. The Human Side of Knowledge Engineering. *Educ. Media Interntl.*, September 1987, *24*(2), 143-148.

Bobrow, D., Sanjay, M., and Stefik, M. Expert Systems: Perils and Promise. *Comm. of ACM*, September 1986, *29*(9), 880-894.

Brown, J., The Low Road, the Middle Road, and the High Road. In *The AI Business*, P. Winston and K. Prendergast, Eds. Cambridge, MA: MIT Press, 1984.

Emond, J., and Paulissen, A. The Art of Deduction. *BYTE*, November 12, 1986, *11*(12), 207-214.

Fellers, J., Key Factors in Knowledge Acquisition. *ACM SIGCPR*, May 1987, *11*(1), 10-24.

Harmon, P., and King, D. *Expert Systems: Artificial Intelligence in Business.* New York: John Wiley and Sons, 1985.

Harmon, P., Maus, R., and Morrissey, W. *Expert Systems: Tools and Applications.* New York: John Wiley and Sons, 1988.

Hayes-Roth, F., Waterman, D., and Lenat, D. *Building Expert Systems.* Reading, MA: Addison-Wesley, 1983.

Hayes-Roth, F. Rule-Based Systems. *Comm. of ACM*, September 1985, *28*(9), 921-932.

Liebowitz, J. Common Fallacies About Expert Systems. *ACM SIGCAS*, Winter/Spring 1987, *16*(4), 28-33.

Myers, E. Expert Systems: Not for Everyone. *Datamation*, May 15, 1986, *32*(10), 28-32.

Prerau, D. Selection of an Appropriate Domain for an Expert System. *AI Magazine*, Summer 1985, *7*(2), 26-30.

Rolandi, W. Knowledge Engineering in Practice. *AI Expert*, December 1986, *1*(4), 58-62.

Romiszowski, A. Expert Systems in Education and Training: Automated Job Aids or Sophisticated Instructional Media? *Educ. Tech.*, October 1987, *27*(10), 22-30.

Sheil, B. Power tools for Programmers. In *Interactive Programming Environments*, Barston *et al.* Eds. New York: McGraw-Hill, 1984.

Sterling, L., and Shapiro, E. *The Art of PROLOG.* Cambridge, MA: MIT Press, 1986.

Waterman, D. *A Guide to Expert Systems.* Reading, MA: Addison-Wesley, 1986.

An Expert System for On-Site Instructional Advice

Elizabeth S. Martindale and Alan M. Hofmeister

Many factors account for the changing nature of our society, but there is general agreement that one of the most dominant forces driving that change is the rapid development and growing sophistication of technology. Technological advancement has affected the workplace. As more information is generated, employees must rapidly assimilate and implement new ideas and techniques. In education, as in other fields, teachers should be informed of current trends and trained to use new ideas and information.

How can administrators ensure that their staff remain knowledgeable about successful strategies and current methodologies? Inservice training and consultant services have traditionally provided exposure to new ideas, but follow-up advice and support on the job is either very costly or not available when most needed.

As in many instructional problems, the missing element is the guided practice necessary for effectively bridging the demonstration of the new skills, and the competent, independent implementation of the skills by the learner. The teacher trying to implement new skills in the classroom needs direction and decision support. In an attempt to provide this on-site, guided practice, an expert system was developed to emulate the role of an on-site practicum supervisor.

Expert Systems Technology

Expert systems technology, a field within the larger field of artificial intelligence, has been developed to capture and disseminate human expertise. In this case the human expertise of interest was that of the practicum supervisor. Expert systems have already demonstrated their utility

Elizabeth S. Martindale is a Research Associate at Utah State University, and Alan M. Hofmeister is Director of the Artificial Intelligence Research and Development Unit, Developmental Center for Handicapped Persons, Utah State University, Logan, Utah, and a Contributing Editor.

in related areas in education where they have enhanced the decision-making ability of teachers and administrators (Parry and Hofmeister, 1986; Hofmeister and Ferrara, 1986; Martindale, Ferrara, and Campbell, in press). In most of the educational applications of expert systems, these computer programs had provided advice on a "one-shot" basis. In a practicum supervision role the "expert" is called upon to provide advice on a continuing basis. Over a period of several weeks, curriculum objectives have to be identified, objectives have to be matched to student needs, instruction has to be implemented, instruction has to be evaluated, and instruction has to be revised based on student performance.

The Problem: A Specific Lack of Expertise

As mildly and moderately handicapped special education students move through the curriculum, an emphasis on academic skills is replaced by an emphasis on non-academic "work" and social skills. In many cases this trend is hastened by student failure in the academic skills. In the final years of high school, important functional academic skills, such as letter writing, are often not taught at all because of the students' earlier failures in this skill area. In many cases students have acquired the necessary prerequisite skills and can now benefit from written language instruction. Many high school special education teachers face two related problems: a limited amount of time and a lack of instructional expertise to teach this complex skill to this challenging group of learners.

Written Language Consultant: An Expert System

An expert system, Written Language Consultant (WLC), was designed to help teachers teach students to write a business letter. Written Language Consultant assisted teachers with grouping students, time management, implementing effective teaching practices, and managing difficult student behaviors. The expert system required an IBM-PC with 512K of RAM and 720K of floppy disk storage.

The teacher consulted with the expert system after each lesson had been corrected. A WLC consultation has three components: (a) entry of the students' test scores, (b) analysis of the teacher's use of classroom time and the teacher's management technique, and (c) the suggestion of specific procedures for assisting individual students to increase their assignment scores.

Student Data Entry

Student scores from a standardized reading and written language test and a domain-referenced test in capitalization, punctuation, and sentence writing were entered into the computer. Based on these data, WLC suggested capitalization, punctuation, and sentence writing lessons which might be appropriate for each student.

Student Grouping

Depending on their student skill level, several grouping procedures were possible. One grouping division was as follows: (a) those ready to begin the business letter lesson, (b) those in need of a modest amount of review, and (c) those needing extensive skill instruction in prerequisite skills in punctuation and/or capitalization.

A second grouping was based on the students' facility with sentence writing. The maximum number of possible student groups was individually determined. This decision was based on the number of groups the teachers could work with in their classrooms.

Characteristics of Effective Instruction

Besides providing consultant help on instructional prescriptions for individuals and groups, the expert systems provided feedback on the extent to which instructional practices were consistent with the findings from the "effective instruction" research literature (Rosenshine and Stevens, 1986). Teachers interacted with the computer every few days and provided information on student progress and teaching practices. The feedback provided by the computer included suggestions on the effective use of time, presentations, practices, and general classroom management.

Time management. Management of classroom time is essential for effective teaching (Rosenshine, 1980). Each teacher was required to log (a) how many minutes elapsed before they started each lesson, (b) how many days they spent teaching the lessons, and (c) how long it took the students to finish the assignment.

If the lesson took longer than the predetermined optimal number of days, the teacher was queried for possible reasons for the excessive time. If the instructional start-up time was longer than two minutes, the teacher was queried for possible causes for the delay. Five options were presented. Based on the response, an appropriate suggestion, designed to help the teacher establish a routine for starting the class, was provided.

Pacing and routine. Pacing and routine are critical components of the experienced teacher's lesson (Berliner, 1986). If the teacher started class promptly but was taking too long to get the students through a lesson, another set of questions was asked. These questions were designed to determine if the problem was related to the teacher's instructional presentation or if the teacher needed help with classroom management. Suggestions in this section included: (a) providing clear directions, (b) setting firm and reasonable standards, (c) stopping inappropriate behavior, (d) praising students and providing encouragement, and (e) circulating among students to make certain they understand the assignment.

The advantage of the expert system providing progressive advice rather than "one shot" advice is that the problems of teachers vary from lesson to lesson. By providing a specific suggestion that relates to the teacher's current problem, the teacher is more likely to implement the technique. The teacher can always return to the expert system for further advice if another problem surfaces in the same domain.

Student performance. Teachers are often frustrated by an individual student's poor performance. One consultation section of the expert system was designed to focus on the performance problems of individual students. The initial pretest scores and norm-referenced scores were paired with the student's performance on each assignment to determine which teacher behaviors or student behaviors might be changed to increase the student's score. Specific suggestions were then provided.

Results and Conclusions

The expert system, Written Language Consultant, was used to provide continued, ongoing support to the teacher. The teacher entered current data regarding student performance and teacher behavior. Written Language Consultant provided suggestions for modifications in teacher behavior to positively impact student performance. A suggestion for change could be tried in a specific problem situation. If this strategy was successful, the new teaching technique might be added to the teacher's repertoire. Each time the teacher returned to the expert system for a consultation, new suggestions were offered, or the teacher was recognized for successfully implementing the strategy.

At the beginning of the treatment, only one of the special education students wrote a business letter above the 69 percent level. At the conclusion of the treatment, 66 percent of the students who were instructed by the six teachers using WLC could write a business letter at the 80 percent or better mastery level.

Teachers' reactions were positive, and the teachers reported professional growth and an interest in further experiences with expert systems. The data on student outcomes and teacher reactions clearly indicated that expert systems delivering practical teaching information can provide on-the-job training and consultant help for classroom teachers searching for advice with difficult instructional problems. ☐

References

Berliner, D.C. In Pursuit of the Expert Pedagogue. *Educational Researcher, 15*(7), 15-13.

Hofmeister, A.M., and Ferrara, J.M. Expert Systems and Special Education. *Exceptional Children*, 1986, *53*, 235-239.

Martindale, E.S., Ferrara, J.M., and Campbell, B.W. A Preliminary Report on the Performance of CLASS.LD2: An Expert System for Classifying Learning Disabled Students. *Computers in Human Behavior*, in press, 1988.

Parry, J.D., and Hofmeister, A.M. Development and Validation of an Expert System for Special Educators. *Learning Disability Quarterly*, 1986, *9*, 124-132.

Rosenshine, B. How Time Is Spent in Elementary Classrooms. In C. Denham and A. Lieberman (Eds.) *Time to Learn.* Sacramento, CA: National Institute of Education, 1980.

Rosenshine, B., and Stevens, R. Teaching Functions. In M.C. Wittrock (Ed.), *AERA Handbook of Research on Teaching (Third Edition).* New York: Macmillan, 1986.

Training NASA Satellite Operators: An Expert System Consultant Approach

Jay Liebowitz and Patricia Lightfoot

Introduction

Training is an important area for computer-based application which has not received much attention over the years. However, with people costs rising and the difficulty of getting experienced individuals growing, tools for helping to train individuals are gradually being created to overcome these problems.

Computer-based training is an area of focus that the National Aeronautics and Space Administration (NASA) sees as deserving attention. Specifically, the ability to have intelligent computer-assisted instruction (ICAI) for helping to train individuals is a worthwhile consideration for NASA to explore. NASA typically builds multi-million dollar simulators to help train, for example, flight operations personnel on observatory performance and operations. To reduce the costs and development times of these simulators, there might be some training functions that could be carried out through ICAI, instead of incorporating all the functions into a simulator.

Computer-based training can take the form of [1]: (1) problem-solving monitors, (2) coaches/tutors, (3) lab instructors, and (4) consultants. Problem-solving monitors check to see if the trainee is thinking in the right manner, i.e., using the correct reasoning process. Coaches or tutors guide the trainee through the process. Lab instructors play a more passive role, as compared with coaches, and they will only help the trainee if he/she has questions. Lab instructors mainly oversee the trainee's work. Consultants go through a series of questions and based upon their knowledge and the trainee's inputs, they will generate a solution.

Jay Liebowitz, a recent ASEE-NASA Summer Faculty Fellow, is with the Department of Management Science, George Washington University, Washington, D.C. Patricia Lightfoot is with the Spacecraft Control Programs Branch, NASA Goddard Space Flight Center, Greenbelt, Maryland.

At NASA Goddard Space Flight Center (GSFC), intelligent computer-assisted instruction systems for training are starting to be developed. These are few in number compared with the expert systems being built at NASA GSFC for scheduling, planning, and fault isolation and diagnosis [2,3]. Having computer-based training aids, however, has been recognized as a needed area for development at NASA GSFC. Some of the reasons for this need are:

- development costs for simulators have been increasing rapidly, and some of these functions could be built using less expensive intelligent computer-assisted instruction;
- most of the training for spacecraft control and operation is done through on-the-job training (OJT) and there are very few training manuals documenting these procedures;
- there is a fairly high turnover rate in the spacecraft operators, which creates a need for preserving their knowledge and having training tools to quickly train the replacement operators;
- on-the-job training takes 3 to 6 months to train the spacecraft operators and training using a simulator takes about 1 year—thus, this process might be speeded up through the use of intelligent computer-assisted instruction;
- it would be helpful to have some way of preserving the "expert" spacecraft operator's knowledge before he/she leaves or retires; and
- many spacecraft operators have only a high school education and they are dealing with very advanced and difficult topics to learn.

This article describes an expert system prototype built for training spacecraft operators on satellite power subsystem contingency operations. It acts as a "consultant" to help the spacecraft operator know what to do in case something goes wrong with a satellite's power subsystem. This prototype uses production rules because [1]:

- they can be used to represent strategies;
- they can provide a clear, simple, transparent structure; and
- they are amenable to automatic manipulation.

This prototype will be described in this article, and future directions for further development and research will be addressed.

Intelligent Computer-Assisted Instruction

An intelligent computer-assisted instruction (ICAI) system should know when to interrupt a student's problem-solving activity, what to say, and *how* best to say it all [1]. They are typically used in domains where [1]:

- expertise in problem solving is a matter of *judgment* gained from experience, not a matter of efficiently applying a deterministic rule;
- this problem-solving judgment depends mostly upon the human's perception of the problem's surface or initial appearance, rather than upon explicitly performing a look-ahead computation and evaluating a succession of transformed results;
- the tutor's best advice does not always lead to a solution;
- if the best advice fails to be productive, then there exists second-best advice, and so on;
- one or more metrics can be devised that provide a goodness ordering on completed solutions to a given problem; and
- the point of the tutor is to stimulate the students to produce better solutions, i.e., to exhibit better judgment.

Besides having the ICAI system meet these problem domain characteristics, it should also be very easy for the student or trainee to use. Error messages should be friendly like "no, have another go" instead of "wrong [1]". Error messages like "warning", "fatal," or "subprocesses error" should be less harsh and more friendly and constructive. The program should intervene if the student has given up. There should be pause-resume and interrupt-restart commands [4]. The system should also give reinforcements to encourage the student/trainee.

There have been various ICAI systems that have been developed over the years. A recent success example is an ICAI built on a microcomputer by the University of Massachusetts-Amherst [8] for training boiler plant operators. This system was built in response to the boiler plant's insurance company's threat to cancel its insurance policy because the boiler plant operators were not being properly trained, which led to various accidents and errors. The boiler plant then contracted with the University of Massachusetts-Amherst, under Beverly Woolf's direction, to develop an ICAI system to train these operators. Part of the problem with the operators was that most of them had only a high school education and they had to deal with such complex topics as physics and thermodynamics. By having an ICAI system, the operators had a better vehicle for being trained than through solely on-the-job training. The system was built in 18 months, and was so successful that the insurance company not only continued its policy with the boiler plant but also reduced their

premiums. Additionally, the insurance company said that if any other boiler plant used this ICAI system, the insurance company would also reduce their premiums as well.

After reviewing the literature, there are several ICAI systems that have been developed from the early 1970s through today. Some of these systems and their domains are shown below:

○ SCHOLAR	Geography
○ SOPHIE	Electronic troubleshooting
○ BUGGY	Arithmetic skills
○ BIP	Programming skills
○ IDEBUGGY	Programming bugs
○ ACE	Complex explanations
○ GUIDON	Case method dialogue
○ IMTS	Troubleshooting skills
○ AIR STRIKE PLANNER	Pilot training
○ STEAMER	Steam vessel propulsion

Over the years, there has been a gradual merging of applying artificial intelligence techniques to simulation [6]. In NASA's situation, simulators to simulate spacecraft and environmental conditions are prevalent and important parts of the space program. It would be beneficial to NASA to make these simulation environments as intelligent as possible. This entails unifying expert systems and simulation. STEAMER and IMTS, as shown above, are graphic simulation systems that provide a user interface which allows the user to manipulate depicted objects directly and then immediately observe graphical consequences in other objects [5]. GMTS (Generalized Maintenance Training Simulator) is another intelligent simulator environment that simulates the behavior of systems through the presentation of static videodisc images in response to student touch inputs [5]. Now that ICAI has been characterized, the next step is to apply the ICAI concepts to the spacecraft operator domain.

Spacecraft Operator Domain

The spacecraft operator or analyst has the responsibility of monitoring the spacecraft health and safety, conducting routine pass activities (i.e., receiving data and transmitting commands), spacecraft commanding, and tape recorder management. The analyst also must be able to handle what to do in event of a system malfunction. The first set of functions is considered *normal* operations, and the latter function deals with *contingency* operations. The most time critical function deals with contingency operations.

There are many factors that could affect the safety and proper operations of a satellite. The spacecraft analyst must be cognizant of these factors when dealing with the satellite's performance and operations. Some of these factors are [4,7]:

Environment:
- Time
- Spacecraft orbit
- Tracking and Data Relay Satellite (TDRS) orbit
- Earth geomagnetic field
- Celestial sphere
- Earth disk
- Gravity gradient
- Solar pressure
- Earth's atmosphere
- Sun position
- Bright objects

Spacecraft:
- Attitude control subsystem
- Power subsystem
- Command and data handling subsystem
- Propulsion subsystem
- Thermal subsystem
- Instruments
- High gain antenna
- Onboard computers

Each of these factors influences the performance of the spacecraft, and the spacecraft analyst has an arduous task in being trained on the effects of these factors on normal and contingency operations.

The next section will describe the current approach of how spacecraft analysts are trained. The Earth Radiation Budget Satellite (ERBS), launched in 1984, is the case study that will be explained.

Training the ERBS Spacecraft Analyst

Training the ERBS spacecraft analyst is predominantly achieved through on-the-job training. This is typical of most training procedures for spacecraft analysts on other projects. It is a labor-intensive training effort which can take from 3 to 6 months.

For training the ERBS spacecraft analyst, there is a training guide that serves as an on-the-job training check-off list [9]. The guide incorporates a trainer/trainee concept in which a qualified individual is assigned as the trainer and is responsible for supplying information and related documentation on the items listed. The list of items that the ERBS spacecraft analyst must know is [9]:

- Tape recorder dump
- Onboard memory load/dump sequence
- Download of daily memory loads
- ERBS instrument calibrations
- Tracking and Data Relay Satellite antenna parameter update
- PB-5 checks
- Contingencies
- Binders
- Spacecraft Subsystem
- Recorder frequency subsystem
- Attitude subsystem
- Command and data handling subsystem
- Power Subsystem
- Thermal subsystem
- Science instruments

For most of these areas, the spacecraft analyst must be knowledgeable on the usage/frequency/background information, current status, and operational considerations of the satellites. The trainer works intensively with the trainee in each of these areas. When the trainer feels comfortable in the performance and knowledge of the spacecraft analyst in each area, the trainer then signs his signature and date for verification purposes.

After the trainer signs all the items in the checklist, the spacecraft analyst then takes an open book certification test [10]. The test is administered on the computer, and the test is divided into modules. The modules for ERBS are: power subsystem section, recorder frequency subsystem section, ERBS instruments section, SAGE-II instrument section, attitude subsystem section, and command and data handling subsystem section. Once in a module, all questions must be answered for that module. Not all modules have to be taken at one time. There are ten questions to each module, i.e., 60 questions in total on the certification test. The questions are true-false and multiple choice questions. The spacecraft analyst must get a percentage score of 85 percent or better to pass the test.

This training procedure has worked successfully, but there are some problems with this method. First, the manuals are very cumbersome and tedious to read. It would be beneficial to have an interactive, automated training tool to aid the spacecraft analyst in learning his material. This would make the learning experience more interesting and challenging for the analyst. Second, for some satellite projects, training manuals do not exist. Thus, for a new analyst being trained, the only way to learn his duties and functions is through individualized contact. To help in this process, an intelligent training tool could free up some of the trainer's time and would supplement the learning experience of the analyst. Last, since the turnover of spacecraft analysts is fairly high on some projects, it would be useful to have a way to encapture some of the analyst's knowledge before he leaves. An intelligent training aid might serve this purpose in building a corporate memory on analyst's functions.

Keeping these points in mind, an expert system prototype was built for training spacecraft operators on ERBS power subsystem contingency operations. This prototype will be explained in the next section.

TOPSCO: Expert System for Training On Power Subsystem Contingency Operations

Developing TOPSCO for ERBS control center analysts followed the traditional rapid prototyping steps of expert systems building. These steps were: (1) knowledge acquisition, (2) knowledge representation, (3) knowledge programming, and (4) knowledge testing, evaluation, refinement, and maintenance. TOPSCO was a one-man effort and was developed on the IBM PC/XT during a 10-week period. Each of the expert system development steps relating to TOPSCO will next be discussed.

Knowledge Acquisition

Before performing knowledge acquisition, it was first necessary to "scope out" the problem. The problem domain selected was the ERBS power subsystem contingency operations. The power subsystem was selected because it is one of the most important subsystems aboard a satellite. The ERBS power subsystem contingency operations domain provided the necessary requirements for expert systems development. These were:

- ○ it was narrow enough in scope for developing an expert system prototype;
- ○ there was an available and willing expert;
- ○ there were plenty of test cases and potential evaluators of the system;
- ○ the knowledge was mostly symbolic, as opposed to numeric, knowledge; and
- ○ a need and strong desire existed for this system.

After selecting and scoping the problem, the knowledge acquisition step could then proceed. The first form of knowledge acquired was from two ERBS manuals which document and flowchart the power subsystem contingency operations. After reading through these manuals, a categorization of the knowledge was easily determined. The first step in this problem domain is to *identify the power subsystem contingency*. The next step is to *determine the contingency procedures to be used* based on the contingency identification. It was apparent from the manuals that there were three major groups of contingencies that could be identified, and these groups could be further decomposed into eight possible power subsystem contingency problems. The major problem with using these manuals, as explained by the ERBS spececraft analysts, was that it was cumbersome and tedious to have to search in the manual for the appropriate power subsystem problem, and then find the contingency procedures to be used by stepping through an elaborate flowchart. If, for no other purpose, TOPSCO could replace the manual and provide the analyst with an interesting and interactive tool for identifying and correcting a power contingency problem, then that alone would make TOPSCO useful. TOPSCO would also help train the spacecraft analyst by giving the analyst some logical construct in which to approach and solve a power contingency problem in a timely and effective way.

After reading through the manuals, an interaction took place with the domain expert to identify his heuristics in solving power contingency problems, and to also identify the correctness of the manuals. By interacting with the expert and other ERBS analysts, some meta-strategies were identified and incorporated into the knowledge base. These meta-strategies increased the level of sophistication of the expert system by representing them as knowledge about knowledge.

After acquiring the knowledge for TOPSCO, the next step was to represent this knowledge.

Knowledge Representation

In reading through the manuals and conversing with the expert, the knowledge seemed to be naturally represented as IF-THEN rules. For example, a description of battery high temperature and overtemperature from the ERBS manual [7] is:

- —If a high battery temperature is encountered, the SPRU will automatically be set to VT2.
- —If an overtemperature is encountered, the charge relay of the battery associated with the overtemperature will be disabled.

These descriptions are in the form of IF-THEN rules, and most of the description on power subsystem contingency operations in the manual or expressed by the expert are in IF-THEN formats. Thus, for ease of development and acceptance by the ERBS spacecraft analysts, production rules were used as the vehicle for representing knowledge.

Figure 1 gives a sample of rules from the knowledge base. Out of the contingency identification and the procedures for the eight possible power subsystem contingencies, the number of rules in the knowledge base devoted to each area is as shown.

Figure 1

Sample Rules from TOPSCO

RULE NUMBER: 57

IF:

    contingency procedure responds to battery overcharge

and either battery is disabled is yes

and SPRU auto kickdown is enabled

and SPRU is in VT mode is no

and SPRU KI level is 1.5 amps is no

THEN:

    PMU output is not working or AHMU full charge pulse is not working Probability=10/10

and switch to the other AHMU — Probability= 10/10

- -

RULE NUMBER: 58

IF:

    contingency procedure responds to battery overcharge

and either battery is disabled is yes

and SPRU auto kickdown is enabled

and SPRU is in VT mode is yes

and Bus V is correct for VT level is no

and levels checkout okay is yes

and kickdown works now is no

THEN:

    PMU kickdown failure exists — Probability= 10/10

and reduce VT level — Probability=10/10

and re-enable charge replay — Probability=10/10

and fly with VT control only — Probability=10/10

- -

contingency identification	6 rules
undervoltage or overcurrent condition on either the Non-Essential Bus or the Control System Bus —	7
battery overcharge —	23
battery high temperature and overtemperature —	2
battery rundown —	24
cell failure/cell balance greater than 0.6 volts —	7
SPRU has no output —	5
SPRU has reduced output —	9
28V instrument regular failure —	8
TOTAL RULES —	91 rules

After representing the knowledge, the next step involved knowledge programming.

Knowledge Programming

In order to quickly develop the prototype TOPSCO, it was determined that an expert system shell should be used. There were several requirements that the shell had to meet, namely:

- the shell had to allow for backward chaining; this is goal-driven reasoning which is used by the spacecraft analysts; and
- the shell had to be affordable and easy to use and learn.
- it had to run on an IBM PC; NASA management felt that since most NASA personnel had easy access to an IBM microcomputer, using a microcomputer would make the development, testing, maintenance, and implementation of TOPSCO easier to accomplish;
- the expert system shell had to allow for production rules.

Based on these requirements, EXSYS [11] was selected as the expert system shell. It runs on an IBM PC, allows for production rules and backward chaining, costs only $395, handles uncertainty, and has an easy-to-use editor for developing, changing, and updating the knowledge base. Encoding the knowledge base began by programming the rules derived from the ERBS power subsystem contingency procedures sections in the ERBS manuals. The knowledge base was set up in a modularized fashion for easy refinement and updating. This was accomplished by characterizing and categorizing the eight possible power contingencies, and then encoding the rules relating to what procedures to take to handle each contingency. Thus, if changes had to be made for a particular power contingency, it was then easy to go right to the part of the knowledge base associated with that contingency. Changes needed to be made to incorporate the expert's comments and his heuristics.

A sample dialogue with TOPSCO is shown in Figure 2. The ERBS analyst would use TOPSCO as an aid for stepping him through the procedures for correcting the power subsystem contingency. At the end of the run, TOPSCO prints out the ordered steps that need to be accomplished in solving the contingency problem.

After encoding the knowledge, there were various features that would have been useful if EXSYS allowed them to be done.

One feature is that EXSYS doesn't allow the "or" logical operator in its rules. Thus, additional rules had to be developed to compensate for the lack of an "or" operator. Second, EXSYS doesn't

Figure 2

Sample Dialogue Using TOPSCO

TOPSCO: Training the ERBS spacecraft analyst On Power Subsystem Contingency Operations

This training aid will help the ERBS spacecraft analyst in understanding what to do when faced with power subsystem contingency operations. Hope you have fun.

contingency aid is
1 analog alarm message
2 discrete state colors in database
3 performance and configuration checks

3
contingency procedure responds to
1 undervoltage or overcurrent condition on either the Non-Essential Bus or the Control System Bus
2 battery overcharge
3 battery high temperature and overtemperature
4 battery rundown
5 cell failure/cell balance greater than 0.6 volts
6 SPRU has no output
7 SPRU has reduced output
8 28V instrument regulator failure

2
either battery is disabled is
1 yes
2 no

1
SPRU auto kickdown is
1 enabled
2 not enabled

WHY

etc.

---

easily allow for free-text comments. For example, if the user is confronted with a term that he doesn't know, it would be helpful to have an attachment like "define term" and the definition of that term (i.e., free-text comment put into the system by the knowledge engineer) would appear on the screen. To circumvent this potential problem, an effort was made to describe the terms as fully as possible when the user first saw the term. Aside from these limitations, EXSYS proved to be an effective, easy-to-use, and easy-to-understand expert system shell for developing TOPSCO.

After encoding the knowledge, the next step involved knowledge testing and evaluation.

Knowledge Testing and Evaluation

By modularizing the knowledge base, the testing of TOPSCO was quite easy to accomplish. After the procedures for a contingency were encoded into the knowledge base, testing was immediately performed to check whether all the paths from the decision points relating to the contingency were covered (i.e., encoded). Since there were numerous paths relating to a contingency, there were invariably some paths and procedures that were not encoded into the knowledge base. These were few in number (about 5 paths out of a total possible 200 paths). By having the ERBS analysts use TOPSCO, other features were incorporated into TOPSCO according to the analysts' suggestions. The major improvement was to give better descriptions of qualifiers (i.e., component functions and descriptions). The analysts also worked through test cases using TOPSCO and the conclusions drawn from TOPSCO were over 95 percent accurate, as compared with the expert's opinions. The analysts felt that TOPSCO was very easy to use, and less cumbersome than following elaborate flowcharts in manuals.

Conclusions

From the assessment and enthusiasm of the ERBS analysts at NASA, TOPSCO proved to be a successful prototype expert system consultant for helping to train analysts on power subsystem contingency operations. The main advantage of TOPSCO is that it steps the analyst through the contingency procedures at the time of the problem (i.e., when faced with the contingency). When a contingency occurs, the analyst is put under great stress to know how to handle the problem.

By using TOPSCO, the analyst would go through the steps in an objective manner to identify and solve the contingency. When placed under stress, the analyst may not be able to think of all the steps, in sequence, as to what has to be done to solve the contingency. TOPSCO is helpful to the analyst in this regard because, by having all the necessary knowledge on ERBS power subsystem contingency operations, the analyst only needs to simply follow TOPSCO's questions to arrive at the procedural steps needed to solve the contingency.

Future enhancements of TOPSCO are planned. Since this version of TOPSCO was successful as a proof-of-concept approach, future versions of TOPSCO will include:
○ a more elaborate man-machine interface than simply a menu-driven approach;
○ incorporate TOPSCO into more of a tutor (instead of a consultant) where a teacher-student role could be played; and

○ determine the generic functions of power subsystem contingency operations so that TOPSCO could be used for other satellite analyst power subsystem training instead of being geared strictly for one satellite (i.e., ERBS).

The rapid prototyping, expert system approach to developing TOPSCO was a quick and inexpensive method for a proof-of-concept. NASA was enthusiastic about this prototype, and TOPSCO proved to be a useful approach for training satellite analysts. □

Notes

1. Sleeman, D., and Brown, J.S. (Eds.). *Intelligent Tutoring Systems*. Orlando: Academic Press, 1982.
2. Lightfoot, P. Special Issue on AI Applications at NASA, *Telematics and Informatics*, Pergamon Press, 1986, *3*(3).
3. NASA Goddard Space Flight Center. *Proceedings of 1987 Conference on Space Applications of AI and Robotics*, Greenbelt, Maryland, May 13-14, 1987.
4. NASA Goddard Space Flight Center. Notes on the Training Simulator for UARS, Code 514, Greenbelt, Maryland, March 2, 1987.
5. Towne, D.M., A. Munro, A., Pizzini, Q.U., and Surmon, D.S. *Representing System Behaviors and Expert Behaviors for Intelligent Tutoring*. Report No. 108, University of Southern California, February 1987.
6. Luker, P.A., and Adelsberger, H.H. (Eds.). *Intelligent Simulation Environments*, Simulation Councils, Inc., 1986, *17*(1).
7. Ball Corporation. *ERBS Contingency Procedures*. Appendix N: Section on Power Subsystem Contingency Procedure, prepared for NASA Goddard Space Flight Center, Greenbelt, Maryland, 1984.
8. Freedman, R.S. (Ed.). Special Issue on Expert Systems that Teach, *IEEE Expert*, IEEE, Summer, 1987.
9. NASA Goddard Space Flight Center. OJT Checklist for the Earth Radiation Budget Satellite Analyst, Greenbelt, Maryland, December 23, 1986.
10. NASA Goddard Space Flight Center. Certification Test—Earth Radiation Budget Satellite Analyst, Greenbelt, Maryland, October 1986.
11. Exsys, Inc. *EXSYS: Expert System Development Package*, Albuquerque, New Mexico, 1985.

The Four Generations of Computerized Testing: Toward Increased Use of AI and Expert Systems

James B. Olsen

This article describes four generations of computerized educational measurement and suggests several emerging applications of artificial intelligence and expert systems to such measurement. Following are some brief definitions of terms:

- "*Artificial intelligence* is concerned with designing intelligent computer systems . . . which exhibit the characteristics we associate with intelligent human behavior - understanding, language, learning, reasoning and problem solving." (Barr and Feigenbaum, 1981).
- "Knowledge based *expert systems* . . . employ human knowledge to solve problems that ordinarily require human intelligence. Knowledge systems represent and apply knowledge electronically. Knowledge based systems simulate human performance." (Hayes-Roth, 1987).
- "*Educational measurement* is the process of specifying the position or positions for educational purposes, of persons, situations or events on educationally relevant scales under stipulated conditions." (Bunderson, Inouye, and Olsen, 1989).

Given these definitions we might logically expect significant relationships to exist among these three professional fields. Each of the fields is concerned with the constructs of human understanding, comprehension, learning, knowledge structures, problem solving, and human performance monitoring. However, there are very few applications of artificial intelligence or expert systems to educational measurement, assessment, and testing.

Personal communications with several professionals in artificial intelligence and expert systems have indicated a critical need for development of both theory and applications of artificial intelligence and expert systems to educational measurement. Literature searches and reviews also showed a lack of research and application articles on these topics.

In response to this need, Bunderson, Inouye, and Olsen (1989) envisioned four generations of computerized educational measurement. Each generation allows for increased use of artificial intelligence and expert systems approaches to improve educational measurement activities. These four generations are as follows:

1. Computerized Testing.
2. Computerized Adaptive Testing.
3. Continuous Measurement.
4. Intelligent Measurement.

Computerized Testing

The first generation, Computerized Testing, involves the translation or conversion of existing paper and pencil tests to a computer administered or computer managed format. This generation includes automation of the traditional educational measurement activities such as test scoring, reporting, and item banking. Computerized testing is hypothesized to provide the following advantages over paper and pencil tests: greater standardization of administration, improved test security, enriched display capabilities, and enhanced response alternatives. Computerized testing also provides the capability for developing new item types, providing equivalent scores with reduced testing time, minimization of certain measurement errors, ability to measure response latencies and patterns, and immediate test scoring and reporting.

Over the past three years the author has helped to develop and deliver more than 100,000 computerized tests of achievement and aptitude. These computerized tests have been focused on district instructional objectives, state assessment objectives, standardized test objectives, and learning aptitude measurement.

Computerized Adaptive Testing

The second generation, Computerized Adaptive Testing, employs computer administered tests in which the presentation of the next task or decision to stop is adaptive or tailored to the specific responses of the examinee to previous tasks or exercises. Computerized adaptive tests have been developed which are adaptive to examinee performance based on presentation speed, item content, item parameters and stopping rules.

In a computerized adaptive test, an item or exercise of average difficulty is presented first. If the examinee answers the exercise correctly, then a

James B. Olsen is Director of Testing and Evaluation for Wicat Systems, Inc., and an adjunct faculty member in Instructional Science at Brigham Young University, Provo, Utah.

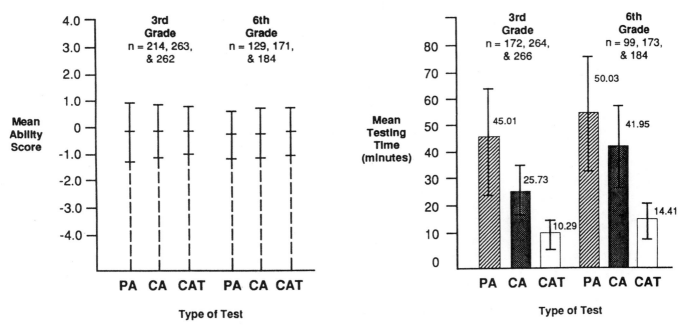

Figure 1

Scores and Test Times for Different Testing Modes

KEY
PA = Paper Administered Test
CA = Computer Administered Test
CAT = Computer Adaptive Test

more difficult exercise is administered. If the examinee answers the exercise incorrectly, then a less difficult exercise is presented. The adaptive testing process continues until a specified stopping rule is reached and the testing process is terminated. Note that an exercise could consist of answers to multiple questions which are then scored as a combined unit.

Figure 1 presents results from a research study which compared paper and pencil tests, computer administered tests, and computerized adaptive tests of achievement. The Figure shows that each of the three testing methods produced comparable test score means and standard deviations; however, significant testing time reductions were found for the computer administered tests (25 to 50%) and computerized adaptive tests (75%).

Computerized adaptive tests are proposed to yield all of the advantages presented above for computerized tests. In addition, computerized adaptive tests provide: increased measurement precision at all levels, equivalent score estimates with reduced testing time by 50% to 70%, and improved test security.

A computerized adaptive test is very similar in purpose to an expert system since it strives to find the most informative item from a large item pool which is closest to the examinee's current proficiency estimate. Research by Frick (1989, in press, 1990) has shown many parallels between expert systems research and computerized adaptive testing research.

Over the past five years, the author has helped to develop over 75 computerized adaptive tests of learning aptitudes and achievement. Computerized adaptive tests have also been developed by American College Testing, American Institutes of Research, Assessment Systems Corporation, Educational Testing Service and The Psychological Corporation (Grist, Rudner, and Wise, 1989).

Continuous Measurement

The third generation, Continuous Measurement, employs calibrated, curriculum exercises or tasks which are embedded within a computerized curriculum and used to unobtrusively estimate dynamic changes in student knowledge and proficiency levels. These dynamic changes may be observed in the amount learned, the proficiency with different tasks, changes in the trajectory of learning throughout the curriculum domain, and changes in the student's profile as a learner. Continuous measurement provides the capability to dynamically specify the learner's position on the simple and complex measurement scales which define the learner's progress space. Continuous measurement makes it possible to prepare a learning progress trajectory over time for the learner in mastering a domain of curriculum knowledge or task proficiency. Measurement is accomplished by assessing performance of each learner on reference tasks which have been calibrated to serve as milestones for progress accomplishment.

The tasks which are to be measured can include items, item clusters, exercises, unit tests, or independent work assignments. Continuous measurement requires that curriculum exercises and tasks be calibrated by difficulty and discrimination and scaled on educationally relevant scales. Continuous measurement will make it possible for teachers, administrators and/or students to receive daily, weekly or bi-weekly reports on reading comprehension, problem solving and reasoning based on measures derived from actual curriculum exercises and tasks. For continuous measurement the curriculum is defined as a broad course of experiences which are intelligently sequenced to monitor the learner's progress toward certain defined educational ends or outcomes. The curriculum also includes a series of course markers or reference tasks that serve as milestones along the curriculum journey.

Continuous Measurement is proposed to yield the following educational measurement benefits: measurement is dynamic, continuous and unobtrusive; measurement tasks are drawn directly from the curriculum; measurement is exhaustive rather than sample-based; and reports can be generated whenever needed.

Both Wicat and the Educational Testing Service have developed some of the preliminary components of continuous educational measurement systems. These continuous measurement systems are often referred to as learning progress systems.

Intelligent Measurement

The fourth generation, Intelligent Measurement, applies artificial intelligence and knowledge based computing to educational measurement issues. The knowledge and expertise of educational testing and measurement professionals can be captured and represented in a computerized knowledge base. This knowledge base can be replicated and distributed to multiple sites in electronic form. Users at each site, both teachers and students, can access the knowledge base and use it for searching, reasoning, and performing educational measurement tasks which require more intelligence or knowledge than they currently have. Intelligent measurement provides a convenient way to package expert testing and assessment knowledge, to replicate that knowledge, and to distribute it to multiple locations for use on multiple occasions. It is possible to implement with a computer system the knowledge base of curriculum and testing experts. Students and teachers could use the knowledge base and an inference engine to explore the knowledge base, to search for information, ask questions, and answer queries based on the expert knowledge base. Students could perform searches and queries of the knowledge base. The system could answer student and teacher queries in a manner approximating that of the curriculum and testing experts.

Similar Theoretical Conceptions Within the Profession

This section presents brief quotations from two instructional technology professionals who also share the vision of advanced technology applications to improve educational testing, assessment, and measurement.

Alan Collins (in press) has recommended that intelligent tutors could be used as intelligent testers to present problem solving and strategic skills tests. These tests could be focused on students' problem solving and planning skills. These tests would evaluate the students' ability to learn in a domain as well as their existing knowledge. The tests would be adaptive to the students' knowledge state and would test their generative abilities instead of just their recognition abilities. Collins also suggests the development of an integrated learning and testing environment through use of computer technology. "Students work with computers either in groups or individually. The teacher's role is that of a coach rather than instructor. The teacher and computer system could suggest activities for the students to engage in, give them advice or help when they need it and monitor how well they are progressing . . . The computer and teacher would be assistants to the student's self learning."

Norman Fredericksen (in press) has noted that, "Testing in the future may not be the special province of the psychometrician. Rather, assessments may be a useful byproduct of problem based instruction. Through trial and error with feedback and with the assistance of a tutor that provides knowledge, hints, examples and practice, the student should acquire automatic processing and recognition skills, improved conceptions of problem structures and meta cognitive skills to control problem solving procedures. Information relevant to the process of learning can be recorded and preserved to provide a continuous record of changes in knowledge, skills and understanding as the student encounters problems of increasing complexity. As our ability to obtain such information during the learning process improves, the need for final exams may disappear."

Preview of Applications of AI and Expert Systems

Following are several potential applications of artificial intelligence and expert systems for improving education measurement. These applications are categorized in the areas of Test Development, Test Administration, and Test Analysis. O'Neil and Baker (1987) have also discussed the development of expert systems for test and item generation, and test reliability analysis.

Test Development
- Computer tools for item development and selection with advisers
- Computer tools for test development with advisers
- Computer tools for developing test specifications with advisers

Test Administration
- Intelligent administration of computerized problem solving and performance based tests with advisors
- Intelligent scoring of complex constructed response tests
- Computer tools for interpreting achievement and aptitude profiles
- Computer tools for generating problem solving and performance based tests and items
- Intelligent advice during continuous measurement
- Dynamic access to intelligent hypermedia databases

Test Analysis
- Computer tools for item and test analysis with advisers
- Intelligent scheduling and on-line calibration of items
- Intelligent data collection and analysis in school settings

Discussion of Applications

The above section has briefly outlined several potential applications of artificial intelligence and expert systems. Three of these applications are described in more detail below.

Intelligent Scoring of Complex Constructed Responses. Knowledge bases which consist of scoring standards and rules can be developed along with automatic inferencing procedures to allow for automated scoring of complex constructed responses. Such procedures can be used for measuring the more complex elements of declarative and procedural knowledge than can be tested with multiple-choice items. The scoring models employed must assign differential values to important variations of the complex constructed response. The scoring models also need to keep results from intermediate as well as final judgments of the constructed response.

Additionally, these scoring models need to keep an increasing database of incorrect or erroneous responses. At present, the scoring of complex constructed responses is conducted by human experts, but is not currently available in automated expert systems. Research studies by Bennett *et al.* (1988, 1989) have examined the agreement of expert systems and human experts scoring judgments of constructed responses to computer science problems. The MicroPROUST program, a microcomputer based expert system, was compared to human reader judgments for two Advanced Placement computer science free-response items. The results showed MicroPROUST to be unable to grade a portion of the solutions; however, the program performed impressively on those solutions which it could analyze. Additional research is currently being focused on improving the production rules for the incorrectly scored items. The researchers indicate that for one of the computer science problems the expert system automated scoring of complex constructed responses might be implemented.

Automation of Individual Profile Interpretations. Psychologists, counselors, and other professionals routinely examine profiles of test scores and provide interpretative commentary on the score profiles to individuals. Such profile analysis is used in career and vocational counseling, diagnosis of learning aptitudes, personality testing, and placement decisions. These profile scoring experts have developed an extensive base of personal experience and knowledge concerning profile meanings and interpretations. This wealth of personal experience and knowledge can be captured in a knowledge base using knowledge engineering principles, reduced to a minimum subset of production rules, and programmed as an intelligent adviser which could mimic their expertise.

Expert systems with a similar focus have also been developed and validated (Thornburg, this special issue; Hofmeister, 1986, Hofmeister and Lubke, 1988). The input to the program would be a profile of scores. Note that these scores could be provided by a battery of tests administered by computer or computerized adaptive testing procedures. The output might include a series of questions for the counselor to ask to clarify information or score discrepancies, and an interpretative commentary could be printed out along with recommended resources or advice to the examinee. The professional could also edit this initial draft and prepare a final interpretative report.

Intelligent Advice During Continuous Measurement. Intelligent advice during the process of learning is one of the most promising contributions of intelligent measurement for both teachers and learners. The goal of the intelligent advice is to optimize the learning process. This will require development of an integrated curriculum and continuous measurement delivery system. The expertise of the best teachers could be engineered into a computerized knowledge base, analogous to the expertise of the counselor who interprets profiles of static scores. The primary difference would be that these new scores would be dynamic and continuous rather than static and discrete. The knowledge base would be complex due to the wide variations of individual learner trajectories and individual learner profiles. The validation of the intelligent system would be considerably easier since the measurement would be continuous, cumulative, and the results of prior decisions would be immediately known at the next level.

"Intelligent advice during continuous measurement is the epitome of computerized educational measurement. The optimization of learning in a growth space of calibrated educational tasks represents a challenge for educational measurement scientists and practitioners that will require a great effort over may years" (Bunderson, Inouye, and Olsen, 1989, pp. 400-401).

For additional reading on these topics please see the following references (Hayes-Roth, *et al.*, 1983; Freedle, in press, Parsaye, *et al.*, 1989; and Wenger, 1987).

Conclusion

This article has discussed the relationships and educational benefits of using artificial intelligence and expert systems to improve educational measurement theory and applications. There are six primary instructional technologies contributing to these developments: (1) low cost, high computation and storage capabilities of advanced technologies; (2) hardware and software necessary for effective computer aided instruction; (3) availability of large capacity digital and optical memories; (4) developments in local area networking technologies; (5) developments of psychometric procedures for calibrating curriculum tasks and estimating positions of individuals and groups on educational measurement scales; and (6) developments in knowledge-based computing and expert systems for building and querying interactive knowledge bases and intelligent hypermedia databases. Together, these advanced technologies expand our human capabilities and permit partial replication of the human abilities of sensing, remembering, deciding, acting, problem solving, reasoning and communicating. □

References

Barr, A., and Feigenbaum, E. A. (Eds.) *Handbook of Artificial Intelligence.* Volume 1. Los Altos, CA: William Kaufmann, 1981, p. 3.

Bennett, R. E., Gong, B., Kershaw, R. C., Rock, D. A., Soloway, E., and Macalalad, A. Agreement Between Expert Systems and Human Ratings of Constructed-Responses to Computer Science Problems. ETS Report RR-88-20. Princeton, NJ: Educational Testing Service,

Bunderson, C. V., Inouye, D. K., and Olsen, J. B. The Four Generations of Computerized Educational Measurement. In R.L. Linn (Ed.) *Educational Measurement, 3rd Edition.* New York: Macmillan Publishing, 1989.

Collins, A. Reformulating Testing to Measure Learning and Thinking. In N. Fredericksen, R. Glaser, A. Lesgold, and M. Shafto (Eds.), *Diagnostic Monitoring of Skill and Knowledge Acquisition.* Hillsdale, NJ: Lawrence Erlbaum Associates, in press.

Fredericksen, J. R., and White, B. Y. Implicit Testing Within an Intelligent Tutoring System. *Machine Mediated Learning,* 1988, *2,* 351-372.

Fredericksen, N. Introduction. In N. Fredericksen, R. Glaser, A. Lesgold, and M. Shafto (Eds.), *Diagnostic Monitoring of Skill and Knowledge Acquisition.* Hillsdale, NJ: Lawrence Erlbaum Associates, in press, 1990.

Freedle, R. (Ed.) *Artificial Intelligence and the Future of Testing.* Hillsdale, NJ: Lawrence Erlbaum Associates, in press.

Frick, T. W. A Comparison of an Expert System Approach to Computerized Adaptive Testing and an Item Response Theory Model. *American Educational Research Journal,* in press, 1990.

Frick, T. W. EXSPRT: An Expert Systems Approach to Computer-Based Adaptive Testing. Paper presented at the Annual Meeting of the American Educational Research Association, San Francisco, 1989.

Grist, S., Rudner, L., and Wise, L. Computerized Adaptive Tests. ERIC Clearinghouse on Tests, Measurements, and Evaluation, Digest 107, February 1989.

Hayes-Roth, F., Waterman, D. A., and Lenat, D. B. *Building Expert Systems.* Reading, MA: Addison-Wesley, 1983.

Hayes-Roth, F. Expert Systems. In S. C. Shapiro and D. Eckroth (Eds.), *Encyclopedia of Artificial Intelligence, Volume 1.* New York: John Wiley and Sons, 1987, p. 287.

Hofmeister, A. M. Assessing the Accuracy of a Knowledge-Based Expert System: Special Education Regulations and Procedures. Logan, UT: Utah State University, 1986.

Hofmeister, A. M. and Lubke, M. M. Expert Systems: Implications for the Diagnosis and Treatment of Learning

Disabilities. *Learning Disabilities Quarterly*. 1988, *11* (3), 287-291.

Olsen, J. B., Maynes, D. M., Slawson, D. A., and Ho, K. Comparisons of Paper Administered, Computer Administered, and Computerized Adaptive Achievement Tests. *Journal of Educational Computing Research*, 1989, *5* (3), 311-326.

O'Neil, H. F., and Baker, E. L. Issues in Intelligent Computer Assisted Instruction. *Evaluation and Measurement*. CSE Report 272. Los Angeles: UCLA Center for the Study of Evaluation, 1987.

Parsaye, K., Chignell, M., Khoshafian, S., and Wong, H. *Intelligent Databases: Object-Oriented, Deductive Hypermedia Technologies*. New York: John Wiley and Sons, 1989.

Thornburg, M. Knowledge-Based Tutoring of Special Education Classification Concepts, this issue.

Wenger, E. *Artificial Intelligence and Tutoring Systems: Computational and Cognitive Approaches to the Communication of Knowledge*. Los Altos, CA: Morgan Kaufmann Publishers, 1987.

A Knowledge-Based System Allowing Formative Evaluation

Marie-Michele Boulet, L. Lavoie, P. Labbe, and D. DeMelo

Introduction

Research on the use of computers in education has enabled the identification of several pedagogical applications. Among these uses there are applications designed to aid the learning process. These uses of computers in curriculum development amount to various modes of interaction between student and computer (Cohen, 1983). Questions form the raw materials for interaction between learner and computer (Alessi and Trollip, 1985). Deciding which questions will be asked can greatly affect how good a job is done by educational software. All the questions and answers help to pace each learner's progress. The idea of pacing implies the use of appropriate remedial measures to help learners get back on track when they run into trouble.

The terms "pacing" and "remedial teaching" are part of the formative evaluation concept defined by Bloom *et al.* (1971). Formative evaluation is defined as a set of measuring instruments designed for the specific purpose of continual intervention in the progress of each learner. Remedial teaching begins with an exact diagnosis of why learners are having problems learning. It then suggests to the learners ways to overcome these problems (Block, 1977). Remedial teaching is based on the diagnosis supplied by formative evaluation. We have integrated these views of formative evaluation and remedial teaching into the knowledge based system described in this article.

First, the theoretical foundations of the system are discussed. Second, a general description of the tool used to produce the knowledge base, the multiple facet sheme, is provided. Third, the steps describing the constructing of a facet test are presented.

Marie-Michele Boulet is a Professor in the Department of Computer Science, Faculty of Science and Engineering, Laval University, Quebec, Canada. Her co-authors are graduate students in this Department.

The Theoretical Choice

Before describing all the characteristics of the system, the learning theory applied has to be presented. The purpose of the system is to help a student learn the writing of minor scales in music. This skill is an intellectual skill. Because of the emphasis he places on intellectual skills, we chose Gagne's learning theory to analyze this task (Gagne, 1977). The implications that Gagne's learning theory has for the acquisition and representation of the knowledge of the system are: rather than modelling this knowledge by doing a list of key words describing potential mistakes of the learners, as per the traditional approach, we organized it into several linked structures that enable the system to take into consideration what a learner can and cannot do. For this purpose, we draw on a formative evaluation tool known as the multiple facet scheme (Scallon, 1988b) to construct a profile of the learner's problems in the computer's memory. On the basis of this profile, remedial teaching can be provided.

The Principle of the Multiple Facet Test

The multiple facet test provides a precise way of measuring how close a subject is to attaining a learning objective of the intellectual-skill type. This model uses facets to define a group of items and derives from them a specifications table having two or more dimensions. A facet is defined as any variation made in the level of the questions used to evaluate a student's performance (Scallon, 1988a). The major investment is made during the elaboration of the test and in processing the results of the many questions making up this test; this processing is made to establish a diagnostic profile for each student. The construction of a facet test and of an analysis chart for the results may be done in three distinct steps.

First step: subject analysis. First, the domain being evaluated has to be identified: Minor musical scales will be used as an example of a domain being evaluated during the following description of the steps. Second, the scope of the domain being evaluated has to be defined: in fact, the following question has to be answered: "What are the difficulties a student could face if he has to write a minor scale?" This question must be repeated until all of the dimensions of the domain have been identified. Two major difficulties can be identified in the present domain (the minor scales): the student should be able to write a melodic minor scale and a harmonic minor scale. This first subdivision allows a determination that a student has difficulty with harmonic and/or melodic scales, if he does not achieve the suitable level of success. The information so far acquired seems insufficient to conclude with a specific diagnosis. Would there not be a way to obtain sufficient information, enabling a more precise diagnosis and thus to construct a more adequate corrective action?

By asking more questions, it could be determined not only whether the student has difficulty with harmonic and melodic minor scales but also whether the problem lies with ascending or descending scales. This could be done by adding ascending and descending dimensions to the initial two dimensions: harmonic ascending, harmonic descending, melodic ascending, and melodic descending.

A third subdivision of the domain evaluation of the initial question can also be identified. We may determine whether the student has difficulty with minor scales possessing flats or possessing sharps. In fact, it is common that some students will only have difficulties with scales possessing flats, while other students will experience difficulty only with scales having sharps. We could add other subdivisions, like the location of tone and semi-tone. Note that we will consider only three subdivisions to illustrate the knowledge representation.

After having established all the different dimensions of the domain of minor scales, we have to establish to which facets each of these dimensions can be related. Then when we have analyzed the students' results, it will be possible to determine with accuracy and fairness the precise domain of difficulties experienced by each student. We now continue with the same example; the dimensions "harmonic" and "melodic" can be grouped in a facet called "type"; the dimensions "ascending" and "descending" can be grouped within a facet called "direction"; and "sharp" and "flat" dimensions in a facet called "breaking," as illustrated in Figure 1.

Second step: writing the test. First, evaluation items have to be produced. For example, as illustrated in Figure 1, under the facets "breaking: 0 to 2 sharps," "type: harmonic," and "direction: ascending," it would be possible to ask the student to write three minor scales (A, B and E). Later, a number has to be assigned to each of the questions; for minor scales, there are sixty possible items.

Third step: constructing the correction tool. In this step, an analysis table of the results has to be produced. As illustrated in Figure 2, the seven following components have to be included in the table: (1) the facets which were identified when the test was developed, the questions to be presented to the student, and the number associated to each of the questions; (2) the total number of questions used for each dimension; (3) the mini-

Figure 1

The Domain Being Evaluated

BREAKING		TYPE			
		Harmonic		Melodic	
		DIRECTION		DIRECTION	
		ascend.	descend.	ascend.	descend.
Sharp	0 to 2	5- A 9- E 60- B	14- A 30- E 36- B	31- A 37- E 42- B	16- A 55- E 44- B
Sharp	3 to 5	2- F# 25- C# 41- G#	7- F# 18- C# 49- G#	4- F# 27- C# 35- G#	12- F# 52- C# 57- G#
Sharp	6 to 7	17- D# 21- A#	29- D# 43- A#	10- D# 51- A#	32- D# 38- A#
Flat	1 to 2	6- D 53- G	22- D 58- G	56- D 59- G	13- D 28- G
Flat	3 to 5	3- C 19- F 39- Bb	8- C 23- F 45- Bb	11- C 26- F 47- Bb	15- C 33- F 54- Bb
Flat	6 to 7	20- Eb 40- Ab	24- Eb 46- Ab	1- Eb 50- Ab	34- Eb 48- Ab

mum number of questions that must be answered correctly—according to mastery learning theory (Block, 1977; Bloom *et al.*, 1981) this minimum can be settled to 80 percent; (4) a place to be used to write the result of the student; (5) a place to be used to write the result of the comparison between item 3 and 4; (6) a place to indicate if a student has mastered the evaluated subject or not; (7) a place to be used to write what is (are) the cause(s) of the difficulty(ies).

Once these steps have been completed, this analysis table could be used by a teacher in order to obtain a better understanding of the specific area that a student did not master and the reason(s) behind the difficulty. The teacher has to apply rules in analyzing the learner's results. Some examples of these rules are listed below. These rules have been implemented into the system.

- Rule 1: If the success level is not attained, then the related element is not mastered.
- Rule 1.1: If an element is not mastered and all related elements down in the tree are also not mastered, then it is not useful to consider elements

Figure 2

Part of Analysis Table

DIMENSION TYPE	Questions	Minimum	Result	Mastered (X)
Harmonic Q- 2- 3- 5- 6- 7- 8- 9-14-17- 18- 19- 20- 21- 22- 23- etc.	30	24		
Melodic Q- 1- 4- 10- 11- 12- 13- 15- 16- 26- 27- etc.	30	24		

DIMENSION DIRECTION/TYPE	Questions	Minimum	Result	Mastered (X)
Ascending/Harmonic Q- 2- 3- 5- 6- 9- 17- 19- 20- 21- 25- 29- 39- 40- 41- 60.	15	12		
Ascending/Melodic Q- 1- 4- 10- 11- 26- 27- 31-37- etc.	15	12		
Descending/Harmonic Q- 7- 8- 14- 18- etc.	15	12		
Descending/Melodic Q- 12- 13- 15- 16- etc.	15	12		

DIMENSION TYPE/BREAKING	Questions	Minimum	Result	Mastered (X)
Harmonic/Sharp Q- 2- 5- 7- 9- 14- 17- 21- 25- 29-30- 36- 41- 43- etc.	16	13		
Melodic/Sharp Q- 4- 10- 12- 16- etc.	16	13		
Harmonic/Flat Q- 3- 6- 8- 19- etc.	14	11		
Melodic/Flat Q- 1- 11- 13- 15- etc.	14	11		

Figure 3

Tree Structures

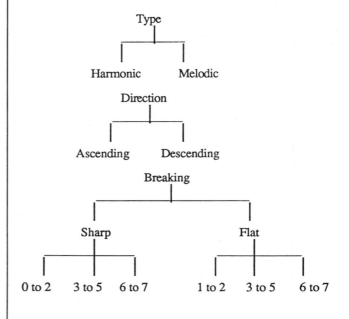

down in the tree: the superior element is declared non-mastered.

- Rule 2: If an element A is not mastered and most of the questions are also related to an element B (the case of an intersection), then element B is implied in the failure of element A.

It can be seen in Figure 1, using a circle, many incorrect answers given by a student; this problem could be easily identified with the analysis table: that is, a student does not master the descending melodic minor scales. From that analysis, it would be possible to provide effective corrective teaching.

The Major Lines of Development of the System

The domain of evaluation knowledge has been expressed in the knowledge base using Prolog relations. The relations can be seen like components of a tree structure in which each item identified in the table corresponds to a node. Three trees corresponding to the three facets were used (Figure 3).

An interactive process is used in order to collect the knowledge to be used to build the relations: a pool of questions, of explanations, and of corrective teaching. The teacher is required to point out the knowledge elements components of each question. The software then determines to which facet(s) a question or an explanation is to be related. So, a teacher can select a knowledge base, describe a domain with "Dimensions and elements" option in the main menu, the system will produce a series of screens. It can be seen in Figure 4 that the teacher entered the name of the dimension "Breaking," and the system asked if there were some subdivisions of this dimension. As the teacher answered "yes," the system has presented another window to allow the capture of the elements of this dimension. It can be seen that the teacher named two elements, "Sharp and Flat." The system is now asking the teacher if there are subdivisions for each of these elements. The process will continue until all the elements would have been collected.

Figure 5 shows one of the screens being used to collect the question subject relations. To produce

Formative evaluation preparation

Figure 4

*Collection of Data Related to
Dimension and Elements*

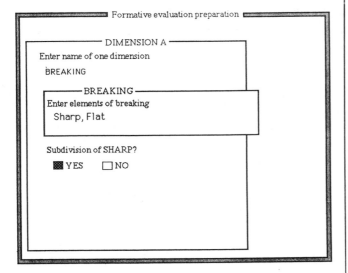

Figure 5

Question/Subject Relation: Dimension "Breaking"

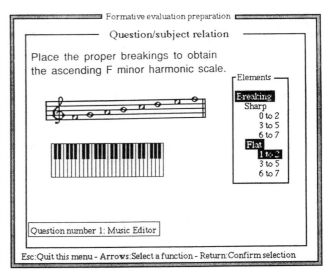

the stave and notes, the teacher has previously used the music editor. The teacher has to point out all the elements related to this question. It can be seen in Figure 5 that the teacher pointed out elements "BREAKING, FLAT, 1 TO 2" as being related to the scale. Other windows will allow to point out whether the question is being related to elements "ASCENDING or DESCENDING," and so on.

When a teacher prepares a test, the system shows all items available into the knowledge base. The teacher can see each of these items and has to select each number of questions that he wants to use within a test. He can decide to not measure a facet or a group of facets.

Here is an example of printed diagnostic and remedial teaching suggested to the student, after she passed a test: "SONIA, you succeeded in writing many scales; congratulations. But you have some problems with the following element: BREAKING, SHARP, 0 and 1. There were 8 questions in the test related to this element. You gave right answers to 6 of these questions. In fact, you failed questions 4 and 13. To allow you to master this element, I suggest that you revise the content of page 56 of Musicontact 3. This revision been made, try solution exercises 1 and 3 proposed at page 61 of Musicontact 3. When you think

that you master this element, you will come back and I will give you another short test to confirm your mastery."

We have only presented the major concepts which are used in the development of the system. The system has many knowledge bases related to formative evaluation and a global knowledge base. This has more general knowledge about the psychology of learning which supervises the use of the other knowledge bases. Furthermore, the student can take control of the lesson whenever he wants. For example, he could be writing a melodic minor descending scale and not remember the meaning of melodic; he could then ask the system to present him this concept. He can also ask the system for advice on his ability to reproduce the ascending minor harmonic scales, on the revisions that he should do, etc. In the same way the teacher could use the system to obtain information about the ability of each of his students or his whole class to achieve an objective.

Conclusion

The important concern of our research is that we used formative evaluation tools not to build pools of items but rather to represent items of knowledge and the ties between these items. Instead of doing a list of key words describing potential mistakes from the learners, as per the traditional approach, our system "thinks," using many tables (diagnostic approach). It can explain the details of its reasoning in giving or suggesting corrective teaching. For each of the different parts of the domain, the author includes explanations, questions, and corrective teaching. The use of the system for the conception of the knowledge base allows the author to be concerned only with his subject and not with the software to be used to produce a lesson. This conception has required the work of many persons specialized in different subjects: a learning psychologist, an educational technologist, a conceptual data modeling specialist, and three specialists in artificial intelligence. The prototype has been made possible with the help of a musician specialist. □

References

Alessi, S.M., and Trollip, S.R. *Computer-Based Instruction: Methods and Development*. Englewood Cliffs: Prentice-Hall, 1985.

Block, J.H. Individualized Instruction: A Mastery Learning Perspective. *Ed. Lead*, 1977, *34*(5), 337-341.

Bloom, B.S., Madaus, G.F., and Hastings, J.T. *Handbook on Formative and Summative Evaluation on Student Learning*. New York: McGraw-Hill Book Co., 1971.

Cohen, V.B. Criteria for the Evaluation of Microcomputer Software. *Ed. Tech.*, Jan. 1983, 10-14.

Gagne, R.M. *The Conditions of Learning*. Third Edition. New York: Holt, Rinehart, and Winston, 1977.

Scallon, G. *L'Evaluation Formative des Apprentissages: L'Instrumentation*. Quebec: Presses de l'Univ. Laval, 1988a.

Scallon, G. *L'Evaluation Formative des Apprentissages: La Reflexion*. Quebec: Presses de Univ. Laval, 1988b.

The research reported in this article was supported by a grant obtained from Canadian Workplace Automation Research Center (CWARC) and from FCAR (Fonds des Chercheurs pour l'Aide a la Recherche).

Expert Systems Technology for Training Applications

Jay Liebowitz

Introduction

One of the biggest problems with organizations is the development and enhancement of the organization's institutional memory. Institutional or corporate memory refers to the accumulation of knowledge about the company's practices, management strategies, and corporate know-how. As people leave the company, a brain drain effect takes place whereby the knowledge of these individuals is not deposited back into the firm. This affects the growth of the organization because new individuals coming into the firm are not able to easily learn from the successes and failures of the individuals who left. As a result, the training of new personnel has to start from scratch instead of building on the experiences of the older employees who left the firm.

In order to build the institutional memory and to facilitate training in the organization, expert systems technology can be used for these purposes. Expert systems [1] allow the capturing of an individual's knowledge and experiential learnings acquired over many years. By capturing this knowledge, the new person coming into the company could be trained through supplementary use of the expert system. The expert system could act as an aid to the trainee in providing a foundation of knowledge and experiences from which to learn a particular activity.

This article explains some examples of where expert systems have been applied for training applications.

Mini-Case Studies of Expert Systems Used for Training

The use of artificial intelligence (AI) for training is not a new phenomenon. Intelligent tutoring systems [2, 3, 4] have been around for many years to help tutor or train individuals. What is new, however, is the application of expert systems or intelli-

Jay Liebowitz is Associate Professor, Department of Management Science, George Washington University, Washington, D.C.

gent tutoring systems to dispersed application areas. Instead of building these systems for the traditional training applications of learning a foreign language, math, or geography, expert systems and intelligent tutoring systems are now being developed for such training applications as boiler plant operations, telecommunications, contracting, and others. RBT [5] is an example of an intelligent tutoring system used to help train new personnel on boiler plant operations. It was so successful that the insurance company, who had grave concerns about the lack of training of boiler plant operators before having RBT, reinstated its insurance policy on the boiler plant.

This section will describe three short case studies of expert systems used for training applications in diverse areas. The first mini-case study describes CESA, an expert system for helping to train the Contracting Officer Technical Representative; the second case study describes TOPSCO, an expert system for training satellite operators; and the third case study explains EVIDENT, an expert system for training a law student in learning evidence. Coincidentally, all three of these systems use Exsys [6] an expert system shell, for prototyping purposes.

CESA

In government contracting, there is a myriad of skills that need to be acquired by the contracting specialist [7]. These skills range from the knowledge required in handling procurement request generation and execution to monitoring and evaluating contractor performance. With a procurement request package, the government contracting specialist assigns the responsibility for the contract pre-award and post-award phases to the Contracting Officer Technical Representative (COTR). To help train the COTR, an expert system prototype called CESA (Contracting Officer Technical Representative Expert System Aid) was developed. CESA aids the COTR in learning about such areas as what's needed in a procurement request package, routing of documents, statement of work preparation, and other pre-award and post-award areas. Such a system is needed due to the difficulty in learning and keeping up-to-date with the contracting material. Also, an interactive aid is more attractive and usable to the COTR than the current practice of sifting through a multitude of contracting instructions and handbooks to obtain answers to COTR questions [8].

CESA followed the rapid prototyping, knowledge engineering approach of problem selection, knowledge acquisition, knowledge representation, knowledge encoding, and knowledge testing and evaluation. For the proof-of-concept version of CESA, the problem domain focused on the pre-award contract phase and the routing of executed documents in post-award phase. The major areas of concern in the pre-award phase which are incorporated into CESA are:

- adequacy of the procurement request (PR) package
    - what is needed in a PR package
    - Justification and Approval (J&A) if requirement to be specified is sole source
    - what type of contract is desired
    - the statement of work
    - evaluation procedures
    - synopsis procedures
    - use of the PPD.
- routing of either the duplicate original (advance copy) of the Procurement Planning Document (PPD) or PR package, or routing of the original PPD, or routing of the original PR

The knowledge for the proof-of-concept version of CESA was acquired in two months. The knowledge was represented as production rules, and the proof-of-concept version of CESA has close to 150 rules, with the average rule having 5-6 antecedents and 2-3 consequents. The knowledge was tested and evaluated to ensure completeness, accuracy, utility, consistency, and good human factors design.

The next system to be described is an expert system prototype for training in telecommunications.

TOPSCO

TOPSCO [9] is an expert system prototype used for training the satellite operator on contingency operations dealing with a particular satellite's power subsystem. Using expert systems for training in telecommunications applications has been rather sparse, as most people have concentrated on the scheduling, planning, fault isolation and diagnosis, monitoring, and network management functions for expert system applications to telecommunications [10, 11]. TOPSCO (Training On Power Subsystem Contingency Operations) was built to aid the Earth Radiation Budget Satellite (ERBS) operator in determining the content and the order of contingency operations to be performed if a problem occurred with the ERBS power subsystem. Because of the high turnover of satellite operators and the complexity and volume of material that needs to be learned on satellite contingency procedures, TOPSCO was built to help train new satellite operators and ameliorate some of these problems.

TOPSCO followed the same knowledge engineering steps as described in CESA's development above. The power subsystem was selected as the area of focus because it is the most important module in a satellite. Contingency operations, as opposed to normal operations, were selected for inclusion in TOPSCO, and greatly aid the satellite operator in determining and stepping through the steps needed when a contingency problem occurs. After narrowing the problem and focusing on ERBS, knowledge was acquired through interacting with an expert and obtaining information from several volumes of material. The knowledge was then represented and encoded in about 100 rules, and was iteratively tested and refined to meet the satisfaction of the users.

The next section looks at EVIDENT, an expert system prototype for training in legal applications.

EVIDENT

Another area where expert systems are beginning to be applied for training purposes is law. Along these lines, EVIDENT is an expert system prototype that has been developed for helping the law student learn admissibility of evidence under the federal rules [12]. Evidence is a difficult topic for the law student because of the many rules, and exceptions to the rules, to know. EVIDENT allows the law student to use a structured, logical approach to determine whether or not a piece of evidence is admissible into court under the federal rules.

EVIDENT was built using the traditional knowledge engineering steps as previously discussed. The problem domain chosen was evidence under the federal rules because there was a need to have some aid to help the law student in this area, and by concentrating on the federal rules, instead of state rules, there would be wider applicability.

(It should be noted that another expert system prototype called OBJECTION! [13] is being developed using VP-Expert, an expert system shell, to handle hearsay exceptions under evidence using Virginia state laws.) After scoping the problem area, the next step involved knowledge acquisition with an attorney and sifting through many books and bar review notes on federal rules of evidence. The knowledge was then encoded using rules, and the system was incrementally tested and refined through interactions with experts and law students.

Observations from Building Expert Systems for Training

There are several lessons that have been learned from a training perspective in building CESA, TOPSCO, and EVIDENT. First, expert systems do not have to be used for only "heroic" tasks; they can be extremely useful for less glamorous tasks that maximize utility. In other words, using expert systems for various kinds of training can have great impact and usability. In the case of CESA, ultimately all COTRs in the Naval Research Laboratory, and perhaps eventually in other parts of the Navy, will be able to use the finished, full version of CESA. Even though government contracting might seem a mundane task for expert systems development, a system such as CESA has the potential for great utility and widespread application.

A second lesson learned from building expert systems for training applications is that feedback on the part of the expert(s) and users is critical to the success of the project. Continual incorporation of their comments will increase the likelihood of individuals using the expert system.

Third, developing an expert system for training into an intelligent tutoring system can be a major undertaking. One rule of thumb typically used in building intelligent tutoring systems is that 60 hours of instruction (which would be about two semesters of a university course meeting once a week for two hours for 15 weeks each semester) takes about five person-years of development effort. Thus, the expert system component (i.e., the expert problem-solving module) is only one of four major modules (the four modules being student module, tutorial module, communications module, and expert problem-solving module) in an intelligent tutoring system.

The last major point learned from building CESA, TOPSCO, and EVIDENT is that the user interface is a very important part of the expert system, as well as in an intelligent tutoring system. For CESA, TOPSCO, and EVIDENT, the user interface needs to be improved to make it more "glamorous" for the user.

With these lessons in mind, expert systems can be built successfully for many training applications. In the near future, great utility will be derived from building these systems for diverse training applications. □

References

1. J. Liebowitz. *Introduction to Expert Systems*. Santa Cruz, CA: Mitchell Publishing Co., 1988.
2. M.C. Polson and J.J. Richardson (Eds.), *Foundations of Intelligent Tutoring Systems*. Hillsdale, NJ: Lawrence Erlbaum Associates, 1988.
3. J. Psotka, L.D. Massey, and S.A. Mutter (Eds.), *Intelligent Tutoring Systems: Lessons Learned:* Hillsdale, NJ: Lawrence Erlbaum Associates, 1988.
4. J. Anderson and A. Lesgold. Intelligent Computer-Assisted Instruction Tutorial, AAAI-86 Conference, American Association for Artificial Intelligence, Menlo Park, CA, August 11, 1986.
5. B. Woolf, and P. Cunningham, Multiple Knowledge Sources in Intelligent Teaching Systems, IEEE Expert, Special Issue on Expert Systems that Teach, IEEE, Los Alamitos, CA, Summer 1987.
6. Exsys, Inc. Exsys: Expert System Development Package, Albuquerque, New Mexico, 1985.
7. J. Liebowitz, L.C. Davis, W.F. Harris, and P. Morgan Development of CESA: Contracting Officer Technical Representative (COTR) Expert System Aid. Submitted for publication to Expert Systems for Information Management, England, July 1988.
8. J. Liebowitz, L.C. Davis, and W.F. Harris. Using Expert Systems to Help the Contracting Officer Technical Representative: A Feasibility Study and Selection Methodology. *Educational Technology*, Educational Technology Publications, Englewood Cliffs, NJ, in press.
9. J. Liebowitz and P. Lightfoot. Training NASA Satellite Operators: An Expert System Consultant Approach. *Educational Technology*, November 1987, *27* (11)
10. J. Liebowitz. Intelligent Computer-Aided Instruction for Training in Telecommunications. *Telematics and Informatics*, 5 (1), 1988.
11. J. Liebowitz (Ed.) *Expert System Applications to Telecommunications*, New York: John Wiley & Sons, 1988.
12. J. Liebowitz and J.S. Zeide. EVIDENT: An Expert System Prototype for Helping the Law Student Learn Admissibility of Evidence Under the Federal Rules. *Computers & Education*, 1987, *11* (2).
13. J.L. Rafferty, J.L. OBJECTION!: An Expert System Approach to Admissibility of Evidence. Presented at the Joint National Meeting of TIMS/ORSA, Washington, D.C., April 25-27, 1988.

Skilling America: The Potential of Intelligent Job Aids

Clay Carr

Introduction

There is a consensus that the United States is headed for a skills shortage of critical proportions.

What will be the results of this skills shortage? The obvious result will be the skills—machining, computer programming, etc.—that we will lack. But this may not be the most significant one. Arguably more significant will be the impact of an unskilled workforce on technology utilization.

As Cohen and Zysman put it in *Manufacturing Matters*:

> • The risk for the United States is that the elimination of the skilled workers may have reduced the dynamic flexibility of the firms—their ability to continuously develop, absorb, and apply new production technology. Equally important, the kind and number of skills that the economy will require will not be determined unilaterally by the distant and disembodied force of technological development driven by competitive pressures. Skill requirements—the market's demand for labor—will also be significantly shaped by skill availabilities, but not in the tautological sense of markets always clearing at some price. Rather, the availability of scarcity of skills may shape competitive strategies as well as the development and application of particular technologies.
>
> ...Today, and more so tomorrow, new degrees of flexibility in application are inherent in the new microelectronics-based technologies. But which of those new technologies are applied—and how—is, in part, a function of available skills.[1]

One might reasonably ask "How did we get into this mess?"

Clay Carr is currently the Chief of the Defense Logistics Agency (DLA) Civilian Personnel Service Support Office in Columbus, Ohio. Among the responsibilities of the office is training design for DLA. The opinions expressed in this article are those of the author and do not necessarily reflect the policies of the Defense Logistics Agency or the Department of Defense.

As with the famous headache tablet, there has been a combination of ingredients. One is the current "Baby bust," which isn't supplying sufficient replacements to the work force. For at least the next decade, there simply will not be enough new workers.

This is exacerbated by the kind of workers that will be available. The highest birth and workforce entry rates are among minority groups and other disadvantaged groups in the population, those who are the least skilled. Since there are not enough even of them, the shortfall will be made up to some extent by immigration—and this, again, is typically a low-skilled group.

Unfortunately, birthrates and immigration do not explain the entirety of the problem. As a nation, we have traditionally looked on mechanization and automation as a means of replacing undesirable humans with desirable machines. Frederick L. Taylor, the father of "scientific management," sounded the keynote of this approach two generations ago:

> The employee is (1) a constant in the production equation, (2) an inert adjust [sic] of the machine, prone to inefficiency and waste unless properly programmed, (3) by nature lazy, and (4) his main concern is self-interest.
>
> ...that other sacred cow of the American economic belief system, the minimization of the role of labor....[2]

Things are not dramatically different today. In his brand-new book, *Thriving on Chaos,* Tom Peters refers to:

> The central idea behind narrow job classifications is the conception of labor as a mechanical tool; cost minimization (low wages) and the widespread application of labor-replacing automation are natural concomitants....
>
> ...Quality and flexibility through skilled labor have never been an American custom."[3]

Many people have been heralding the new computer technologies such as Artificial Intelligence (AI), and particularly Expert Systems, as an answer to the shortage of skills. Perhaps. One might want to recall at this point that twenty-five years ago computers were going to banish human drudgery and grunt work, and then observe the real-world impact of data processing on individual skills and job interest.

I see no reason for application of current computer technology to have a different result—unless a sizable body of influential people force it in a different direction. No one is better placed to spearhead this effort than those who will be in the forefront of applying this technology to training goals. In all probability, that's you.

The Function of an Expert System

As a way into the problem, we can look briefly at expert systems and what they do. Many training designers are already working on expert-system-based Intelligent Tutors. Elsewhere, I have described the concept of a Master System based on some of the functions of an Expert System.

And what is the function of an expert system? It is really quite simple:

The function of an expert system is to replace a human expert.

Many will deny this. Some of those closest to expert system development stress that they are advisory, making recommendations instead of decisions. I do not doubt the sincerity of the individuals who say this. Consider this, however:

Your family doctor says to you: "My expert system says that there's a 90% probability that Johnny has acute appendicitis. I just don't feel that way, though. Take him home and give him some Pepto Bismol, and call me in the morning if he's not feeling better."

Or your stockbroker says to you, "Eleanor, our expert system says that there's a 75% probability of a serious price drop in the next eight days. I really think it's being too conservative, though, and I think you ought to take a strong position in . . . ."

Or take one closer to home. A few days ago, I heard a presentation of an instructional design expert system. The system asks a series of questions, then makes recommendations about the most effective media for course presentation.

The presenter was asked if the system did not in fact make the decision. He replied that it did not; it presented the user with the top two choices and let him pick between them.

So much for human choice.

The Virtues of Expert Systems

Actually, when expert systems are used correctly they have redeeming virtues, at least two of them. To understand and put these virtues into perspective, we might compare them with a major technological invention familiar to everyone: the electronic calculator.

I was working in a research and development facility when electronic calculators first became feasible. Primitive by today's standards, they were a technical marvel at the time. Within a few years, these little boxes had transformed slide rules from everyday tools into quaint curiosities.

An expert system is significantly different from an electronic calculator in the result it produces for the user. An electronic calculator presents a valid result (if used rightly, of course), but no explanation of why the result is valid. An expert system, on the other hand, can give a detailed explanation of why it reached the conclusion it did.

That is an important distinction. Even where expert systems are used to replace human experts, their ability to make their reasoning clear can make them useful trainers. An individual working with an expert system who takes the time to query the system about its conclusions will learn a great deal about how to make proper decisions in that domain. It is not unlikely that he or she could begin to pick up the reasoning herself and bypass the system in familiar situations. No electronic calculator has the capability to do this.

That was the difference. There is also an important similarity, and this concerns the way in which both electronic calculators and expert systems can be used.

Either can be used in ways that will reduce human skills. Because children have access to calculators at an eary age, their skills at doing arithmetic are almost certain to suffer. Witness the check-out clerk with a barcode-driven electronic cash register. (While this is actually a terminal on a computer system, from the user's point of view it is a fancy electronic calculator.) His or her primary computational skill is now the ability to count the change the machine says to give back to you.

The impact of electronic calculators on engineers, though, was nothing like this. Are they less skilled? No—Quite the reverse. They now have the time to spend on much more demanding and fruitful endeavors than the computation of a cube root.

Why the difference? To the supermarket, the electronic cash register is a way to minimize human error and lower the skill requirements (and hopefully the cost) of the checker's job. To the engineer's boss, the calculator is a way to free him from mathematical grunt work so he can apply his primary skills more fully. In other words, to the engineer the electronic calculator is a *tool*.

A tool, of course, is an artificial contrivance which expands the abilities of its user. Perhaps we will get a greater payoff from AI if we conceptualize its primary function as that of a tool.

(A quick note before we explore that notion. There is an alternate way of looking at the impact of electronic cash registers on checkers. If the job of the checker is to punch prices in and do computations, the register has certainly taken away his skill. But what if the primary function of the checker is really to see that the customer is satisfied? If this is a valid way of looking at the situation, then the barcode-reader-driven cash register becomes a most useful tool.)

An Intelligent Tool?

If we approach the use of AI from the point of view of a tool, what do we do? Where do we start?

Actually, a point of departure already exists. Many managers and high-level knowledge workers already have a tool called a "Decision Support System." This is a brief look at what it is and how it functions.

A Decision Support System (DSS) is a tool which helps decision-makers and their support staffs access, analyze, and synthesize information in unpredefined ways. A typical decision support system (DSS) has four basic components:

1. **A Database.** The user has access to a relevant subset of the organization database. For instance, if the DSS is serving the Marketing Department, it will contain all of the company's data relevant to marketing—but nothing about personnel or accounts receivable.

A database is little help if the necessary data can't be gotten at quickly. In the case of a DSS, there is another requirement; the database must also permit the user to access it flexibly—in *ad hoc* ways. One of the great virtues of DSS's is that they let their users "poke around" and "play with" the data, looking for the information latent in it. The basic purpose of a DSS is defeated if the user cannot get at data in this way.

2. **A Model Base:** Since most DSS's deal heavily with quantitative data, they require a set of tools to work on this data, usually called models. Perhaps the most common tool is a spreadsheet, which permits the user to develop a wide variety of models easily. There may also be a variety of statistical models, and even such sophisticated models as linear programming or queueing models.

3. **A User Interface.** Since the users of DSS's are not usually programmers or other computer professionals, it is critical that they have a comfortable user interface. A word that is often used to describe an effective user interface is "intuitive"—meaning that it does things in a way that the user *expects* it to.

4. **Output Software.** When the user has found meaningful information in a database, he or she needs to capture it. This is most commonly done on paper, so the DSS is equipped with an editor or word processor, a graphics package, and a printer and/or plotter.

How does the functioning of a DSS compare with an Expert System? Since my background is in human resources work in the Department of Defense, here is an example of an Employee Rela-

tions Specialist advising a supervisor on a disciplinary action.

If the specialist were working with an expert system, the system would take the initiative and ask questions relevant to the action: what was done, what its consequences were, whether there were prior offenses, etc. The system would ask these and other questions to search its rule base until it found the appropriate rule(s) for the situation, and provide that to the specialist. The specialist could inquire "why?" and the system would respond by listing the rules it had used.

Suppose the Specialist were using a DSS. Its database would be the relevant laws, court decisions, and human resources policies and procedures at various levels in the organization. The database would have a highly flexible structure, making it easy to navigate among the various components. There would not be a highly mathematical model base, but there might well be a variety of tools for creating and examining alternate ("what if") approaches. The interface would make it easy for the user to find and link the relevant information, perhaps using a variety of "Hypertext" (see below). Ideally, the product would be the disciplinary action itself, ready to be signed.

The difference between the two approaches should be clear. In the first, the system retains the initiative, and the user learns only what the rules communicate. In the second, the user has the initiative, and the system responds to this initiative. Because the user is much more active, much more learning occurs.

Hypertext

An automated tool, similar to a decision support system, is one way that programmed intelligence can be used in support of human skill-building. Since a "hypertext" system might well be one component of such a system, it is worth a quick detour to look quickly at it.

Hypertext is a term and idea coined in the late 60's by computer expert Ted Nelson. The basic idea is simple: organize data so that it can be accessed in a non-linear fashion. A full-fledged system would include not only text but graphics, perhaps even video footage. What makes it hypertext, though, is that the user can "browse" through the information, moving from one place or idea to another through a web of associations. At least in theory, this more closely supports the way the human mind works than conventional, linear database managers.

While this technology is still in its infancy, there are actually working hypertext systems; the most notable are Guide for the Apple Macintosh or IBM

PCs (and compatibles), Hypercard for the MacIntosh. The next year or two should give a very good indication of how well the idea works in practice.

The Master System

The detour over, it is time to look at the application of decision support system concept to the skills shortage we face. Here, the concept needs to be modified. By taking the components of a DSS and adding some aspects of AI to them, we come up with—viola!—a *job aid*. In short, we have here a tool which teaches its user how to utilize itself.

A number of individuals are already experimenting with facets of this idea. One of the ideas being explored, for instance, is that of an Intelligent Tutor. I call my own concept a "Master System."

My analogy here is a master in the old guild structure. He was himself recognized as a master, or expert, who was familiar with the most difficult aspects of his craft. Along with this, he was responsible for training and developing apprentices to be full journeymen as they worked. If he was fully successful, in fact, he would produce not only journeymen but more masters.

I see the Master System as the core of the support system, and the element absolutely necessary to transform a tool into a job aid. The Master System knows and understands both the database and the tool base. It is also an expert in the skills required by the occupation (whether it is data entry clerk or systems analyst).

When the human user is new and untrained, the Master System operates much like a human tutor, explaining all of the aspects of the process and the data and tools available. It can call up data, explaining how it found it; it can call up tools, explaining how to use them.

At this stage, the Master System is very active, tutoring the user, checking on his performance, repeating steps as necessary. As the user becomes more proficient, however, the initiative moves gradually to him. The Master System slips into the background, reappearing only when asked, or when an error is made. Finally, the Master System transforms itself into a help system and scorekeeper.

An interesting question arises at this point, by the way. When the user is proficient and makes an error, what does the Master System do? Logically, it should interrupt the user at that point and identify the error. If it does this, however, there is the risk that the operator will never become fully independent—depending instead on the System to catch his mistakes for him. If it does not, it permits errors to get at least partway into the system. As I said, it's an interesting question.

Feasibility

Could such a system be developed now? Probably. Several Intelligent Tutors are under development and a few have reached the prototype stage. An extensive hypertext system is up and being tested at the Cornell University Medical College. The integration of the two could present problems, but not insuperable ones.

Would it be feasible? It is probably much too early to tell. The applications of AI for training developed so far are considerably more expensive than older technologies. But that is characteristic of almost any new and developing technology. What the capabilities and costs will be five years downstream from now is not clear.

Should we be doing it? The integration of a database, tool base and Master System into an integrated operating/learning environment is one approach to the problem of the growing skills shortage. I believe it should be considered carefully, and something like it tested.

Conclusion

AI offers the hope that human skills and intelligence can be amplified significantly. The form of AI which seems most relevant is the Expert System, though the idea of a Hypertext may prove equally as useful. There is at least the possibility that these and other techniques could be combined into an electronic tutor and job aid, the purpose of which is to move the human user from neophyte to expert.

My concern, though, is not with any specific system or technology. It is with the skills shortage itself and the tendency of this country to continually downgrade the human element in productivity. My goal is for those of us who design and develop training to keep the shortage—and the imperative for dealing with it—in the forefront of our thinking and planning. Our job is developing human skills, not substituting dependable and cheap machines for unreliable and expensive human beings. We are uniquely situated to make a dramatic contribution to the quality of life and productivity during the next few decades. □

Notes

1. S.S. Cohen, and J. Zysman. *Manufacturing Matters: The Myth of the Post-Industrial Economy.* New York: Basic Books, 1987, p. 174.
2. Quoted in G.L. Lippitt, *Organization Renewal: A Holistic Approach to Organization Development*, 2nd edition. Englewood Cliffs, NJ: Prentice-Hall, p. 124. No reference is given to the source of the quotation.
3. T. Peters. *Thriving on Chaos: Handbook for a Management Revolution.* New York: Alfred A. Knopf, 1987, pp. 20-21, 22.

Using Expert System Job Aids: A Primer

Clay Carr

Introduction

In "Skilling America: The Potential of Intelligent Job Aids" (*Educational Technology*, April 1988), I described how highly automated job aids based on knowledge-based technology could support human beings in their jobs. This was a speculative article, one based not only on current technology but on that which may be developed in the coming five to ten years.

But what about the present? Can knowledge-based technology—and especially expert systems—be used now as job aids? The answer is clearly "yes." This present article then is as practical as the April 1988 article was speculative. Its purpose is to show how current, off-the-shelf expert system technology can be used to create useful job aids.

For someone who hasn't worked yet with expert systems, this may sound like a tall order. As I hope to show in the next few pages, it need not be. After a brief discussion of what an expert system is, we'll look at:

1. the situations in which an expert system job aid will be most effective;
2. how to select an appropriate expert system "shell"; and
3. how to develop a working expert system job aid.

What Is an Expert System?

In order to hunt snipes, it helps to know what a snipe is. In order to create an expert system job aid, it's useful to know what an expert system is.

An expert system is almost exactly what it sounds like: a computer program which performs the same role as a human expert. It has detailed knowledge of some specific area (called a "domain"). It asks the user questions and then provides an answer. It might advise a user on where to look for minerals, identify why a car won't start, or diagnose an infection.

Clay Carr is Chief of the Defense Logistics Agency's Civilian Personnel Services Support Office and is a frequent writer on the implications and applications of artificial intelligence.

It's important to understand that expert systems are "expert" only within a very limited area. An expert system for picking stocks, for instance, isn't able to advise on what bonds to buy, much less whether to invest in gold. Expert systems are never general experts; they always know a great deal about only one small area. This concentration on a limited area is what makes them so effective; in fact, it's what makes them possible at all.

Expert systems are a form of "knowledge-based" system. Traditional ADP systems store data; knowledge-based systems store facts (another name for data), too, but they also store the knowledge of how to use these facts to make decisions.

The most common way that an expert system stores knowledge is in rules, such as this one:

> IF Weather is Wet
> AND Temperature is Cold
> AND Car is Outside
> THEN stay inside.

The expert system will request the facts it needs to make a decision (What is the weather? What is the temperature? Where is the car?). When it finds a rule that matches the facts, that rule "fires" and provides the answer for the user. In the example above, if the weather is wet, the temperature is cold and the car is outside, the expert system will fire the rule that recommends staying inside. If even one of the facts doesn't match the rule, it will look for another rule to fire.

Expert systems, though, aren't the only kind of knowledge-based systems. This technology can be used to build systems which perform a variety of different roles. For instance, knowledge-based systems can be built to function as assistants, or librarians, or coaches, or even tutors. For the present, though, we'll stick to expert systems—since they're easy to describe and comparatively easy to create.

Creating them requires a specific piece of software, called an "expert system shell." These shells make it possible to write expert system job aids, useful ones—even for people who've never programmed a computer and don't intend to start. They vary widely in expense, from $29.95 to over $50,000. Later in the article we'll discuss how to select an expert system shell that's right for producing job aids.

When Is an Expert System a Good Job Aid?

Expert systems have become quite popular, even faddish. This doesn't mean that they can be used as job aids in every situation, simply replacing written materials. The truth of the situation is quite different; there are only a limited number of situations in which an expert system job aid is effective. Here are some of the basic considerations in making the decision of whether or not to use one.

Type of Job Function. First, an expert system (by definition) does something instead of its human user. It takes a former job skill and replaces the human in exercising it. It's fairly obvious common sense, then, that you don't want to use an expert system as a job aid when the process it's expert in is required for the person to do the job effectively.

For instance, if you were training librarians in how to use the Dewey Decimal cataloging system and then gave them an expert system which used it instead of them, you'd be doing them a real disservice. Part of being an effective librarian is knowing how to use the Dewey Decimal system. If an expert system did it instead of the human librarian, the human would lose a skill necessary for the job.

On the other hand, suppose you're training data processing professionals how to order automated equipment. Is knowing how to do it an intrinsic part of their jobs? Hardly—it's a requirement imposed on them by an external system. In this situation, an expert system which selected the correct procedure for them would be entirely appropriate. (In fact, they would probably love you for it.)

There's one more situation in which you might consider an expert system as a job aid: where the task is performed so infrequently that the individual can't remember how to do it correctly. On the one hand, an expert system is a natural for a situation where a human can't remember all the relevant considerations. On the other, if it's an intrinsic part of the job, putting it on an expert system removes the skill from the job.

The best answer to this is to build a knowledge-based system which functions as a coach rather than an expert. In a future article, I hope to discuss how this is different and how it creates more choices for the training designer. For now, if the task is essential to the job but done very infrequently—you'll just have to pay your money and make your choice of whether to create an expert system job aid for it.

Kind of Process. The next consideration concerns the kind of process that an expert system is to embody.

Expert systems are used for a number of different purposes: they can diagnose, design, plan, schedule, control and perform other functions. When planning an expert system as a job aid, though, the best choice is one which uses the system for diagnosis.

This may sound a bit strange. After all, most training designers don't create a lot of courses in diagnosis. That's true—but we do develop a lot in which something has to be classified or the correct way of doing something has to be found. And these are the same thing—where an expert system is concerned—as diagnosis.

Diagnosis consists in starting with one or more symptoms and finding the "cause" of the symptoms. Classification consists in starting with an item and finding the correct "slot" to put the item in. Identifying the right way to do something consists in starting with a variety of alternatives and finding the right one. Where an expert system is concerned, these are all processes for finding something.

You would use this kind of process to find the right kind of expert system "shell" to use to develop an expert system for a job aid, or the right performance rating to give an employee, or the right purchasing method to use to buy a new computer.

Impact of Errors. A third factor, if present, could override one or both of the factors above. If mistakes are made in the process which are very costly or very difficult to correct, an expert system may be justified. In this case, it may well be more complex than you would want to start with, and you might want to save it until you have a few others under your belt.

Simplicity. The next consideration is a common-sense one: don't try to write an expert system as a job aid unless the process it embodies is relatively simple.

There's nothing absolute here. If the process is too simple, an expert system is trivial and a paper-and-pencil job aid will work just as well—at a lower cost. If it's too complex, writing the expert system will be an overwhelming chore.

Here's an example. If making a decision requires you to consider three factors, each of which can have two values (is or is not expensive, is or is not durable, is or is not convenient, for instance), there are potentially eight rules to apply. If it's just a little more complex, say four factors, each with three values (expense is low, medium or high, etc.), the potential number of rules is 81.

The actual number of rules won't be as great as the potential; often only a fraction of the number. The basic point is valid, though: the more factors that have to be considered, the more complicated an expert system is going to be.

Just as a ball-park estimate, you should begin with a process which requires about 15 to 30 rules —say one which uses 4 or 5 factors to select among the same number of outcomes.)

Limited Input. Just as there should be a limited number of rules (for your sake), there should be limited input needed (for the user's sake).

Not a great deal needs to be said about this. If a worker knows he will have to spend 15 minutes just putting information into the expert system, he'll try to find an alternative that doesn't require as much work. If he has to make a dozen or fewer entries, though, he'll probably think it's practical.

Frequent Computer Use. The next consideration is another commonsense one, but one that's easy to skip or to make invalid assumptions about: expert systems will be good job aids only when students use computers regularly in their jobs. This really means that all four of the following conditions are true:

• Employees use personal computers (PCs), not terminals on larger systems. Starting by developing an expert system for anything larger than a PC is almost certainly going to be too time-consuming.

• Employees routinely use PCs and have easy access to them. Many organizations have PCs on everyone's desk, but they're seldom if ever used. It's almost as bad if employees can use computers, but have to leave their immediate worksite to do so. In either case, the chance that an expert system job aid will be used is minimal.

• The organization encourages computer use as part of the job. We're not that far from the time when the only people who used personal computers at work were the "hackers," and many organizations retain a deep suspicion of them from that time. If this is the case, most workers won't feel comfortable using an expert system.

• The employees are "computer literate." They're comfortable with the PC and use it for a variety of job tasks. Many people who have personal computers at their desks use them for just one function, such as word processing or financial worksheets. They may think of the computer as a machine which does this one function, and not be open to using it as a job aid.

There's a fifth computer-related factor which may encourage employees to use an expert system as a job aid: when the organization wants to introduce knowledge-based technology. That's not requisite for the use of a job aid, but it can be quite helpful.

Development Time. This is the final consideration: don't commit to an expert system as a job aid unless you have time to do it.

There aren't any absolute guidelines for this. If you are familiar with PCs and use a relatively simple expert system shell, you could probably start from scratch and produce a useful expert system job aid in a day or so. If you're unfamiliar with PCs and use a more demanding shell, it may take several days even to produce a relatively simple expert system.

Here, again, the best approach is the commonsense one. Pick a good application, allow yourself plenty of time, and have a more traditional job aid available as a backup just in case.

All of this may sound quite complicating and limiting. Actually, you'll find that there are a surprising number of situations in which an expert system job aid is appropriate. It's a little bit like driving a Cadillac: you don't notice how many other people drive Cadillacs until you own one yourself. If you start designing expert system job aids, you'll quickly see how many opportunities there are to use them.

Expert System Shells

I've used the term "expert system shell" before, and now it's time to explain it. The first expert systems were written in specialized languages like Lisp and required a very experienced programmer months or years to do. Now that expert technology has become popular, though, companies are producing software which permits a non-programmer to complete a small expert system in a matter of hours. These products are called expert system shells, and if you want to write expert system job aids you need to start with the right one of them.

How do you tell which one is right? Here are some of the points you would want to consider.

1. First, the shell should be *inexpensive.* There are two sides to this. The first is the obvious one: the initial cost. But a second cost—the charge for a run-time package—is even more significant.

Most expert system shells produce a "knowledge base" which requires an additional piece of software to run it. This is called a "run-time" package, and is normally a simplified version of the shell itself. If the cost for each run-time package is very high, the cost of distributing expert system job aids will be high.

Here's an example: *VP Expert* is a good, flexible expert system shell which is also inexpensive ($149 or so). Once you've written an expert system in it, though, you have to buy a run-time license: for $300 a year, you can produce as many run-time copies of your systems as you want. If you're going to produce a number of expert systems, this is a good buy. For a few, it's expensive.

2. Particularly when you're just starting out, the shell should also be *easy to learn and easy to use.* This means several things. It means, for instance, that you shouldn't have to know anything about computer programming to use it effectively. It means that it should be easy to create each part of the system (building the rules, asking for input, etc.) And you should be able to learn it well enough to create a simple expert system in a matter of hours.

3. The other side of this is that the shell should be *comfortable for the user* as well. In the jargon of the day, it should be "user friendly." "User friendly" is often taken to mean the same thing as

"easy to use." Certainly a user-friendly program should be easy for the user. But it really means more than this. Basically, user-friendly means that the user can do everything he needs to do while using the system without having to think a lot about it. He should be able to concentrate on getting what he wants from the system, not on what he has to do to get it.

4. The next feature is one that means one thing when you're first starting and another when you've become experienced at building expert systems. The shell should be *powerful* enough to do what you want done.

There's a general conflict here between simplicity and ease of use on the one hand and power on the other. The conflict isn't absolute; a shell can be powerful and still relatively easy to use—or difficult to use and still not very powerful. In general, though, the more powerful a shell is the longer it will take to learn to use it fully.

This is why it's good to start with a fairly simple expert system. That way, you can also start with an easy-to-use but limited expert system shell. As you become more proficient, you'll probably outgrow your initial shell—but by then you'll be much more proficient at developing expert systems and have a much clearer idea of what you want in the shell.

5. Finally, the company that makes the expert system shell should be *reliable* and provide at least some technical support to you. And here we run into a conflict again. Companies which sell low-cost shells simply can't afford to provide extensive support. But even they should be willing to answer questions from users who're obviously trying to use the product intelligently.

Surprisingly enough, there are three expert system products for less than $100 that—in two different ways—are quite impressive.

The first of these is *Easy Expert,* available from Park Row (4640 Jewel Street, Suite 101, San Diego, CA 92109, 619/581-6778) for the princely sum of $49.95 (no shipping charge if prepaid). Easy Expert is very limited, but it will produce highly usable systems quickly and (as its name implies) easily. The run-time system is included in the purchase price, so you can make and distribute as many copies of expert system job aids as you want for free. Even if you have only minimal experience with a PC and none with expert systems, you can learn to use Easy Expert effectively in a matter of hours.

The second is even less expensive, though not quite as easy to use. It's *XXXPert,* available from many electronic bulletin boards or from Stephen Thurber, 1926 Labrador Lane, Vienna, VA 22180

for $29.00. Again, there's no charge for the run-time system.

The third product is very different from the other two. It's *If/then,* available for $69.95 plus shipping from If/then Solutions, P.O. Box 52097, Palo Alto, CA 94303, 415/322-3430. It consists of a 160-page text on expert systems and a disk with a number of programs. It runs only with Lotus 1-2-3, Version 2. If you produce training on and about spreadsheets, *If/then* could be a way to design effective job aids.

(*VP Expert,* mentioned above, falls above the $100 ceiling I arbitrarily set for this article. It takes a little practice to get comfortable with it, and you have to pay a run-time fee. However, if you expect to produce a number of expert systems, it might be a good investment.)

Building an Expert System Job Aid

Once you've selected the right application and the shell to use for it, the time has come to actually do it. And this is a lot more like designing effective training than you might think at first glance.

You've probably already analyzed the process that the expert system will perform—as part of the training design itself. Presumably, it's part of the content of the course. That means that all you need to do to create an expert system job aid is to turn the process into a series of rules.

This isn't all that difficult, if you do it before you start working on the system itself. One of the besetting faults of people who work with computers is that they want to get started punching stuff into the computer before they've thought through just how to organize what they're punching in. (Training designers would never do that, of course.) As anxious as you may be to get to work on the rule base, you need to work out all of the logic before you touch the first key. If you do, the rest will be relatively easy.

(There are many different ways to work out the logic of a process, and choosing between them is largely a matter of local practice and/or individual preference. A new product which helps build automated decision logic tables can be helpful for making sure that all of the alternatives are covered. The product is **Logic Gem**, $199 from Sterling Castle (702 Washington Street, Suite 174, Marina del Rey, CA 90292, 213/306-3020). It's designed for computer programmers, but will work well in any situation which requires the logical analysis of a process.)

When you're sure you have the process logic down, it's time to pause and ask if you really need an expert system. After all, people have gotten by for years with pencil-and-paper job aids. An expert system will almost certainly take longer to develop.

If you spend the time and effort on it, you need to make sure that the payoff for the user will be worth it.

If the expert system is still appropriate, you're almost ready to create the system. I say "almost" because there's one important step left: putting the rules in the best order.

There's a very simple guideline here:

> An expert system should be built so that the user has to provide the minimum amount of data necessary to get a decision.

Nothing will turn a user off to expert systems more quickly than one which asks him for information which he knows isn't needed to make that specific decision. In general, this means that the rules should be organized so that the ones which require the smallest amount of input are examined first.

Here's an example. I've been working on an expert system to help supervisors deal with people problems. It happens that the factor which drives what a supervisor can do more than any other is the amount of trust between him and the employee. Consequently, the system tries to determine how trusting the relationship is early in the session. Depending on the input, it may then need only one or two more questions to arrive at a recommendation.

Back to you. You've reduced the essentials of the process to a series of rules, and you've organized the rules so that they don't waste the user's time asking for unnecessary input. What now?

Well, if you really have done steps 1 and 2, you've come to the easy part: actually building the system. How you do it will depend on the shell you're using, but these are the major steps:

1. Create the rule base.
2. Create the questions to ask which will get the information required for a decision.
3. Provide help screens that the user can access if he doesn't understand what he's to do.
4. Provide a glossary of terms or some other device which defines any technical terms used.
5. Provide information about why a given bit of data is needed.
6. Provide an explanation of how the system reached the conclusion it did.

When the first pass of the system is done, you do with it what you do with a training module: you try it out on the sort of people who will be its users. How extensively you need to do this depends on the complexity and unfamiliarity of the process the expert system is performing. At the very least, it should be tried out on one or two individuals, and their feedback used to modify it as necessary.

And this leads to another important point about expert system job aids. One of the strengths of expert system shells is that if they're used properly it's comparatively easy to modify the expert system you create. You can incorporate user feedback quickly and easily.

When the system has been tested, it's time to put it into final form. Some of this is technical, a question of following the vendor's instructions for creating a run-time version.

Beyond the technical, though, is the necessity to put it in the form that's as easy for the user to use as possible. Here are three tips.

• Some workers these days still have PCs with only floppy disk drives. If this is true for some of the employees you're preparing the job aid for, make sure they can run the program easily from a floppy.

• If some or all of the users have computers with hard disk drives, prepare an INSTALL program which will create a subdirectory on the drive and load the expert system job aid(s) into the subdirectory. I suggest that you name the subdirectory JOBAIDS, or something similar—to reinforce the idea that this is a permanent, growing part of the computer's function. You might also want to put a batch file in the root directory that will run the system from there.

• Finally, don't make the user enter a long or pretentious name to run the system—or even a short one that's too cutesy or unclear. Make everything he has to do as simple and clear as possible.

Conclusion

Well, this is the end of the primer. Hopefully, it's whetted your appetite and persuaded you that building expert system job aids is something you might want to try. With the low cost of usable expert system shells, the cost of experimentation (and occasional failure) is relatively low—and the payoff is potentially high. This makes it easy to try expert systems job aids in a variety of situations.

The fact of the matter—and you already know this—is that knowledge-based technology is only a tool. It may turn out to be a very powerful tool; I believe that it will. But it is only a tool. Just like a power drill, it's really helpful sometimes and completely useless a lot of the time. As with so many other tools, the true art isn't just in knowing how to use it, but knowing when to use it. □

If you're interested in seeing what a small expert system job aid might be like, you can download JOBAID. ARC from the CompuServ, GEnie, or ExecPC electronic bulletin boards and try it out.

Part I
Section Three

Expert Systems and Instructional Design and Development

Artificial Intelligence Techniques: Applications for Courseware Development

Brian L. Dear

Introduction

Applying research from the field of artificial intelligence (AI) to education and training has become the goal of an increasing number of computer-based instruction (CBI) practitioners and developers. Research investigating AI's potential in education has steadily evolved since the early 1970s. Most of this research has dealt with intelligent tutoring systems (ITS). Recently, the research has begun to explore another application for AI: improving the development, or authoring, of instructional software (courseware).

This article introduces some general concepts and techniques of AI and investigates ways we might apply these techniques to the analysis, design, development, implementation, and evaluation of courseware. Applying AI techniques will require a change in the way authors do things. Before AI techniques become accepted as useful development tools, authors may need to break some habits and traditional conceptions of what courseware is and what it takes to develop it.

AI Research

Feigenbaum and Feldman (1963) define the goal of AI research as: "to construct computer programs which exhibit behavior that we call 'intelligent behavior' when we observe it in human beings."

There are various sub-disciplines that comprise the overall AI research effort: vision systems, robotics, speech and natural language systems, knowledge representation and expert systems, intelligent tutoring systems, and problem-solving systems.

In the parlance of instructional designers and developers, one might approach AI from the

Brian L. Dear is a Senior Courseware Developer at Hazeltine Corporation, Training Systems Center, Reston, Virginia.

standpoint of a performance objective. For example, a "performance objective" of AI research might be:

> Given any problem, a machine will *create goals* to solve the problem, then *solve* the problem, then be able to *explain how* it solved the problem, and then be able to *apply* this problem-solving experience to future problems.

To "master" such an ambitious objective would require a good set of tools. Numerous hardware and software systems have been created and improved upon to aid AI workers in their research. Much of this research is done in sophisticated computer-based "laboratories" using such programming languages as LISP or Prolog. These rich environments give AI researchers a large set of tools and techniques with which to work.

Before we consider how these techniques might be applied to the CBI work environment, let us first examine the techniques themselves:

- natural language interfaces
- expert systems
- knowledge bases and knowledge representation
- heuristics
- user-interface metaphors
- object-based environments.

Natural Language Interfaces

"Natural language" (Rauch-Hindin, 1984; Rich, 1984) means "any language that humans learn from their environment and use to communicate with each other" (Harris, 1985). The purpose of a "natural language interface" is to allow natural language communication between a computer and a human: this communication might be spoken or typewritten. Most intelligent tutoring systems make use of some form of natural language interface which supports student-tutor dialogues. Another popular application involves database inquiry systems that allow a user to request, in English, information from a database.

Expert Systems

An expert system (Hayes-Roth, 1984; Hayes-Roth, 1985; Kearsley, 1985; Parsaye, 1985; Rauch-Hindin, 1983; Thomas and Sykes, 1985) is a computer program that:

(1) allows for the acquisition of expert knowledge of a certain, usually technical, field, and

(2) allows for non-experts to then consult with the system for advice and recommendations.

Expert systems are becoming the most well-known AI application outside of the AI research community. Business, industry, and government are investing millions in expert systems development (Reinhold, 1984; Harmon and King, 1985). Such commitment signifies that expert systems are past the drawing-board stage and are ready to be given real-world applications.

Intelligent tutoring systems are expert systems that contain a base of knowledge about a particular domain, or subject area, and, using their tutoring rules and heuristics, help the student to master the domain.

Knowledge Bases

A knowledge base (Hayes-Roth, 1984; Hayes-Roth, 1985) is a computer file which contains knowledge about a domain such as behavior descriptions, vocabulary definitions, relationships between objects, rules, constraints, heuristics, and facts (Fikes and Kehler, 1985). The "expertise" in expert systems comes from its knowledge base. Knowledge-based expert systems may be the first AI techniques to be applied in the CBI field. But before such techniques can be introduced, a new way of thinking about courseware development is required. A discussion of this concern will follow later in this article.

Heuristics

The literature refers to a "heuristic" (Barr and Feigenbaum, 1981) as a "rule of thumb," "hunch," or "judgment." A heuristic is a decision to act in a certain way based only on a guess as to whether the action is appropriate or correct for a given situation. For example, teachers and tutors use heuristics when they sense that one instructional strategy might be more effective than another.

An intelligent tutoring system might make use of heuristics to adapt itself to the learner; a natural-language interface might use heuristics to help clarify an ambiguous statement such as "The man with the moustache that held up the store is being sought by the authorities" (Meng, 1985).

User-Interface Metaphors

Computer users often adopt some kind of metaphor or set of metaphors which allow us to more comfortably understand a system and its man-machine interface (Wong, 1983) and more easily explain it to others, once we have figured it out for ourselves. Computers are exotic gadgets and are sometimes difficult to conceptualize. Just what are we doing when interacting with a computer, when programming instructional material on line? In CBI we have adopted what could be termed the "book metaphor." In recent years this book metaphor has been criticized. As Merrill (1985) stated,

"we are often trapped by our metaphors."

As we shall see, the introduction of AI techniques to the development of CBI may require replacing old metaphors, ideas, and habits with a more appropriate set of metaphors and perspectives.

Object-based Environments

Objects in this sense are icons, pictures, or symbols, that a computer user manipulates for various purposes. Goldberg and Robson (1983) state that "an object consists of some private [computer] memory and a set of operations" that act upon the memory.

One of the most well-known yet simple object-oriented environments is the LOGO system (Papert, 1980), where a user manipulates a "turtle" to create graphics and displays.

Whereas LOGO represents an object-oriented environment using *one* object, there are other environments which make use of *multiple* objects.

Xerox Corporation's Palo Alto Research Center (PARC) has contributed greatly to the object-based approach in software development. Two of Xerox PARC's more well-known object-based systems are the Smalltalk environment (Kay and Goldberg, 1977; Goldberg and Robson, 1983) and the Rehearsal World environment (Finzer and Gould, 1984). I say *environment* and not *programming language* because these systems require a whole new way of thinking about programming a computer.

In the Rehearsal World environment, for instance, a user interacts with a collection of "performers" on the screen. The user may send messages (text, numbers, pictures) to performers, tell performers to do specific things (display a message, calculate a number, retrieve some data), or instruct them to order other performers to do something. This is a *theatrical* user-interface metaphor, and the user is a kind of *playwright*, or *director*, and as such tells the performers what to say and what to do.

Another user-interface that Xerox has developed is the desk-top metaphor, which the Apple Computer company took notice of and implemented on their Macintosh computer. Public acceptance of the desk-top metaphor has been overwhelmingly positive.

The desk-top and theatrical metaphors should be considered by designers of courseware development systems; both may aid in gently introducing sophisticated AI techniques to the user.

Current Methods of Courseware Development

When we think of a courseware developer, or author, we often picture someone working at a computer, typing at the keyboard, transferring instructional material from paper script to computer memory, either by programming in a computer language, or by using one of the many "authoring systems" available in the marketplace.

There is a growing sentiment in the CBI and educational research literature that insists that courseware development really encompasses a lot more than just the entering of material into the computer.

Many suggest that the major problem with courseware development, indeed, CBI in general, is that too much emphasis is placed on the *computer*, and not enough on the *instruction*. Perhaps CBI should actually be termed IBC: *Instruction-based* computers. Many suggest that to view courseware development in its proper perspective, one should view it more like instructional systems design (ISD) (Bunderson, 1981; Montague and Wulfeck, 1984; Heaford, 1985). In the context of this article, "courseware development" is a set of activities like those in ISD: analysis, design, development, implementation, and evaluation.

Instructional Systems Design (ISD)

Educational researchers established a systematic method for creating instruction called Instructional Systems Design (Gagne and Briggs, 1979) to aid instructional developers in their job of creating effective instruction efficiently. Computers have already been considered for automating some of the more tedious and routine ISD tasks (O'Neal, 1985; Brecke and Blaiwes, 1981; Kearsley, 1985). AI techniques are being considered for use in automating some ISD tasks, as well as (and perhaps more importantly) in creating computer-based "intelligent assistants" for instructional developers.

AI applied to ISD is an increasingly debated issue. One of the major areas of concern is to first determine the correct way to perceive ISD: is it a procedure? Is it organized common sense? Is it an art? How we perceive ISD affects how we can consider applying AI techniques to it.

ISD has been described as an art (Davies, 1981; Sachs, 1981), as a science (Gibbon, 1981; Reigeluth *et al.*, 1981), or as some combination of both (Bunderson, 1981; Noel and Hewlett, 1981; Schrock and Coscarelli, 1981). Some say it's common sense, some say it's not. In the AI field, one thing is for sure: common-sense, artistic, and intuitive things are very hard to model on a computer; strict, procedural things are easier (Rose, 1984).

This concern for applying AI to ISD was echoed at a 1984 conference on Intelligent Authoring Aids (Proceedings, 1984):

If ISD is conceived as common sense made systematic, then it may be anomalous to consider AI as a promising approach to ISD, since the common lament among AI workers is their inability to capture "common sense."

Regardless of the perspective agreed upon, there are tasks in the instructional development process where AI techniques may be effectively applied.

The ISD model is primarily oriented to the curricular level of development. Some claim that one of its major shortcomings for CBI is the "lack of detail it provides individual lesson development" (Alessi and Trollip, 1985). Many have complained that the ISD model tells what to do, and in what order to do it, but not how to do it (Bunderson, 1981; Montague and Wulfeck, 1984; Schulz, 1977).

Most authoring systems include an on-line "help" program to aid authors in the programming of the courseware, yet few, if any, offer assistance in the analysis and design of the instruction. To provide courseware developers with on-line instructional guidance and assistance, a set of sophisticated programs must be created. These programs can and should make use of AI techniques, such as expert systems, heuristics, and natural language interfaces.

Applying AI Techniques to Courseware Development Activities

Following the design of the ISD model, I have grouped the many and varied activities that go into developing courseware into five common areas (see Figure 1).

Definition and Analysis Activities

Before one can design and develop courseware, one must define the purpose of the courseware. What is (and equally importantly, *what isn't*) the subject? What are the needs? Who is the audience? These questions must be answered before one can ask "How will this topic be taught?" or "How should I present this to the students?"

The computer is usually not used until the development and delivery of the courseware; rarely is it used in the early stages of a CBI project. While budgetary and resource concerns might be the causes of this phenomenon, it should also be noted that most CBI systems lack the tools needed to assist developers in the early phases of courseware definition and analysis.

There is enormous potential for applying the computer from the earliest project phases onward. An expert system whose knowledge base contained a large collection of CBI rules, facts, guidelines, algorithms, and even theories is but one possibility. The computer has already demonstrated its versatility in the so-called "idea processors" now

Figure 1

Courseware Development Activities

Definition and Analysis:
*   Defining the purpose of the courseware .
*   Identifying needs
*   Identifying the subject(s) to be taught
*   Defining the audience

Design:
*   Defining goals and outcomes
*   Creating course and lesson plans
*   Identifying instructional strategies
*   Creating storyboards and scripts of lessons

Development:
*   Transferring design material onto computer
*   Programming and debugging lessons

Implementation and Delivery:
*   Installing hardware and software
*   Allocating system resources
*   Registering and scheduling students
*   Delivering the courseware
*   Collecting student data

Evaluation:
*   Analyzing student record data
*   Updating outdated or obsolete material
*   Revising where needed

---

available in the personal computer marketplace. For example, many writers now use idea processors to *brainstorm*; these programs facilitate getting the ideas on-line as quickly as possible.

Many definition and analysis tasks are algorithmic and procedural in nature, and are hence worth considering for automation and "expertizing" (by "expertize" I mean "create an expert system for some process"). By "algorithmic" I mean that flowcharts can be drawn up and the procedure clearly stated and defined.

Feasibility analysis offers interesting prospects for "expertization." A computerized forecasting tool would allow potential CBI users to predict how much a courseware development project might cost, and how much it might cost if implemented in a different way and for different topics. This might consist of a "first-draft" knowledge base to be later modified and enhanced in the design and development groups.

There are many resources available in the literature to assist in the definition of instructional

goals. The important word here is *assist*. Expert systems, such as MYCIN (Shortliffe, 1976), a medical diagnosis program, are generally designed to assist people; their creators are not concerned with creating machines that think, but rather tools that help *humans* think. With the advent of AI technology, we can now consider implementing some on-line instructional tools to assist in the definition and analysis of instruction.

Design Activities

There are already automated tools to help in the writing of performance objectives, such as the J/T Pak program from GP Courseware Company. Perhaps something more is needed—an advisor—a guide—to verify the appropriateness of the objectives written. Here is another case where we might want to "expertize" the task.

Merrill (1985) suggests that the next generation of courseware development systems should offer a set of what he terms instructional "transactions." Whereas authoring systems usually support some standard set of interactions, such as multiple-choice, short answer, and matching, there are no authoring systems which offer guidance in selecting transactions and strategies and suggest which might best match a particular objective (Merrill, in press). In other words, what is appropriate and when? When should one use multiple choice? When short answers? Current CBI systems lack this needed guidance.

Some researchers (Wager, 1982) have suggested that courseware developers use the nine events of instruction as outlined by Gagne and Briggs (1979). Gagne, Wager, and Rojas (1981) have drawn up guidelines for the CBI author that take these nine events into account. These nine events are:
1. Gaining attention
2. Informing the learner of the objective
3. Stimulating recall of prerequisite learnings
4. Presenting stimulus material
5. Providing learning guidance
6. Eliciting the performance
7. Providing feedback about performance correctness
8. Assessing the performance
9. Enhancing retention and transfer.

An on-line "expert" program whose knowledge base consisted of a wide accumulation of ISD principles could greatly benefit courseware developers, especially in sites where ISD specialists are scarce.

Intelligent tutoring systems take advantage of the ability to support some of the more sophisticated transactions that are usually difficult to implement on standard authoring systems (see below).

Some New Strategies and Transaction Modes

- "Mixed-initiative" dialogues (Merrill, 1985; Carbonell, 1970)
- "Coaching" (Burton and Brown, 1982)
- "Socratic Dialogue" (Stevens, Collins, and Goldin, 1982)
- Discovery or "Learning by Doing" (Papert, 1980)

The "mixed initiative" dialogue is a two-way conversation. For example, the following conversation (taken from a hypothetical lesson on the Fifty States of the United States) illustrates the concept of "mixed-initiative dialogue":

Computer: What is the capital of Maryland?

Student: Baltimore

Computer: No, the correct answer is Annapolis. Annapolis lies adjacent to what large body of water?

Student: The Cheasapeake Bay

Computer: Right. And what state lies directly east of Maryland and the Chesapeake Bay?

Student: Where did the word "Chesapeake" come from?

Computer: Chesapeake is an Indian name. Now answer the question.

Student: Does the Chesapeake Bay have fresh or salt water?

Computer: First answer the question.

And so on. The student could get quite carried away with digressions! The computer needs to know how to teach, when to say "no," when to say "let's get back on track." The computer needs to have tutorial expertise.

A "Socratic" dialogue, explored in the experimental WHY system (Stevens, Collins, and Goldin, 1982; Barr and Feigenbaum, 1982) makes use of heuristics that affect the direction of the student-computer dialogue. According to Stevens and Collins (1977), human tutors use heuristics to attempt to correct student misconceptions and "bugs" (errors). A computer program would simulate these heuristic methods when tutoring a student. Because computers can interact with much larger numbers of students than a single human tutor, the possibilities for the system gaining more and more tutoring expertise and experience are phenomenal.

A computerized "coach" has been explored by Burton and Brown (1982). For informal learning environments, such as games, simulations, and the LOGO system (an example of "learning by doing"), a computer coach monitors a student's actions and progress through a program and interrupts the student if there is an indication that the student has made a "poor move." In a similar sense, the TICCIT Advisor program (Merrill, 1985;

Bunderson, 1981) can be considered a "coach" that watches the student's progress through a CBI course and makes recommendations when necessary.

An important concept to consider is the *student model*, which many suggest is a necessary component of any intelligent tutoring system. There is much discussion of the student model in the literature (Carbonell, 1970; Barr and Feigenbaum, 1982; Merrill, 1985; Dallman, 1986).

In brief, the "student model" is a program on the computer that draws up some image of how the student is performing in a lesson. The model of the student is compared with a model of an expert, and thus some conclusions may be made about the student.

The model of the expert sometimes turns out to be merely the "knowledge base"—if the student model and the ideal, expert model matched, then the system might say the student had achieved perfect mastery. One of the problems with this model is that it is dangerous to assume the student reasons as the expert or teacher does (Barr and Feigenbaum, 1982).

Other uses for a student model involve (1) gathering data about the student's learning styles and behavior, (2) recognizing patterns in a student's progress through a course, and (3) recognizing patterns in a student's response (Tennyson, 1984; Tennyson, Christensen, and Park 1984; Barr and Feigenbaum, 1982).

Development Activities

How the author interacts with the computer is just as important as how the student does so. Intelligent tutoring systems research concentrates on the student-tutor interaction. I believe that a parallel can be drawn between the author-computer interaction and the student-computer interaction. Whereas intelligent tutoring systems include a model of the student, I propose that authoring systems include a *model of the author*, which would include information such as:

1. Intentions and goals of the author (i.e., "What I want to accomplish" and "What I want this lesson to do" and "What routines and code I plan to use").
2. Recognition of the author's misconceptions—from pedagogical misconceptions to programming misconceptions.

Researchers at Yale are studying the "intentionality" of computer programmers (Johnson, 1985; Johnson and Soloway, 1985). This research suggests that by giving the computer a sense of what the programmer "has in mind," the process of debugging code can be simplified. Miller (1982) suggests that systems should emphasize to novice programmers the plan instead of the code. Genesereth (1982) has also researched plans. Although these researchers have had students in mind in their research, the idea of plans and intentionality should be explored more by designers of authoring systems.

Some form of natural language interface between the author and the computer might ease problems of (1) the user not understanding the computer, and (2) the computer not understanding the user (Schank, 1984).

Improving Authoring Systems

While it is nice to think that better programming tools make for better courseware, there is little or no evidence suggesting that courseware is actually improved (Heaford, 1985; Merrill, 1985). Perhaps the emphasis should be shifted from mere programming tools to instructional design tools—by first making authors aware of the fact that they are creating instruction, not mere computer programs.

The Myth of "Easy to Use" Authoring Systems

Much in vogue lately is the idea that a good authoring system means an easy-to-use authoring system (Pollock, 1985). Easy-to-use authoring systems often wind up churning out unsophisticated courseware. Vendors of so-called "programmerless" systems often cite the long hours needed to train a novice author in using an authoring language which requires programming. However, if the author stays on the project for any length of time, he or she will soon no longer be a novice (Heaford, 1985). He or she will soon be saying, "Why can't I get the system to do this?" or "I want to do something more sophisticated!" This problem is being recognized by some in the field, and steps are being taken to create "multi-level" authoring systems, such as ADAPT (Mudrick, 1985; Mudrick and Stone, 1984).

Time to Phase Out
the "Frame-Based" Approach to Authoring

Merrill (1985) has stated that almost all authoring systems share the "frame-based" mentality (Carbonell, 1970), or, as this article terms it, the "book metaphor." The key words are "frame," "page," "chapter," "table of contents," "index," and, of course, "author." It is time to consider a new user-interface metaphor.

Instead of interacting with the computer on a one-to-one basis perhaps we should consider an interaction with a set of object-based "performers" or "characters," each a specialist in one area of developing instruction.

Imagine you could call on an Instructional

Strategy Expert character, who could make recommendations about and review your work; or perhaps an on-line subject matter expert, which in effect would be the knowledge base. Imagine another performer, a "go-fer," which could be called on to do repetitive tasks or mundane work, such as checking for proper spelling, verifying the reading level of text, searching for text or pictures from an on-line library, or actually generating program code based upon the author's goals and intentions and on the instructional strategies selected.

There are serious implications in such an environment. At first glance, one might say that such an environment promotes the "one-man band" courseware development phenomenon: one person does everything. The intent is not to create such a system: this proposed environment would be used by a team of instructional designers, courseware developers, and subject matter experts. This environment would encourage each person to share his or her expertise and skills with other members of the team. The performer icons on the screen might actually be doorways into the individual "knowledge bases" of the humans working on the project.

Rapid Prototyping

One of the emerging benefits of object-based systems is that prototypes of the final program can be rapidly created. Scripting and storyboarding activities could be made more productive with such tools. A common lament among instructional designers is that they wish they had been able to see "what it looked like" on the screen earlier on (Dick, 1985). It is difficult to prototype a lesson or group different lesson scenarios because most authoring systems are not as simple to use as claims state.

The Content Vs. the Code

There is a trend developing in the world of computers: the change in the relationship of the *content* and the *code* (see Figure 2). In the case of authoring languages, the content, that is, what is being presented on the computer, is quite often the code, or the authoring language. This is most often the case with languages such as TUTOR (and its offspring, TenCORE and ACCORD), PILOT, and IBM's Coursewriter. In fact, when CBI is developed using a general-purpose programming language like PASCAL or BASIC, most likely, the content and the code are one and the same.

Clearly, the trend is towards a separation of the content with the code. Most AI researchers now agree that it is highly beneficial to separate the massive amounts of knowledge ("content") from the so-called "inference engine" (the "code").

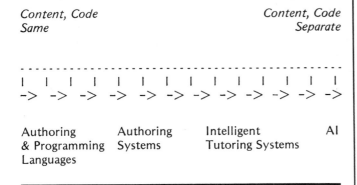

Figure 2

The Content and the Code

Content, Code Same		Content, Code Separate

```
- - - - - - - - - - - - - - - - - - - - - - - - - - - - -
 |   |   |   |   |   |   |   |   |   |   |   |   |
->  ->  ->  ->  ->  ->  ->  ->  ->  ->  ->  ->  ->
```

Authoring & Programming Languages	Authoring Systems	Intelligent Tutoring Systems	AI

A parallel can be drawn to database systems, especially those on personal computers of today. What we now have are generic tools, the "code," which allow for the acquisition, storage, and retrieval of data ("content"). Without such generic tools, no-one but programmers would bother using databases on computers. Separation of the database program from the data base allows users the level of flexibility they want.

In intelligent tutoring systems and expert systems, the "knowledge base" is equivalent to the "content" and the "inference engines" are the "code." Already, researchers have begun designing prototypes of knowledge-based authoring systems, such as OBIE-1-KNOBE (Freedman, 1984) which lets the courseware developer create sophisticated representations of content without the drudgery of programming.

CBI with Programming Languages

There are some who use and recommend general-purpose programming languages as development tools for courseware (Bork, 1985). In fact, one of the designers of a large authoring system has admitted that his own work is done in Pascal (Merrill, 1985).

The $50 million CBI project going on at MIT, called Project Athena, is made up of software that is almost exclusively being developed in C, Fortran, or LISP, not TUTOR, ADAPT, or PILOT (Project Athena, 1985).

Obviously, many think that the job can be done just as well, even better, without an authoring system. Sometimes, though, the very reason for criticism of an authoring language or authoring system is that it does not aid the developer in creating good pedagogical material (Bork, 1985). The critics then go off to do their work in a language such as Pascal or C. Yet Pascal and C and other general-purpose programming languages face the same problem: where is the good pedagogy in Pascal or C?

Improving the On-line Environment

A current trend in the personal computer world is to improve the "on-line environment." This on-line environment now includes such things as "integrated" software, including word processing, database management, accounting and project management, telecommunications, and graphics design.

In the AI computer world, researchers have come up with some interesting tools that might also turn out to be of benefit to courseware developers.

The AI Programming Environment
- DWIM (Do What I Mean) (Barr and Feigenbaum, 1982; Teitelman and Masinter, 1981)
- Intelligent Assistant (Barr and Feigenbaum, 1982)
- WIMP (Window Icon Mouse Program) (Blackburn, 1985)

DWIM, or, Do What I Mean, is a facility in the INTERLISP-D LISP programming environment that tries to "figure out what the programmer really meant to say (Barr and Feigenbaum, 1982)" when he or she typed in an uninterpretable command. DWIM also corrects spelling errors. I think DWIM would be a welcome addition to any courseware developer's set of tools.

An intelligent assistant "watches" the activity of a programmer and, when requested, it can repeat a command or set of commands, or undo something just entered. These types of facilities have already made their way into personal computer software—word processing programs are becoming more and more sophisticated while maintaining ease of use.

Windows, icons, and mice (Blackburn, 1985) are other facilities that are receiving wider and wider acceptance in the marketplace. The Macintosh computer did much to make such technology household words.

To improve courseware development we should look to other computer applications and determine whether there are worthwhile tools that would benefit courseware developers. The AI programming environment, the Smalltalk environment, and even the emerging, "integrated" software environments of personal computers offer many such tools that should be examined.

Implementation, Delivery, and Evaluation

Implementation, delivery, and evaluation of courseware might also benefit from "expertization." Software debugging, logistics planning, computer resource allocation, student registration and scheduling, and data interpretation activities all have room for improvement.

Expert "troubleshooting" programs should be accessible to the actual teachers and proctors who work in the CBI classroom. A courseware development system should include tools to create advisory programs that come bundled with the final delivered product. Such programs, which could be "hidden" behind a non-threatening "performer" interface, would assist teachers, proctors, and even students in making best use of the system and its capabilities.

Another potentially useful tool for the courseware evaluator is an expert program that assists in the analysis of the student data records. Many CBI systems provide course evaluators with large "dumps" of student data: yet there is never enough time to analyze it completely, and often an analysis of the data requires custom programming. An object-based "evaluation performer" could assist in the early stages of a courseware project by helping a team generate a list of hypotheses, predictions, and algorithms which would be used to verify the hypotheses and predictions by analyzing the student data automatically.

Conclusions and Summary

The next generation of courseware development systems must take heed of these technological developments. Users are going to demand such powerful, yet more intuitively natural computing environments.

I believe the next generation of courseware development technology will be much more powerful than what we now use. Some of the techniques mentioned in this article are certainly going to take a lot of effort and money to implement for the CBI field. Other techniques, though, can be implemented sooner.

There is a great need for research in this area. With such sophisticated courseware, capable of mixed-initiative conversations with students, and instant access to huge amounts of knowledge, how will this change the way we learn? How will this change students' attitudes towards computers? More importantly, how is this going to change students' attitudes towards their teachers?

By adding such sophistication to the courseware development process, we are finally beginning to tap into the computer's enormous power and potential. It will reshape the way we think about in-structional design. It will reshape the way we do things in general. We need to be prepared.   □

References

Alessi, S., and Trollip, S. *Computer-based Instruction: Methods and Development.* Englewood Cliffs, NJ: Prentice-Hall, 1985.

Barr, A., and Feigenbaum, E.A. *The Handbook of Artificial Intelligence, Volume 1.* Los Altos, CA: William A. Kaufmann, Inc., 1981.

Barr, A., and Feigenbaum, E.A. *The Handbook of Artificial Intelligence, Volume 2.* Los Altos, CA: William A. Kaufmann, Inc., 1982.

Blackburn, L.N. For CBT Read SBT—System Based Training. Paper presented at the 1985 Multi-Media Authoring Systems Conference, London, England, June 18-20, 1985.

Bork, A. The Computer in Education in the United States: The Perspective from the Educational Technology Center. *Computers & Education*, 1985, *8*(4), 335-341.

Brecke, F., and Blaiwes, A. CASDAT: An Innovative Approach to More Efficient ISD. *Journal of Educational Technology Systems*, 1981, *10*(3), 271-283.

Bunderson, C.V. Courseware. In H.F. O'Neil (Ed.) *Computer-Based Instruction: A State of the Art Assessment.* New York: Academic Press, 1981, 91-125.

Burton, R.R., and Brown, J.S. An Investigation of Computer Coaching for Informal Learning Activities. In D. Sleeman, and J. Brown (Eds.), *Intelligent Tutoring Systems.* New York: Academic Press, 1982, 79-98.

Carbonell, J.R. AI in CAI: Artificial Intelligence Approach to Computer-Assisted Instruction. *IEEE Transactions on Man-Machine Systems*, 1970, *11*(4), 190-202.

Dallman, B. Intelligent Tutoring Systems Research. In *1986 Air Force Conference on Technology in Training and Education Proceedings.* Montgomery, AL: Air University, 1986.

Davies, I.K. Instructional Development as an Art: One of the Three Phases of ID. *NSPI Journal*, 1981, *20*(7), 4-7.

Dick, W. The Design and Development of the U.S. Army Computer-Based Job Skills Training Program. Paper presented at the Multi-Media Authoring Systems Conference, London, England, June 18-20, 1985.

Feigenbaum, E.A., and Feldman, J. (Eds.) *Computers and Thought.* New York: McGraw-Hill, 1963.

Fikes, R., and Kehler, T. The Role of Frame-Based Representation in Reasoning. *Communications of the ACM*, 1985, *28*(9), 904-920.

Finzer, W., and Gould, L. Programming by Rehearsal. *BYTE*, 1984, *9*(6), 187-210.

Freedman, R. Knowledge-Based Authoring Systems. *Training Technology Journal*, 1984, *1*(2).

Gagne, R.M., and Briggs, L.J. *Principles of Instructional Design.* New York: Holt, Rinehart, and Winston, 1979.

Gagne, R.M., Wager, W., and Rojas, A. Planning and Authoring Computer-Assisted Instruction Lessons. *Educational Technology*, 1981, *21*(9), 17-26.

Geneseth, M. The Role of Plans in Intelligent Tutoring Systems. In D. Sleeman and J. Brown (Eds.), *Intelligent*

Tutoring Systems. New York: Academic Press, 1982.

Gibbons, A.S. The Contribution of Science to Instructional Development. *NSPI Journal*, 1981, *20*(7), 23-25.

Goldberg, A., and Robson, D. *Smalltalk-80: The Language and Its Implementation*. Reading, MA: Addison-Wesley, 1983.

Harmon, P., and King, D. *Expert Systems: Artificial Intelligence in Business*. New York: John Wiley and Sons, 1985.

Harris, M.D. *Introduction to Natural Language Processing*. Reston, VA: Reston Publishing Company, 1985.

Hayes-Roth, F. The Rule-Based Expert System: A Tutorial. *IEEE Computer*, 1984, *17*(9), 11-28.

Hayes-Roth, F. Engineering Systems of Knowledge: The Great Adventure Head. In K.N. Karna (Ed.), *Expert Systems in Government Symposium*, McLean, VA, October 24-25, 1985, 678-692.

Heaford, J. Technical and Instructional Considerations in Using Multi-Media Authoring Tools. Paper presented at the 1985 Multi-Media Authoring Systems Conference, London, England, June 18-20, 1985.

Johnson, W.L. PROUST: A System Which Debugs Pascal Programs. In K.N. Karna (Ed.), *Expert Systems in Government Symposium*, McLean, VA, October 24-25, 1985, 157.

Johnson, W.L., and Soloway, E. PROUST. *BYTE*, 1985, *10*(4), 179-190.

Kay, A., and Goldberg, A. Personal Dynamic Media. *IEEE Computer*, 1977, *10*, 31-41.

Kearsley, G.P. The CBT Advisor: An Expert System for Making Decisions About CBT. *Performance and Instruction*, 1985, *24*(9), 15-17.

Meng, B. Natural Language Ambiguity, or Is the Turkey Ready to Eat? *Digital Design*, 1985, *15*(11), 51-58.

Merrill, M.D. Where Is the Authoring in Authoring Systems? *Journal of Computer-Based Instruction*, 1985, *12*(4), 90-96.

Merrill, M.D. Prescriptions for an Authoring System. *Journal of Computer-Based Instruction*, in press, 1986.

Miller, M.A. A Structured Planning and Debugging Environment for Elementary Programming. In D.L. Sleeman and J.S. Brown (Eds.), *Intelligent Tutoring Systems*. New York: Academic Press, 1982.

Montague, W.E., and Wulfeck, W.H. Computer-Based Instruction: Will It Improve Instructional Quality? *Training Technology Journal*, 1984, *1*(2), 4-19.

Mudrick, D. Human Factors in the Design of User-Friendly Authoring Systems. Paper presented at 1985 Multi-Media Authoring Systems Conference, London, England, June 18-20, 1985.

Mudrick, D., and Stone, D. An Adaptive Authoring System for Computer-Based Instruction. *Journal of Computer-Based Instruction*, 1984, *11*(3), 82-84.

Noel, K.L., and Hewlett, B. Plying Your Craft: Instructional Development and the Use of Aeuristics. *NSPI Journal*, 1981, *20*(7), 15-48.

O'Neal, A.F. The Current Status of Instructional Design Theories. Paper presented at the 1985 Multi-Media Authoring Systems Conference, London, England, June 18-20, 1985.

Papert, S. *Mindstorms*. New York: Basic Books, 1980.

Parsaye, K. The Evolutionary Road to Expert Systems. In K.N. Karna (Ed.), *Expert Systems in Government Symposium*, McLean, VA, October 24-25, 1985, 68-69.

Pollock, J. Authoring Courseware: No Skills Necessary? *Educational Technology*, 1985, *25*(11), 44-48.

Proceedings, Intelligent Authoring Aids Conference, University of California at Los Angeles, June, 1984.

Project Athena: Faculty/Student Projects. Cambridge, MA: Massachusetts Institute of Technology, March 1985.

Rauch-Hindin, W. Artificial Intelligence: A Solution Whose Time Has Come. *Systems & Software*, 1983, *2*(12), 150-177.

Rauch-Hindin, W. Natural Language: An Easy Way to Talk to Computers. *Systems & Software*, 1984, *3*(1), 187-206.

Rose, F. *Into the Heart of the Mind: An American Quest for Artificial Intelligence*. New York: Harper & Row, 1984.

Reigeluth, C., Van Patten, J., and Doughty, P. Science Approach to Instructional Development. *NSPI Journal*, 1981, *20*(7), 19-22.

Reinhold, R. Machines Being Built to Emulate Reasoning of Human Experts. *New York Times*, March 29, 1984, p. 1.

Rich, E. Natural Language Interfaces. *IEEE Computer*, 1984, *17*(9), 39-47.

Sachs, S.G. Practicing the Art of Instructional Development. *NSPI Journal*, 1981, *20*(7), 8+.

Schank, R. *The Cognitive Computer*. Reading, MA: Addison-Wesley, 1984.

Schrock, S.A., and Coscarelli, W.C. Some Sources of the Art, Craft, and Science Views of Instructional Development. *NSPI Journal*, 1981, *20*(7), 26+.

Schulz, R.E. On-Line Authoring Aids for Developing Tests and Instruction. In H.F. O'Neil (Ed.), *Procedures for Instructional Systems Development*. New York: Academic Press, 1977.

Shortliffe, E. *Computer-Based Medical Consultation: MYCIN*. New York: American Elsevier, 1976.

Stevens, A., and Collins, A. The Goal Structure of a Socratic Tutor. *BBN Report No. 2518* from Bolt, Beranek, and Newman, Inc., Cambridge, Massachusetts, 1977.

Stevens, A., Collins, A., and Goldin, S.E. Misconceptions in Students' Understanding. In Sleeman, D., and Brown, J.S. (Eds.), *Intelligent Tutoring Systems*. New York: Academic Press, 1982, 13-24.

Teitelman, W., and Masinter, L. The INTERLISP Programming Environment. *IEEE Computer*, 1981, *14*(4), 25-33.

Tennyson, R.D. Artificial Intelligence Methods in Computer Based Instructional Design. *Journal of Instructional Development*, 1984, *7*(3), 17-22.

Tennyson, R.D., Christensen, D.L., and Park, S.E. The Minnesota Adaptive Instructional System: An Intelligent CBI System. *Journal of Computer-Based Instruction*, 1984, *11*(1), 2-13.

Thomas, D.E., and Sykes, D.J. The Impact of Artificial Intelligence on Maintenance Training. *Proceedings of the 7th Interservice/Industry Training Equipment Conference*, November, 1985, 14-23.

Wager, W. Design Considerations for Instructional Computing Programs. *Journal of Educational Technology Systems*, 1982, *10*(3), 261-270.

Wong, P. MMI: The Man-Machine Interface. *Training and Technology Journal*, 1983, *1*(1), 19-35.

Expert Systems: Instructional Design Potential

Joellyn Pollock and R. Scott Grabinger

The versatility of the computer permits educators and students an almost unlimited variety of computer-based instructional technologies. One of the newer computer technologies finding its way into instruction is the expert system.

Viewed as a product of research in artificial intelligence and cognitive processing, an expert system is a program that uses inference techniques to arrive at problem solutions in a specific area of knowledge. The program asks questions of a user in order to guide that user through the problem-solving process to reach presumably the same conclusion a consensus of experts would reach. This interaction between expert and non-expert within a specific domain of knowledge has attracted the attention of education and industry in the anticipation that this "new" software technology will provide applications not produced with traditional procedural-based computing.

Expert System Components

An expert system is comprised of two major components: a knowledge domain and an inference engine. The knowledge domain, or knowledge base, consists of a set of related facts organized by rules and goals that define relationships among the facts. The inference engine uses facts, rules, and goals from the knowledge base to solve problems for a user. Figure 1 shows an extremely simplified knowledge domain for selecting instructional media.

Facts in the knowledge base are simple statements that define objects and conditions. Rules provide a structure that leads to specific decisions—decisions that an expert would make under similar conditions. For example, the facts in Figure 1 define several factors used in the selection of a specific instructional medium: media, learner control,

Joellyn Pollock is an external design consultant for Instructional Innovators, Inc., and a doctoral student at Arizona State University, Tempe, Arizona. **R. Scott Grabinger** is Assistant Professor, Division of Instructional Technology, University of Colorado at Denver.

Figure 1

Knowledge Base Example

Facts

A book is a medium.
A slide/tape is a medium.
Computer-assisted instruction is a medium.
Video tape is a medium.

Low is a level of learner control.
Moderate is a level of learner control.
High is a level of learner control.

Verbal abstraction is a type of instructional message.
Simulation is a type of instructional message.

Individual is a group size.
Small group is a group size.
Large group is a group size.

Rules

1. If content is primarily verbal abstractions
    and high level of learner control is necessary
    and group size is small
   Then appropriate medium is a book.

2. If a moderate level of learner control is desired
    and group size is large
    or group size is small
    or group size is individual
   Then appropriate medium is slide/tape.

3. If a high level of learner control is desired
    or a moderate level of user control is desired
    and instructional method is simulation
    and group size is individual
   Then appropriate medium is CAI.

4. If a high degree of learner control is desired
    and group size is individual
   Then the appropriate medium is CAI.

types of message, and class size. Facts define and limit the problem and its attributes. In this case, the facts list four attributes that an expert would use when deciding which medium to use in an instructional situation. The rules in Figure 1 establish the relationships among the facts. In other words, the rules describe the decision-making process. A novice user, one who does not possess the expert's knowledge, may ask the system for the most effective medium to use with individualized instruction when a high level of user control is desired. The inference engine, the computer code that directs the decision search, examines the knowledge base until it finds a rule that matches the user's conditions—computer-assisted instruction (Rule 4).

Although on the surface there may appear no differences between conventional programming languages and languages derived from artificial intelligence research, there are important distinctions. While both are capable of reasoning and inferencing processes, traditional programming languages such as BASIC, FORTRAN, or Pascal require a step-by-step procedural approach in an "IF A THEN B" format. Programs written in these languages use algorithms which follow a precisely defined path to produce a guaranteed solution and the same solution each time.

Expert systems, on the other hand, attempt to approach the solution of a problem using heuristics or "rules of thumb." In this context, programming takes on an "IF A OCCURS TO X DEGREE THEN B HAPPENS TO Y DEGREE AND IF THAT DOESN'T WORK TRY Z" format. Heuristics do not always point to the most efficient solution nor always result in the same solution. Heuristics reflect the ambiguity of real world situations. The system can go back within itself to find alternatives, to ask for more information—just as an expert does. For example, when playing chess, neither the expert nor the novice analyzes every possible move. Each uses heuristics to limit the possible number of moves based on past instruction or experience. The move chosen may be poor, average, or excellent, given the facts available.

The advantage of this type of system is that not every possible option need be anticipated. An algorithmic system has a single discrete path for each solution. This is a memory-intensive means of programming and one reason why computer use in instruction has been limited to new versions of programmed instruction. It is impossible to devise a program to anticipate every response for every condition. However, artificial intelligence, in general, and heuristics in specific, provide us with the opportunity to design programs that would react more like a real teacher. The use of heuristic techniques permits us to build smaller programs that can react to more diverse situations. It may not always be the best response, but a teacher doesn't do that either. One of the practical programs based on artificial intelligence techniques is expert systems. Both large and small expert systems use artificial intelligence techniques to solve complex tasks. It is only recently that "small" expert systems have been made available for microcomputers.

Expert System Languages and Shells

The actual creation of expert systems takes many forms. Like programming languages and authoring courseware, tools to construct expert systems lie along a continuum of flexibility and ease of use. Languages for programmers are at one end of the continuum while systems or "shells" for the non-programmer are at the other end. The difference between shells and languages can be compared to ways of making model boats. A sophisticated model builder may begin with blocks of wood and tools to create the model while the novice model maker will use a plastic kit with preformed pieces and glue. The sophisticated expert system developer will use a language to create the system from "scratch"; the novice will begin with a shell.

One of the most popular languages for developing expert systems is Prolog (PROgramming in LOGic). Prolog ". . . is a declarative language that allows the programmer to make direct statements and assertions about objects and relationships. . ." (Burnham and Hall, 1985, p. 1). Most languages are "prescriptive," but Prolog is "descriptive." This means that the programmer describes facts and relationships about a problem rather than prescribes the steps to be taken to solve a problem (Clocksin and Mellish, 1984).

Using the simplified instructional media selection knowledge domain in Figure 1 as a starting point, the instructional designer using Prolog would begin to go into detail and create a larger knowledge base. What other media should be considered? What other factors affect the media selection decision? What concepts should be defined to clarify concepts and increase the accuracy of the recommendation? For example, what is a verbal abstraction and how does the system know the parameters of "primarily" in the rule, "If instructional message is primarily verbal abstractions. . ."?

Another level of relationships must be developed. If a term is too difficult to define, Prolog has the capability to accept instances. Assume that "complexity" of the instructional presentation was a factor added to the knowledge domain. A rule could be written that defined complexity as "requiring detailed graphics." Inherent in the language is a great deal of power and flexibility for the designer, though this power and flexibility is coupled with the difficulty of learning the specifics of a programming language.

Most instructional designers will use "shells" to construct expert systems. Shells can be compared to authoring systems that are used to simplify the production of computer-assisted instruction. A typical expert system shell contains a menu-driven editor for inputting the knowledge domain, an inference engine for arriving at conclusions, and a parser to verify the correctness of the statements for that particular shell language. However, depending on the sophistication of the shell, power and

Table 1

Media Selection Matrix

	Book	Slides	Overheads	Video	Film	Audio	CAI	Slide/tape
Large group?		X	X	X	X	X		X
Small group?		X	X	X	X	X		X
Individualized?	X	X		X	X	X	X	X
Visual only?	X	X	X	X	X		X	
Audio only?						X		
Audiovisual combined?				X	X			X
Print only?	X							
Photographic only?	X	X	X					
Graphic only?	X	X	X				X	
Graphic & photographic?	X	X	X					
Still only?	X	X	X				X	X
Motion only?				X	X			
Simulation?							X	
Still/Motion combined?				X	X		X	
Verbal abstractions?	X							
Prepared before?	X	X	X	X	X	X	X	X
Prepared during?			X					
High level of user control?			X				X	
Moderate level of control?		X					X	X
Low level of user control?	X			X	X	X		

flexibility may be sacrificed for simplicity of programming and ease of use.

Expert-Ease (Human Edge Software), is an example of the "do-it-yourself" approach to expert systems. One begins to use Expert-Ease, a shell, by determining the answers to a problem such as determining the most effective media to use under certain conditions. Next, the problem attributes for discriminating among different examples of the problem are listed with questions that will permit the user to assign values to problem attributes. This generally results in a decision table or matrix like the one in Table 1.

Next, most expert system shells will "induce" the rules from the solution/attribute matrix. This eliminates the time-consuming step of writing out all the rules for the programmer. The logic that selects the presentation of pertinent questions with which the user interacts with the expert system is inherent in the software and based on the induced rules. As the user responds to the questions, the logic leads to an "expert" solution.

Although shells are relatively easy to use, the original problem area must be well-defined and rather simple. However, a shell is useful in modeling simple versions of complex problems before moving onto the development of an expert system by using a language.

Expert System Uses

Only problems that meet several general criteria are suitable for small expert system solutions: (a) someone with the necessary expertise to solve the problem successfully must be available; (b) well-defined problem domains for which a well-developed knowledge base already exists; and (c) situations that require basic reasoning skills but do not turn out the same predictable way every time lend themselves to use of expert systems (Harmon, 1986). Helping university students determine a plan of study, diagnosing a patient's illness, and troubleshooting a computer system are all examples of appropriate problems to warrant the development of an expert system. Developing a storyboard for a videotape production, searching for broadly defined geographical data, or learning correct tennis strokes are not appropriate problems for expert system development.

It may seem that the problems of instructional technology do not meet the criteria. Yet, expert systems that perform needs analysis, guide course design and development, manage instruction, and serve as job aids have been developed or are currently in the process of being developed.

Dear (1986) suggests that expert systems could facilitate needs analysis with a knowledge base that would determine the feasibility or cost-effectiveness of a project. Computer-Based Training Analyst, developed by Kearsley (1986), is one such program on the market. As its title suggests, Computer-Based Training Analyst guides a needs analysis on the cost-efficiency of using computer-based training over other instructional media.

Expert systems as instructional management aids in computer-based training are a powerful tool for instructional designers. Findings from the research on the effects of learner control (Tennyson, 1980; Tennyson, 1981) consistently indicate that conditions in which learners are provided continuous, updated advisement on their progress and instructional needs produce the greatest achievement. The Minnesota Adaptive Instructional System (MAIS), while technically considered an intelligent tutor rather than an expert system, is an example of using artificial intelligence techniques. It manages the amount of instruction, sequence of instruction, display time, advisement of learning progress, refreshment of prerequisite knowledge, and adjustments of instruction for individual differences (Tennyson, 1984). Credibility or diagnosis by machine is a hurdle that is overcome by providing the user access to the inference process and by including reports on the rationale for the diagnosis.

Use of an expert system that directs goals, learning strategies, and screen prototypes will greatly facilitate the design and development of instructional programs. While some attempts were started on such a project using traditional authoring tools (Merrill and Wood, 1984), expert system technology made the project more feasible. Using the Component Display Theory as the theoretical framework, Merrill (1987) and colleagues are currently developing an expert system that works in conjunction with authoring systems. The expert system will guide instructional designers through each step as the instructional sequences are developed on line.

The use of knowledge-based systems as "smart" jobs aids (Wilson and Welsh, 1986) is developing rapidly. Job aids, such as flow charts and decision tables, are common and effective means for solving performance problems. Expert systems can explain and guide non-experienced performers through decisions and procedures that require judgmental conclusions. Welsh and Wilson (1987) note that the advantages of expert systems over traditional job aids are the abilities to engage in dialogue with the user, handle ambiguous situations, and explain choices, decisions, or procedures involved in doing a task.

Harmon (1986) cites Campbell Soup Company's "Cooker Maintenance Advisor" program developed with Texas Instruments' Personal Consultant expert system as an example of a currently used smart job aid. This expert system aids in the diagnoses of the cooker machinery when it malfunctions and provides suggested steps an expert would take to correct the problem. Another example of a smart job aid is a program used by First National Bank of Chicago as a credit decision aid to junior lending officers, created on a small expert system from Teknowledge, Incorporated. And, finally, designers of interactive video may refer to IMSATT for prescriptions of instruction. The use of computer expert systems often means that expert knowledge can be disseminated cheaply since disk duplication, distribution, and updating is easier and faster than with other media such as video or print.

Educational uses of expert systems tend to be small scale, well-defined systems. Expert problem solving systems have been used by teachers and counselors for such tasks as classifying, diagnosing, and categorizing student performance. The Diagnosis of Reading Difficulties Expert System, for example, is used to help diagnose reading problems (Colbourn and McLeod, 1983). Expert advice is given on the type of data needed to determine whether the student has a reading problem. Once the data are collected and entered into the expert system, diagnostic findings are available to aid in placement or development of an instructional program for the student (Thorkildsen, Lubke, Myette, and Parry, 1985).

The use of expert systems in direct instruction is not as well developed as their use in analysis, management, development, and job aid functions for several reasons. Prior to recent refinements in artificial intelligence-based products and increased power in personal computers, education and training facilities lacked the equipment necessary to implement strategies utilizing expert systems. There have also been programming problems. The complex artificial intelligence (AI) languages, Prolog and Lisp, require programming skills which are beyond most instructional developers. Finally, there is a lack of people in instructional development who understand or are even interested in this new technology. However, as the development of expert systems becomes easier, moves are being made to include expert systems within direct instruction.

An immediate use of expert systems in instruction is as a feedback/evaluation system. One such program developed by Grabinger and Pollock (1987) used an expert system in guiding students to analyze and criticize their own instructional media design and production work. The system asked questions of the students that forced them to look for production flaws and strengths. The questions encouraged the students to produce their own feedback by leading them through a structured analysis procedure. The program insured consistent feedback and encouraged a more active student role in settings where there are a large number of undergraduate students and only minimally qualified teaching assistants.

Lippert and Trollip (1986) encourage student design of knowledge bases for expert systems, suggesting that such work will facilitate greater depth of cognitive processing of content as the students explore the how, why, and what of instruction. Some words of caution are in order, however. Knowledge bases constructed by only one subject matter expert will yield the idiosyncratic reasoning of that individual. Ideally, the reasoning of several experts should be encoded in these programs to give consensus solutions. Furthermore, Roberts and Park (1983) question whether the expert models used in expert systems are, in fact, the best models. They fear that as models become simplified so do their applications.

Finally, teachers and trainers are not Renaissance people. Development of effective programs takes an enormous amount of time and requires a team approach. It takes an instructional technologist to extract the program's content and processes from a subject matter expert and fashion it into a usable format for a computer programmer. □

References

Burnham, W.D., and Hall, A.R. *Prolog Programming and Applications.* New York: John Wiley & Sons, 1985.

Clocksin, W.F., and Mellish, C.S. *Programming Prolog.* New York: Springer-Verlag, 1984.

Colbourn, M., and McLeod, J. Computer Guided Educational Diagnosis: A Prototype Expert System. *Journal of Special Education Technology,* 1983, *6*(1), 30-39.

Dear, B. *How Artificial Intelligence Techniques Can Be Used in Developing Courseware.* Paper presented at the 27th Annual Association for Development of Computer-Based Instructional Systems Conference, New Orleans, February 1986.

Grabinger, R.S., and Pollock, J.C. *Graphics.* An Expert System for Diagnosis of Graphic Design Problems [computer program]. Lincoln, NE: University of Nebraska-Lincoln, 1986.

Harmon, P. Expert Systems, Job Aids, and the Future of Instructional Technology. *Performance and Instruction Journal,* 1986, *25*(2), 26-28.

Kearsley, G. *Applying Expert Systems to CBT.* Paper presented at the Association for the Development of Computer-Based Instructional Systems Convention, Washington, DC, November 1986.

Lippert, R., and Trollip, S. *Building Knowledge Bases for Expert Systems.* Paper presented at the Association for the Development of Computer-Based Instructional Systems Convention, Washington, DC, November 1986.

Merrill, M.D. *Can Computers Deliver Effective Instruction? Trends for Computer-Based Instruction Research.* Paper presented at the Association for the Development of Computer-Based Instructional Systems Convention, Washington, DC, November 1986.

Merrill, M.D. *President's Forum: Issues in Artificial Intelligence and Education.* Presentation at the Association for the Development of Computer-Based Instructional Systems Convention, Oakland, CA, 1987.

Merrill, M.D., and Wood, L. Computer Guided Instructional Design. *Journal of Computer-Based Instruction,* 1984, *11*(2), 60-63.

Roberts, F.C., and Park, O. Intelligent Computer-Assisted Instruction: An Explanation and Overview. *Educational Technology,* 1983, *23*(12), 7-11.

Seigel, P. *Teaching Problem Solving with Expert Systems.* A pre-session at the Association for Computer-Based Instructional Systems, Oakland, CA, 1987.

Stubbs, M., and Piddock, P. Artificial Intelligence in Teaching and Learning: An Introduction. *PLET,* 1985, *22*(2), 150-157.

Tennyson, R.D. Instructional Control Strategies and Content Structure as Design Variables in Concept Acquisition Using Computer-Based Instruction. *Journal of Educational Psychology,* 1980, *72*(4), 525-532.

Tennyson, R.D. Use of Adaptive Information for Advisement in Learning Concepts and Rules Using Microcomputer-Assisted Instruction. *American Educational Research Journal,* 1981, *18*, 425-438.

Thompson, B., and Thompson, W. Inside an Expert System. *BYTE,* 1985, *10*(4), 315-330.

Thorkildsen, R.J., Lubke, M.M., Myette, B.M., and Parry, J.D. Artificial Intelligence: Applications in Education. *Educational Research Quarterly,* 1985-86, *10*(1) 2-9.

Welsh, J.R., and Wilson, B.G. Expert System Shells: Tools to Aid Human Performance. *Journal of Instructional Development,* 1987, *10*(2), 15-19.

Wilson, B.G., and Welsh, J.R. *Something New Under the Instructional Sun: Small Knowledge-Based Systems as Job Aids.* Paper presented at the American Educational Research Association Convention, San Francisco, April 1986.

Winograd, T. *Understanding Natural Language.* Edinburgh, Scotland: University Press, 1972.

Computer Courseware: Frame-Based or Intelligent?

Jodi Bonner

We often hear that computer-based instruction (CBI) is a disappointment because it has failed to exploit the capabilities of the computer. Because most CBI (with or without videodisc) is frame-based, i.e., each screen display is planned, computer delivery systems have been similar to other delivery systems such as programmed text. Frame-based approaches have earned their poor reputation from the page-turning nature of courseware with limited or meaningless interaction. Intelligent CAI, or intelligent tutors to use the preferred terminology (Anderson, Boyle, Farrel, and Reiser, 1984), promises to exploit the capabilities of the computer. Instead of screen specifications, intelligent tutors rely on models of the student, knowledge base, and tutor (Fletcher, 1985) to generate screens.

Some seem to view intelligent tutors as the ultimate form of CBI. However, another view is that there will always be a use for the frame-based approaches as well as intelligent tutors. Of course, by frame-based approaches, I am referring to meaningfully interactive courseware.

With this view, computer courseware can be conceptualized on a continuum from least to most sophisticated system (see Figure 1). If this is the case, then we will be required to make decisions about which kind of CBI system is appropriate for various instructional situations, a fine-grained media selection decision. As with other media selection decisions, instructional designers should endeavor to be theory-based. With this in mind, I will contrast some aspects of frame-based CAI and intelligent tutors that may have an impact upon media selection.

Frame-Based CAI

Frame-Based CAI has been characterized as usually taking one of three forms, which are most easily described using Gagne's instructional events and kinds of learning (Gagne, Wager, and Rojas, 1981):

Jodi Bonner is a Senior Scientist, Human Resources Research Organization, Alexandria, Virginia.

Figure 1

Computer Courseware Continuum

| Frame-Based Drill & Practice | Frame-Based Tutorial | Frame-Based Simulation | Expert System | Intelligent Tutoring |

- Drill and practice consists of eliciting performance and providing feedback. These events are particularly appropriate for practicing rule using, discriminations, and concepts.
- Tutorial consists of presenting new stimulus material, providing learning guidance, eliciting performance, and providing feedback, at a minimum. This combination of events is particularly useful for information and concept learning when the material is new to the learner. Tutorials are generally more expository than interrogatory, to use Tennyson's (1984) terminology. A tutorial may include drill and practice and simulation.
- Simulation consists of presenting the objective, presenting the stimulus, eliciting performance, and providing feedback. This form of instruction is especially useful for teaching rule using and problem solving.

The key to frame-based CAI has been interactivity; this is no surprise since learner involvement is the key to any successful delivery system. It has probably been stressed with CAI because learners are less likely to tolerate the various computer media without a great deal of interaction. Learning research and experience have provided us with guidelines for implementing the instructional events for a lesson. These guidelines may or may not be specific to any one medium. See, for example, Carey and Briggs (1977), matching conditions of learning to instructional events and types of learning; Ellis and Wulfeck (1978), presentation consistency and adequacy; HumRRO (1979), job aids for specifying learning events/activities; and Gagne, Wager, and Rojas (1981), guidelines for CAI authors.

Intelligent Tutors

Intelligent tutors have been based on the idea that the most natural way to learn is in the context of doing (Anderson *et al.*, 1984; Collins and Brown, n.d.), through problem solving in a tutor-tutee situation. In a computer tutoring system, the instruction takes the form of simulation in which explanations are embedded. It consists of a problem-solving environment where explanations are provided to the student when the student is diagnosed as having difficulty. Two concerns for intelligent tutoring are when to interrupt the student with an explanation and what to say in giving the explanation (Burton and Brown, 1982). The emphasis has been on a discovery approach to learning, though there is interest in accommodating different styles, such as by allowing the learner to choose a discovery approach (problem first) or an explanation first (problem second) approach. When tutor building comes from computer scientists, we should watch for instructional soundness. When tutor building comes from cognitive science, we assume that cognitive theory is translated into the tutor, though this translation is sometimes not explicit. We should be concerned about this issue of carrying theory into practice because there are still many gaps in cognitive theory. Some tutor builders have explicated tutoring principles, see Burton and Brown (1982) and Anderson *et al.* (1984); and some have studied teaching methods to derive instructional strategies, see Collins and Stevens (1983) and Collins and Brown (n.d.). These are positive efforts, but demonstrate a lack of involvement of instructional designers. Several people have noted the desirability of an interdisciplinary approach to the application of cognitive theory to instruction (Low, 1980-81; Wildman and Burton, 1981; Wildman, 1981).

In addition to the emphasis on problem solving, intelligent tutors are concerned with teaching metacognitive skills—the cognitive strategies and learning strategies traditionally ignored in instruction. In intelligent tutoring systems, these metacognitive skills are treated as domain specific, and are taught along with other cognitive skills.

Frame-based CAI has dealt with motivation through the use of visuals, questions, humor, sound, learner control, sequencing, and other techniques. Intelligent tutors deal with motivation through the discovery approach where curiosity and inquiry are inherent aspects of the learning strategy.

Subject matter experts have been used in the development of frame-based CAI, as they have been used in the development of instruction for other media—to define content and review material. In building intelligent tutors, cognitive psychologists are interested in studying the differences in experts and novices. Knowledge about how both groups approach problems assists tutor developers in defining the novice's entry skills and knowledge so they can design instruction that will change novice behavior to expert behavior.

Place for Both

Even if we could replace all frame-based CAI with intelligent tutors, we should consider that both kinds of CBI have a place in training. We need to use frame-based CAI for those kinds of learning tasks for which it is suited. Frame-based CAI is a sound choice for teaching simpler knowledge and skills early in a curriculum when students have a minimum of knowledge about a subject, i.e., they need to learn information, concepts, discriminations, and rules. This is a situation where the instructional designer can anticipate enough of the students' responses to provide minimal limitations in interacting with the knowledge.

Intelligent tutors are a good choice for more complex kinds of learning, when the student knows enough about a subject to work with it in a problem solving context, or knows enough about one subject to generalize to a different subject, i.e., the student is ready for problem solving and metacognitive skills. An on-the-job training (OJT) situation where some basic training has already occurred is an excellent place for intelligent tutors. For OJT, intelligent tutors offer some of the same advantages of frame-based computer simulations, such as safety from physical danger and equipment breakage, and provision of seldom-seen occurrences and unseen aspects of equipment.

Frame-based tutorials and drill and practice courseware may be the most efficient and economical for simpler learning tasks. What is difficult is deciding whether a simulation is best as frame-based or intelligent. To make this decision, we need evidence about how individualized instruction needs to be and how complex the cognitive task is. The more complex the task, the more difficult it is to specify the responses required to keep a frame-based approach individualized enough. It is unfortunate that we don't get a grasp on the research and application of theory to one technology before we begin to use a new one, since many of the same questions (such as this one about what is enough individualization) apply to a variety of media.

Instructional Designer's Role

The role of instructional designers (IDs) in the development of frame-based CAI is quite clear compared to their role in intelligent tutor development. What does an instructional designer need to know or do to participate in the design of intelligent tutors? One answer is that the ID should probably begin with a good understanding of the concepts of cognitive psychology that influence instruction. Some of these concepts are discussed by Gagne and Dick (1983). IDs can work with cognitive psychologists in developing the details

Table 1

Cognitive Concepts and Instructional Systems Development

Model Component	Cognitive Concepts
Analysis	
Basic Needs Assessment*	
Task Analysis	information processing
Entry Characteristics	schemata
Design	
Objectives	
Taxonomy	domain specific cognitive skills
	generativity and transfer
Sequencing	stages of skill acquisition
Testing	likeness of stimulus-response situation in practice and testing
Instructional Strategies	problem-solving context
Development	
Formative Evaluation	cognitive principles of instruction for design guidelines
	emphasis in collecting data about non-observable cognitive tasks in learner tryouts

Summative Evaluation*

*Components that should remain theory-free.

---

of an instructional systems design model for developing intelligent tutoring systems. Table 1 illustrates where some cognitive psychology concepts can be applied to the components of an instructional systems approach.

There are some areas where cognitive psychology can be applied directly or combined with other instructional theory or practice, and there are some areas that should remain theory-free, namely basic needs assessment (not task analysis) and summative evaluation, since they are concerned strictly with relating training performance to job performance, and remain free of theory bias.

Cognitive task analysis will identify the cognitive structures and processes required to perform a job. It should also identify motivational components of performance because of the emphasis on the learner's information processing activity (Wildman and Burton, 1981). Work on the design part of the model should lead us toward the development of instructional theories.

If cognitive task analysis tells us what occurs internally that we want to influence, instructional theories should provide us with the tutoring principles (and a framework for these principles) we should employ to manipulate the environment to influence cognition positively so people learn. Instructional models should tell us about learning analysis, i.e., how to move from the cognitive task analysis to the design of instruction, answering questions such as how to select tasks for training, how to select or adjust problems encountered on the job so they are suitable for use in training, and how and what objectives to write.

Learning taxonomies may reflect domain-specific skill taxonomies, with particular emphasis on objectives for problem solving and metacognitive skills, with sequencing addressing the integration of individual skills and automaticity.

Discovery learning and learning in the context of problem solving are instructional strategies consistent with the cognitive approach.

Formative evaluation can take the guidelines approach (see *IQI*, 1979-80) or the learner tryout approach (see Dick, 1977). Guidelines should reflect the theory base, and data obtained during learner tryouts should be examined in view of theory.

As IDs have worked with software engineers to develop CAI authoring systems, these two can also work together to produce intelligent design environments. Pliske and Psotka (1986) describe current work sponsored by the Department of the Army in this area. In the actual development of an intelligent tutor, one would expect the ID to work with the development of the student and tutor models.

Summary

There is a place in training for a variety of kinds of instruction, including a variety of kinds of CAI. The development of intelligent tutors is adding a new delivery system to our list of media selection alternatives. Instructional designers have a role in tutor building that neither they nor the tutor builders should overlook. □

References

Anderson, J.R., Boyle, C.F., Farrell, R., and Reiser, B.J. *Cognitive Principles in the Design of Computer Tutors.* Office of Naval Research Tech Report No. ONR-84-1, 1984.

Burton, R.R., and Brown, J.S. An Investigation of Computer Coaching for Informal Learning Activities. In D. Sleeman and J.S. Brown (Eds.), *Intelligent Tutoring Systems.* NY: Academic Press, 1982, 79-98.

Using Artificial Intelligence in Education: Computer-Based Tools for Instructional Development

Ray S. Perez and Robert J. Seidel

Today's US Army is faced with the situation whereby it is asked to train less qualified soldiers to operate and maintain more complex and highly sophisticated equipment in a shorter period of time with less money! The combination of several factors (e.g., modernization of equipment, demographics, and rapid changes in training doctrine) has forced the Army to modernize its training development procedures. Force modernization is predicted to alter substantially the quality and quantity of equipment used by the Army.

This decade will mark the end of the U.S. Army's "modernization blizkrieg." The Army has fielded over 400 new or improved systems that are composed of 249,000 major communications and electronics items (Kitfield, 1986). The introduction of this modernization has had a severe impact on the type and amount of training required to operate and maintain these new and modified systems.

Coupled with the increasing equipment complexity there is a decline in available quality high school graduates. It is estimated that the available pool of potential recruits will decrease by 20 percent from 1980 to 1995 (McGrath, 1984).

Current Army doctrine, which describes the way the Army will fight, requires an increase in the self-reliance of individual soldiers and their units on the future battlefield, so that individual units will be responsible for performing their own maintenance. In 1987 DOD spent about $18 billion on formal residential training as reported in the "Military, Manpower Training Report For FY1987, Volume

Ray S. Perez is Senior Scientist and Team Leader of the Automated Training Development Team, the Automated Instructional Systems Technical Area, and Robert J. Seidel is Chief, Automated Instructional Systems Technical Area, U.S. Army Research Institute for the Behavioral and Social Sciences, Alexandria, Virginia.

IV: Force Readiness Report." That figure does not reflect on-the-job training activities, where expenditures for training are almost impossible to determine. In addition to these factors, the available dollars for training are predicted to shrink over the next decade.

On the other side, development of training materials is highly labor-intensive, costly, and slow. For example, official Army training documents for collective and individual training reach the user two-plus years after changes in doctrine and training standards. Staff responsible for training development have high turnover rates and low levels of experience; therefore, automated tools for design, development, and production of training offer a real promise of quicker, cheaper, and less labor-intensive training. Therefore, techniques which make the development or delivery of training more efficient would be readily welcomed.

Computer-Based Training

One innovative approach to efficient delivery of training is the use of computer-based instruction. The goal of modern educational computing is to capture the pedagogical advantages of effective instruction and deliver it, via computers, to students. The promise of computer-based training has been to provide to each student high quality, inexpensive, individualized instruction. The research on the effectiveness of computer-based instruction indicates that computer-based training is more cost-effective, requiring on the average 30% less time to train students for achieving an equivalent or higher levels of performance than conventional training methods (Orlansky and String, 1976).

In the last decade, artificial intelligence (AI) has evolved from research laboratory prototypes to become a principal component in many areas of high-technology development (e.g., robotics). Artificial intelligence techniques and methods have been applied to education and training and show promise to further increase the effectives of training. Developers of intelligent tutoring systems (ITS) have combined traditional computer-based instructional techniques with artificial intelligence methods and techniques to provide training in a variety of technical domains, such as medical diagnosis, computer programming, and electronic troubleshooting.

The goal of providing high quality, inexpensive training is not limited to the delivery of instruction on a computer. High quality training is needed in other types of instructional delivery media, e.g., platform instruction, simulators, and other training devices. The development of AI techniques, however, requires sophisticated computer and instructional design personnel. Unfortunately, there are

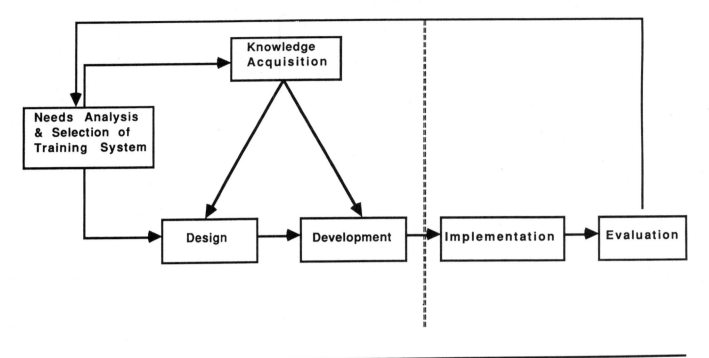

Figure 1

Training Development and Implementation

not enough experienced training developers in the Army to meet the current demands of production. As indicated above, the process of training development in the Army is slow, inefficient, and labor-intensive, and requires personnel.

Application of AI to Training Development

A solution to this problem is the automation of the training development process itself. This includes the development of various software tools and decisions aids that can be used by relatively inexperienced training personnel to develop intelligent training systems and training materials. Tools would reduce the time and expertise needed to produce high quality training. These tools and decision aids would consist of editors, authoring systems, expert systems, and on-line intelligent help systems. They range from off-the-shelf desktop publishing packages including word processing programs, to custom tailored expert systems that aid training developers in the design of training programs (e.g., lessons plans). Examples of software tools for training development are CBI authoring systems, desktop publishing software packages, graphics editors, and relational data base management systems (RDBMS).

AI based tools are software systems that represent and use knowledge to perform complex reasoning tasks. These tasks are typically performed by a human and presumably require intelligence (Barr and Feigenbaum, 1982). Examples of AI-based systems are intelligent tutoring systems (ITS) also referred to as knowledge based tutors (KBT) and expert systems. The specific AI techniques that can be used to design and build decision aids and software tools are: search techniques, knowledge representation methods, inferencing techniques, machine learning, and natural language dialogues.

AI Research in Training Development

In response to the need to develop innovative approaches to training and the development of training materials, personnel at the U.S. Army Research Institute have been conducting a program of research for the exploratory development of AI tools to aid efficient and effective training development. As part of this comprehensive program we are also conducting research on instructional strategies to teach complex problem solving skills and on the formulation of a cognitive model of the expertise required in the process of developing training materials. This process is referred to as the Systems Approach to Training (SAT) as defined by TRADOC Regulation 350-7 and shown in Figure 1.

Prior to a discussion of the automated training development tools and decision aids under development in our laboratory, we would like to present our view of the requirements and expertise needed for training development. This curriculum development model is based on a general systems theory. The SAT model is comprised of five processes: Analysis (includes Front-End Analysis), Design, Development, Implementation, and Evaluation. This model is systematic and iterative, characterized by evaluation as an integral process at each step of the cycle. Although the SAT process provides a set of high level procedures to be followed in the development of training materials, it does not provide much guidance on *how* to design and develop specific instructional elements (e.g., how to sequence instruction). Additionally, training developers in the Army, for the most part, are subject matter experts who are skilled technicians or instructors. Few have received formal training in instructional design. The overall goal of our research is to develop, test, and evaluate software tools and decision aids for each phase of the SAT process in order to help these relatively untrained developers.

Training Development Expertise

An initial task prior to the development of tools for training development is the specification of the cognitive requirements (problem solving skills) of the training development process. To do this we propose a model of the expertise requirements in this process, which in turn implies attributes of the developer (see Figure 2). A primary goal of our research program is to model the expertise of an expert training developer. This cognitive model would then serve as the conceptual framework for the design and development of training development tools and decision aids.

In the formulation of this model we have used an expert-system building technique called "knowledge acquisition." Expert systems are software programs designed to address problems in a similar manner and with similar results as a human expert. In the process of building an expert system the designer must first identify an expert, then extract knowledge from him/her, and then transfer that knowledge to a computer program. This process is called knowledge (or more generally domain) engineering. The technique used to extract knowledge is referred to as acquisition or elicitation. Knowledge acquisition techniques have been used to build not only expert systems but also intelligent tutoring systems. The resultant cognitive model is comprised of three functionally separate components (see Wiggs and Perez, 1988, for a detailed discussion): (a) a knowledge base, which contains domain related facts; (b) problem solving strategies that are the means of using the knowledge base to solve a problem, inference mechanism; and (c) working memory or monitoring processes, used to record the input data and progress for each problem.

Expert knowledge consists of declarative knowledge (i.e., facts, concepts, and principles), formal rules (i.e., on how to use these facts), meta-rules (i.e., rules used in applying formal and procedural rules), heuristics (i.e., rules of thumb) and the relations among all these. Hart (1986) has pointed out that of all the components of expertise, an expert's reliance on heuristics rather than algorithms when solving problems is the key distinguishing characteristic.

In the use of an algorithm, a single goal or solution is assumed, and problem solving involves executing a series of predetermined series of steps which represent a single-solution, specific path to the goal. However, some problems have more than one solution. Within this framework, an expert's expertise consists of the ability to select the best path from a variety of paths that are adequate in meeting all the conditions of the problem.

The knowledge acquisition process not only provides a model of the cognitive processes and knowledge base used by the expert, but also identifies the decision rules that the expert uses in performing a task. More specifically, the model characterizes the problem solving behavior by representing domain related facts that are widely shared knowledge, such as that written in textbooks. Heuristics (rules of thumb) gained through experience are used by the expert in problem solving that represents the knowledge of good practice and good judgment. The process of training development, as described above, is a difficult subject matter of study. Relatively little research exists detailing exactly what an expert training developer does in designing instruction; perhaps more importantly, we do not know how these experts acquire their skills.

Domain Expertise

A primary factor to be considered in the development of an instructional system or instruction is the structural characteristics and learning requirements of the content domain to be taught. In the previous section we have discussed our generic view of the nature of training development expertise. This expertise would be somewhat modified depending on the structural characteristics and learning requirements of the subject matter domain. In general most training content domains can be classified into two: (a) procedural tasks domain and (b) a structural knowledge domain. Training of a specific procedural task requires the student to learn only skills that are specified in the task pro-

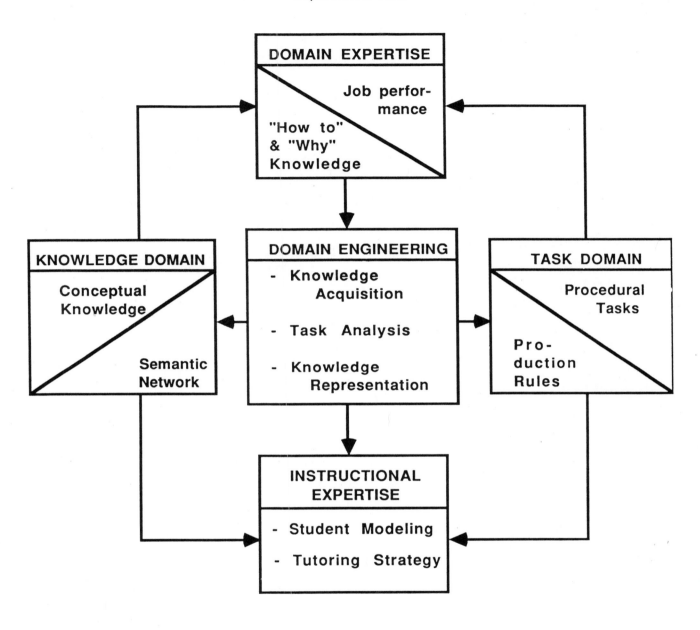

Figure 2

Expertise for ICAI

cedures (e.g., procedures for operating and trouble-shooting a specific weapon-system); in this view the student is not required to understand the conceptual knowledge underlying the use of these procedures. In contrast, training for structural knowledge requires the student to learn the conceptual knowledge about the structure and functions of the system, and perhaps an understanding of theoretical principles controlling the system's be-

havior. From the development perspective, the domain expertise requirements of expert developers are analogously implied.

The upper halves of the two side boxes in Figure 2 represent these two types of training content domains. Figure 2 depicts the expertise requirements needed to build an intelligent tutoring system (see Seidel, Park, and Perez, 1988 for a more detailed discussion of this model). It also captures and provides a context for the expertise requirements for the development of training. The five boxes map out needed expertise and the relationships among them. The model presumes that a team of experts will be needed to build an ITS system. These experts would include: a domain expert, expert instructor, instructional psychologist, and AI expert. The development of training in other media could very well benefit from these cooperative efforts. In fact, many of the training development projects presently underway include teams of experts, such as a domain expert, expert instructor, and instructional psychologist or technologist in producing training materials.

The center box for domain engineering lists the methods and techniques (i.e., knowledge acquisition and task analysis) that should be used in analyzing the domain (front-end analysis) to obtain the needed expertise for the development of training. Once the domain expertise is extracted, then the designer will have to decide how to represent that knowledge to students.

The top box for domain expertise depicts the two types of criterion expertise needed. The expertise of a procedural task domain is represented in the expert's actual job performance (e.g., a technician troubleshooting a specific system). The expertise of structured knowledge domain is represented in the expert's "what" and "why" cognitive knowledge (e.g., an engineer's theoretical understanding of the system). Depending on the objective being taught, one or both types of expertise may be needed as the basis for the development training.

The bottom box for instructional expertise identifies the skills that comprise the instructional designer's expertise. These include the use of instructional strategies, identification of meaningful learner characteristics, specification of potential student error patterns or misconceptions, identification of procedures for diagnosis of learning needs, listing of important learner variables, and the use of tutoring strategies. In previous boxes for domain engineering (e.g., representation of domain knowledge) and domain expertise (e.g. matching the domain expertise with training objective) of the model, we have identified activities that are important for the design and development process. This box presents the decision-making processes that closely emulate the expertise of the instructional designer.

The decisions that are made by instructional designers consist of the selection of what to teach for what objective, how to organize and structure it, and how to present instruction. These decisions are not only guided by learning theories and instructional design principles, but also by knowledge of good practice acquired by expert practitioners. These decisions are influenced and based on the contents of the others boxes in Figure 2. Our research program described below on tools for aiding development is guided by this approach.

Research Approach

Our research approach is depicted in Figure 3 for the development of automated training development tools and decision aids. This approach combines cognitive science and instructional design research with AI techniques and methodologies. It is an iterative approach that emphasizes design, development, testing, and evaluation. It utilizes empirical research, training requirements analysis, and the selection of advanced training technology. The need for the development of new training or the modification of existing training, as depicted in Figure 3, can be triggered by the identification of a new threat (e.g., a new enemy tank), a change in training doctrine, or the identification of a performance deficiency.

A training requirements analysis is conducted to determine new training requirements. These requirements are used as the basis for the design of the tool or decision aid. An analysis of emerging or existing advanced training technologies is conducted and an election of a candidate technology (or in some cases off-the-shelf tools or tools developed under our basic research program) are identified for the development of the potential tool or decision aid. The candidate tool or decision aid is then designed and developed in accordance with training requirements and potential user characteristics. The prototype tool decision aid is then tested and evaluated at one of two local university laboratories using curriculum developers and evaluated with a set of empirically generated criteria and user requirements. The purposes of this testing and evaluation phase is "proof of concept" and to insure that the tools are free of software bugs, meet the evaluation criteria, and user needs.

The information collected during the testing and evaluation phase is then used to revise the tools, as necessary. The refined prototype tools are then field-tested and evaluated at U.S. Army schools and units. The results of the field-testing evaluation are used to make recommendations for the modifications of the tools for operational versions.

Tools and Decision Aids for Training Development

The overall goal of our research is to develop, test, and evaluate software tools and decision aids for each phase of the SAT process. In a similar vein, we are in the process of developing, testing, and evaluating decision aids and tools to help or incorporate expertise described in Figure 2. We are

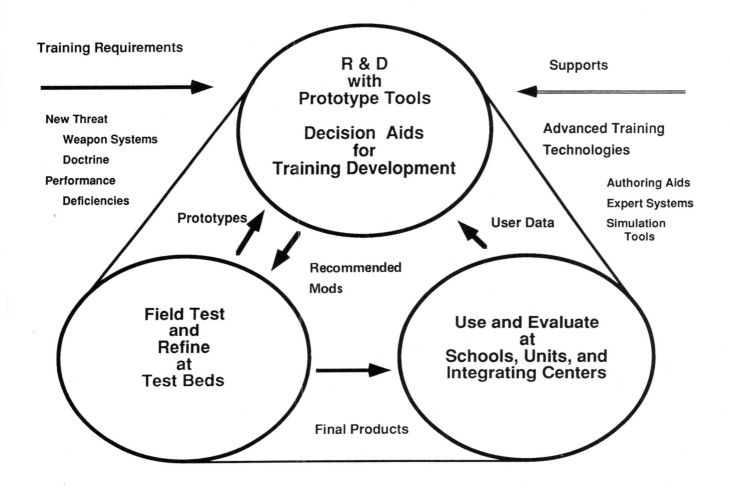

Figure 3

*Automated Training Development
Research Approach*

Training Requirements

New Threat
   Weapon Systems
   Doctrine
Performance
   Deficiencies

R & D
with
Prototype Tools

Decision Aids
for
Training Development

Supports

Advanced Training
Technologies

Authoring Aids
Expert Systems
Simulation
   Tools

Prototypes

Recommended
Mods

User Data

Field Test
and
Refine
at
Test Beds

Use and Evaluate
at
Schools, Units, and
Integrating Centers

Final Products

---

currently evaluating a number of decision aids/ tools. Some of these tools have been developed under contract, others are either inhouse developed products, or commercially available or have been developed by other military organizations. These tools involve the following:

1. **Prototype Automated Knowledge Acquisition Tool (AKAT).** This is designed to streamline the process of eliciting expertise from a subject matter expert. The information elicited is of a procedural task domain in the expert's actual job performance (e.g., a technician troubleshooting a specific system); and expertise of a structured knowledge domain, the expert's "what" and "why" cognitive knowledge (e.g., the systems engineer's theoretical understanding of the system). This tool is used to elicit information found in the upper halves of the two side boxes in Figure 2.

2. **Instructional Design Expert (ID Expert).** The ID Expert is an on-line expert system that uses prompts and questions to guide both experienced and inexperienced instructional designers in the task of designing a lesson. It is described in greater detail elsewhere in this special issue. The ID expert was developed on the basis of M. David Merrill's Component Display Theory and utilizes information characterized in the top box of Figure 2.

3. **Automated Test Development Aid (ATDA).**

This is a PC computer-based job-aid designed to help training developers prepare written test items, with specific examples, guidance, and references. This job-aid uses information from the upper halves of the two side boxes, the top box, and the center box of Figure 2.

4. **Simulation Design Tool for Training Development (SDTD).** This software tool consists of graphics editors and a library of icons to aid in the design, and development of interactive computer simulations. This tool is designed to provide training developers with the means for developing effective and efficient simulation based training. These training simulations would be used to depict a model of complex equipment and would represent structural knowledge from the upper half of the left side box in Figure 2.

5. **The Automated Systems Approach to Training (ASAT).** This is an effort sponsored by the Army's Training and Doctrine Command (TRADOC); as the name implies, it is an automated system designed to support the SAT process. ARI is serving as technical advisors and monitoring this project. ASAT will provide software tool prompts, helps, and a relational data base management system to aid training developers in conducting collective and individual front-end analysis, design, and the development phases of the SAT process. The ASAT system would use as input all of the contents of the five boxes in Figure 2.

6. **Intelligent Automated Systems Approach to Training (ISAT).** This system represents the prototypic integration of the expert systems for each phase of the SAT process and other tools for the development of training. It will consist of a natural language interface, an intelligent on-line help system for multi-level users, an authoring system for development, and a relational data base management system. It is anticipated that the results of the testing and evaluation of ISATs will be the basis for recommendation for enhancements of TRADOC's ASAT system. We are currently in the process of exploring ways to integrate our tools with complementary efforts at Navy and Air Force laboratories. The product of this project would be an automated system for training development consisting of an integrated set of modular software tools sufficiently generic to be used by the different services in the production of training materials.

Research Issues

We have summarized an ongoing program of research that has as its goal the application of AI and cognitive science methodologies and techniques and instructional design theories and principles to the design, development, and evaluation of computer-based tools and decision aids for training development. We have presented a model of the expertise needed for the development of training materials and a brief description of the tools and decision aids currently under development in our laboratory.

It may be that the model of expertise that we have described is differentially useful according to the target domain and the task being taught. Different applications may demand different expertise than those specified by the model. Varying levels of expertise across training developers will also require different computer interfaces for each of the tools. The model may be viewed therefore in the practical sense as a heuristic or "strawman."

Within this area of research, there are nonetheless at least three issues that need to be addressed. (A) What are the domains of expertise for training development? (B) How are the domains of expertise for training development acquired? (C) How should knowledge be represented and is this representation sufficient to train with? Then, for a fourth issue, (D) How complete should the cognitive model of the training developer be in order to be considered adequate for the design software tools and decision aids?

In an expert system, the expert's knowledge (expertise) is represented as domain related facts and heuristics in the knowledge base and formal rules in the inference mechanism. However, it is not clear how accurately this represents the thinking and problem solving process of human experts. The implication is that human thinking follows a given set of rules and, in fact, our observations are that experts do not typically reason using a logical set of rules, nor do they approach a problem in a stereotypic way. Their thinking process is often fraught with "gaps" in the problem solving process, and their solutions are generally context bound. Systematic research is needed to ensure the validity of these models, to assess how well they emulate the workings of the expert's mind, and to determine their general applicability.

The acquisition of expertise of training development has not been studied in a systematic way. Charting the course of the development of this expertise would provide guidance: in the design of the tools and decision aids, in the design of the interfaces, and in the type of help systems needed. Further, a descriptive model of the evolution of this expertise would also be prescriptive in providing guidance in how to train training developers. This is an extremely important part of any training development program that purports to make the process more efficient and effective.

The issue of how to organize and structure instruction to optimize learning has been an issue of great concern for instructional developers and researchers. The designers of intelligent tutoring systems (ITS) or knowledge based tutors (KBT) have taken the approach of designing their instruction around a cognitive model of the expert's performance. How the task is represented is based on the modelling of how the expert performs the task and/or job. The efficacy of this instructional approach is yet to be demonstrated empirically. The notion of presenting to a novice a mature model of the cognitive processes involved in the successful completion of a task, although appealing, may not make much sense given the current literature on cognition and learning. A series of empirical studies is needed to investigate the efficacy of this approach to training.

Using an expert's cognitive model of how to develop training to design tools and decision aids requires that the model be explicit enough and complete. The resultant cognitive model that is represented in a computer program must contain explicit representations of proposed mental processes and knowledge structures, so that changes in the internal state of the model reflect changes in the internal state of the human mind. Thus, for the cognitive model of a training developer to be useful, it must accurately model the human cognitive structures: the model must be complete. How to determine the completeness of the model is problematic. It, however, could be verified empirically, by systematically comparing the results of experts with and without the use of the decision aids that are built with the cognitive model. Our program is designed to provide some answers and practical guidance for Army developers. □

References

Barr, A. and Feigenbaum, E.A. *The Handbook of Artificial Intelligence* (Vol. 1), Los Altos, CA: William Kaufman, 1982.

Hart, A. *Knowledge Acquisition for Expert Systems.* New York: McGraw-Hill, 1986.

McGrath, M. The Need for Improvements in Weapon System Maintenance: What Can AI Contribute? In *Artificial Intelligence in Maintenance: Proceeding of the Joint Services Workshop, Technical Report* (AFHRL-TR-84-25). Brooks AFB, Texas, 1984, 15-22.

Kitfield, J. High Tech's Missing Link. *Military Logistics Forum*, 1986, p. 43.

Orlansky, J., and String, J. The Performance of Maintenance Technicians on the Job (IDA paper P-15970). Alexandria, VA: Institute for Defense Analysis, 1976.

Orlansky, J., and String, J. Cost-Effectiveness of Computer-Based Instruction in Military Training (IDA Paper P-1375). Alexandria, VA: Institute for Defense Analysis, 1976.

Seidel, R.T., Park, O.K., and Perez, R.S. Expertise of ICAI: Development Requirements. *Computers in Human Behavior*, 1988, *4*, 235-256.

Wiggs, C.L., and Perez, R.S., The Use of Knowledge Acquisition in Instructional Design. *Computers in Human Behavior*, 1988, *(4)*, 257-274.

TRADOC Regulation 350-7, Systems Approach to Training (SAT). Ft. Monroe, VA, 1987.

Military Manpower Training Report for FY1987, Volume IV. Force Readiness Report, Department of Defense, 1987.

The Second Generation Instructional Design Research Program

M. David Merrill
Zhongmin Li
Mark K. Jones

Introduction

The high demand for education and training, and the shortage of qualified personnel to develop and deliver that education, has resulted in a dramatic increase in the use of interactive, computer-based technologies to provide education and training.

Current instructional design theory (which we term First Generation Instructional Design, or ID1) has a number of shortcomings when applied to the development of applications using these interactive technologies. Principal among these are:

- **coherence:** instructional analysis and design focuses on knowledge and skill components in isolation, and not on the integrated wholes necessary for the understanding of complex, dynamic phenomena;
- **utility:** prescriptions for pedagogic strategies are either superficial or lacking altogether;
- **comprehensiveness:** existing theory does not provide any means of incorporating fine-grained expertise about teaching and learning, gained from research, and applying this in the design process.

As a result, the potential of instructional design is not being met. The Second Generation ID Research Program, currently underway at Utah State University, has as its goal the development of a second generation instructional design theory (ID2), which while building on prior work will address the shortcomings of ID1. The projects in this program aim to produce an integrated system that includes the following components:

- a theoretical base that organizes knowledge about instructional design and defines a methodology for performing instructional design

for interactive technologies, and a prototype instructional design system that implements and demonstrates the theory;
- a methodology for representing domain knowledge for the purposes of making instructional decisions, and a prototype knowledge acquisition and analysis system that demonstrates and implements the methodology;
- a collection of "mini-experts," distributed rule-based expert systems, each contributing a small knowledge base relevant to a particular instructional design decision or a set of such decisions;
- a library of instructional transactions for the delivery of instruction, and the capacity to add new or existing transactions to the library;
- an online intelligent advisor program that dynamically customizes the instruction during delivery, based on a mixed-initiative dialog with the student.

Project Design

Overall Design

An important part of this work is the specification of theory. How does one go about developing theory? Does one sit at a desk and ponder?

We suggest that there are two aspects to theory development. The first is the selection, or discovery, of a small set of ideas which become the foundation for the theory. One endeavors to find the smallest set that is sufficiently powerful to account for the available data. This should be tied to some research base, in our case, cognitive psychology.

Once the foundation of a theory is in place, the next step is to explore all the ramifications. Can the theory accommodate what we empirically know about instruction? Can it actually generate the prescriptions we anticipate? How does it accomplish this? And (in a final step) how valid are these? Are the basic concepts sufficient, robust, and coherent?

We believe that one problem underlying many of the shortcomings of existing theories is that they are insufficiently precise and consistent. In our work to date in developing knowledge acquisition and representation methods, we have found that the translation of theory into a computer program forces a more complete, precise, and internally consistent explication that would be done otherwise. This occurs partly in the programming, a process which is intolerant of fuzzy thinking, and then later in the exercise of the program, which serves to test aspects of the ideas. We are in the process of developing a number of such programs,

M. David Merrill, a Contributing Editor of this magazine, is Professor of Instructional Technology at Utah State University, Logan, Utah, and Director of the Second Generation ID Research Program in the Department of Instructional Technology. **Zhongmin Li** and **Mark K. Jones** are research associates in the Department of Instructional Technology.

Figure 1

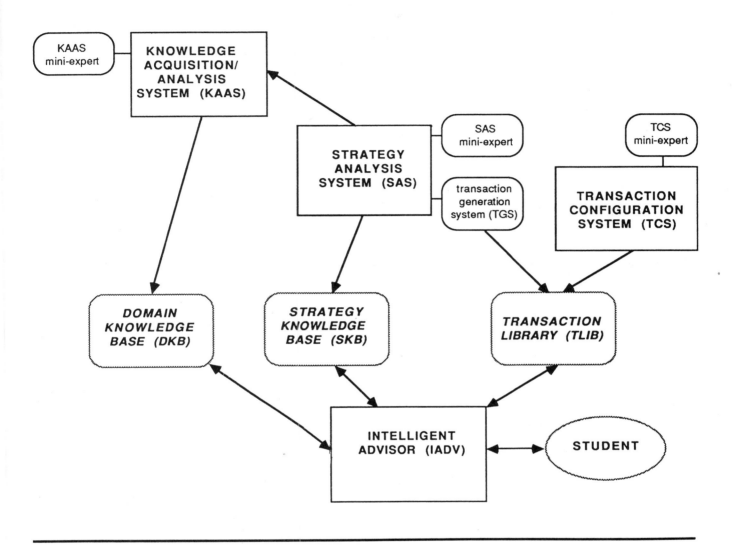

Configuration Chart for Principal ID₂ Tools

as tools for performing various aspects of instructional design, using the theory we develop.

There is another advantage to tool development as a theory-building methodology. A tool, even a prototype tool, can be put immediately to work by someone else both to test the capability of the tool, and to demonstrate in practice the meaning of the theory. For this purpose it is far more effective than a simple presentation of the theory.

Finally, tool development will be necessary to the implementation of the theory. The driving force behind this project is the insufficiency of present theory to teach integrated goals. We believe that while the final instruction need not be more complex, the analysis and design of that instruction must be more complex in order to take into account a wider range of variables related to content, audience, and setting. We will need these tools in order to manage this analysis and design, and we believe that practitioners who use the theory will likewise require these tools.

For example, one tool to be created is a Strategy Analysis System to assist the designer in the identification of instructional goals, and the selection of transactions to deliver instruction to achieve those goals. There are several advantages to using such a tool. First, ID₂, if it is to include rules for the above, will likely contain far more prescriptions than is the case for ID₁. Learning all of these rules would comprise a considerable task for an instructional designer. Taking into account all of these rules during the development process would be a significant task and it is likely that many rules will be overlooked or forgotten in the press of practical development. Finally, it is unlikely, once a design decision has been made, that an instructional designer could consider a very large set of alternative course organizations, knowledge acquisition prescriptions and filters, or interaction sequences. There are so many decisions to make that once a reasonable design has been selected it is likely to be implemented. A Strategy Analysis System would relieve the instructional designer of much of the burden of this large set of rules. The system would systematically consider all of the relevant rules. The idea of an *instructional spreadsheet* emerges. The designer could easily change a few assumptions about the learner, the course goals, or the environment and see the recommended changes in course organization and transaction sequence. Thus a much wider set of alternatives could be considered with a likely result of far more appropriate instruction.

In the following sections we outline the principal tools under development as part of the Second Generation Program.

Knowledge Acquisition and Analysis System (KAAS)

A fundamental component of ID2 is a means to acquire and represent course content. The basic representational unit is the frame, an object that has both an internal structure consisting of slots into which values are placed when the frame is instantiated, and an external structure of links to other frames. The structural elements are termed elaborations of the frame, of which there are four kinds: the internal slots, containing properties; and three external elaborations, abstraction, components, and associations. The set of all elaborated frames together, which contains all the knowledge to be instructed by a course, is called an elaborated frame network (Merrill, Li, and Jones, 1990).

The knowledge analysis and acquisition system guides the designer in representing the course content in terms of an elaborated frame network. The properties of the frames determine the kinds of knowledge that must be acquired. The designer is guided to identify the frames, frame abstraction level, frame components, and frame links which describe the subject matter content to be taught. In addition KAAS knows how to propagate knowledge from one frame to a linked frame, so that some portions of the knowledge acquisition are done automatically. The outcome of the KAAS is a domain knowledge base, representing the content for which instruction should be developed.

Transaction Library and Transaction Configuration System (TCS)

A transaction is defined as a mutual, dynamic, real-time give-and-take between the instructional system and the student in which there is an exchange of information. The purpose of a transaction is to promote the acquisition of one or more mental models. Instruction designed using ID2 is in terms of a sequence of these transactions.

An ID2 system achieves design efficiency in part by having available to the designer prepared instructional units which have already been coded and which can be easily adapted and included in a course under development. A *transaction instance* is a segment of computer code which when executed causes a given transaction to take place. Transaction instances are domain independent, in that they are each designed to instruct a particular type of content, but are not tied to any given content domain.

Transaction instances are in effect the structure of instruction. They are customizable, both at design and run-time. Parameters to transaction instances include the degree of learner control, the pedagogic method (tutorial to experiential), the mode (inquisitory or expository), the degree of learner guidance, and the instructional function (overview, familiarity instruction, basic instruction, example, practice, assessment, remediation). In addition, the strategy contained within the instance depends upon global variables, such as those contained in student profiles (level of expertise, past performance, learning goal, etc.), and environmental data (available resources, time and cost constraints, etc.).

Once a transaction has been selected or prescribed, it must then be configured and authored. Configuration involves setting the parameters, modifying the strategy, and attaching the content. Authoring involves attaching domain specific instructional materials to the instructional structure set up by the transaction. For example, in concept learning by compare/contrast, the transaction would contain all the elements to generate examples, practice, and assessment items for concept learning. However, it would require that images of the different concepts, with the defining attributes indicated, be provided by the designer. Each transaction instance knows what domain specific data it requires, and will guide the designer in preparing and entering that data.

Each transaction instance has default values for each of its parameters, including its strategy elements. While most practical instruction will require the modification of these parameters, the acceptance of default values allows the rapid prototyping of instruction incorporating the content and instructional strategies identified. This rapid prototyping allows the designer to get a feel for the structure and look of the finished course while still early enough in the design process to easily change design decisions. The effects of making different design choices can also be easily compared.

Transaction instances reside in a *transaction library*. In addition, configured and authored components are also stored in the library. The library supports the reuse of components, and is a key element in improving the efficiency of the design process.

Strategy Analysis System (SAS)

The strategy analysis system provides a strategy link between knowledge acquisition and transactions. SAS queries the user/designer to obtain specific information about subject matter goals, learner characteristics and environmental constraints. Using its built-in strategy rules and the information provided by the user/designer, SAS also knows how to recommend course organization. Course organization is a sequence of transactions, each instantiated with appropriate knowledge and configured for the specified goals, environment and learner audience. SAS also knows how to provide the necessary course management information. Management information provides the control of sequence at the various decision points in the course, either between transactions or between individual interactions within a transaction. This control can vary from learner control via a menu, to system control via some performance criteria. Note that this control is much more than simple branching between displays as is typical of much CBI or programmed instruction. The criteria used here may consist of a history of response over a transaction or a set of transactions, as well as a single response to a single display. Furthermore, the decision is between complete interaction sequences rather than between individual displays.

Prescriptive Mini-experts

Instructional design expertise is distributed throughout the system in a number of *mini-experts.* Similar to conventional expert systems in the way in which expertise is encoded as production rules, these mini-experts differ in that instead of a single, large, monolithic expert system designed to produce a single decision, the expertise is broken into a myriad of small, narrow-focus knowledge bases each capable of making a single decision, or providing a piece of data to a tool. This reflects the nature of the instructional design process, which is composed of a large number of individual decisions at different stages of the process.

The expertise that is encoded in the mini-experts is theoretical and empirical data relevant to the particular decision to be made. The self-contained and distributed nature of the knowledge bases makes this expertise easy to modify and update. Thus the mini-experts are the means by which the latest knowledge about instructional design is linked into the ID$_2$ design process. Because the mini-experts may be modified without change to other components of ID$_2$, an ID$_2$ development process can evolve painlessly as new instructional design knowledge becomes available.

Intelligent Advisor (IADV)

The prescriptions made at design time are based on the designer's best estimate of the learner population. During the delivery of instruction, information about the learner, his or her aptitude, specific goals, motivation, familiarity, and other factors, as well as the learner's expressed preferences, may be taken into account to modify those prescriptions.

An intelligent advisor program would extend the capability to customize instruction into the delivery phase. The advisor would have access to the knowledge base, both for the domain and the pedagogic prescriptions. In addition, it would maintain a student model that contained information about the learner. Using the information gathered about the student, the advisor would adjust design decisions to customize the instruction to more adequately meet the characteristics of the student. The advisor could also engage in a mixed-initiative dialog with the student which would allow the student to participate in this decision-making.

Additional Tools

A fully functional system will require additional tools:

- TAQS, the transaction acquisition system, will provide the capability to capture existing instructional transactions, not developed under ID$_2$, and describe them in ID$_2$ terms, so that they may be added to the transaction library and prescribed for instruction;
- SAQS, the strategy acquisition system, to support modification of the pedagogic rule base underlying the SAS;
- IADM, the intelligent administrator, to manage the administrative aspects of course delivery;
- IDMS, the instructional development management system, to aid in managing the development effort;
- IDES, the instructional development explanation system, to provide an explanation facility for the reasoning incorporated in the prescriptive mini-experts and the SAS rule base.

Previous Prototypes and Current Work

From 1987 until 1989, in cooperation with Human Technology, Inc., and supported in part from funds from the Army Research Institute and the U.S. Office of Personnel Management, we explored the construction of an Instructional Design Expert System. For this previous project we built two prototype systems, ID EXPERT v1.0 and ID EXPERT v2.0 (Merrill 1987a, 1987b, Merrill and Li, 1988, 1989a, 1989b).

ID EXPERT v1.0 was implemented on a VAX computer using the expert system shell *S.1*. This prototype was primarily rule based with a linear interface. It did, however, demonstrate the feasibility of an instructional design expert. This v1.0 prototype is able to guide a limited content analysis, make reasonable recommendations for course organization and make reasonable recommendations about possible transactions within this course organization for a limited domain of subject matter. This prototype explored various rule structures including the accumulation of evidence using certainty factors for decisions involving a large number of attributes.

ID EXPERT v2.0 transported the expertise to a desktop platform using Macintosh SE computers and the expert system shell NEXPERT with a HYPERCARD interface. This prototype shifted from a rule based system to a hybrid system which is primarily frame-based. The object-oriented programming characteristics of HYPERCARD, together with the object-oriented implementation of NEXPERT were exploited to represent instrucal objects. We first experimented with a frame-based representation in v2.0. Content analysis was expanded to a preliminary version of a knowledge acquisition system. Transactions were investigated and several sample transaction instances were constructed. Furthermore, the interface was improved to be more graphic and interactive allowing a non-linear navigation through the instructional design process.

Current work focuses on the KAAS, SAS, and the transactions. On a project funded by IBM Corporation, we are completing the conceptual and design work on the KAAS, and developing a stand-alone KAAS tool. Under a separate contract, we are continuing conceptual work on the SAS. We have been working with the Air Force Academy on integrating ID2 with an instructional data base. And, on a currently unfunded project, we are continuing conceptual development on transactions, with the expectation of developing a representative set of transactions at some future time.

Applications of ID2

The domain of ID2 is instruction; it is not restricted to a particular focus (education vs training), a particular audience (e.g., secondary, higher education, adults), or a particular delivery system (e.g. lecture, computer-based training, video). Rather, ID2 is intended to support the development of effective instructional applications whatever the focus, audience, or delivery system.

The design of instruction using ID2 is computer-based, but the delivery need not be. For example, a classroom teacher could deliver an ID2 designed lesson, and benefit from the careful identification of content and performance, the prescriptions for instructional strategies, and the generation of instructional outline, guide, and aids from a transaction instance appropriate for that delivery method.

However, if the delivery is computer-based, the knowledge bases of ID2 can be utilized during instruction. The customization process, under control of an intelligent advisor program, can continue during delivery. This has benefits for a variety of applications. For example:

- Computer-based training and interactive video would benefit from improved interaction between student and program; enhanced opportunities for learner control; and reduced development costs.
- Self-directed learning would benefit from the ability to customize the learning experience yet retain a structured learning environment.
- A new form of instruction would be feasible: *just-in-time instruction*. J-I-T instruction is a form of embedded training, defined as the delivery of the instruction required, and only that instruction, at exactly the time needed. This form of instruction is useful for operators of complex, high-technology systems, for whom ongoing training is a necessity. The J-I-T concept suggests that such training should be integrated with operation, in small, customizable segments, rather than being a separate activity. The knowledge representation of the domain as part of ID2 makes J-I-T instruction feasible, in that it is possible to select any goal as a starting point of instruction, to construct instruction to bridge from current knowledge to that goal, and to be able to continue instruction in a manner beyond that goal, upon demand. □

References

Merrill, M.D. The New Component Design Theory: Instructional Design for Courseware Authoring. *Instructional Science*, 1987a, *16*, 19-34.

Merrill, M.D. An Expert System for Instructional Design. *IEEE Expert*, Summer, 1987b, 25-37.

Merrill, M.D. Applying Component Display Theory to the Design of Courseware. In D.H. Jonassen (Ed.), *Instructional Designs for Microcomputer Courseware*. Hillsdale NJ: Lawrence Erlbaum, 1988.

Merrill, M.D., and Li, Z. *Implementation of an Expert System for Instructional Design* (phase 2). Army Research Institute Technical Report, 1988.

Merrill, M.D., and Li, Z. *Implementation of an Expert System for Instructional Design* (phase 3). Army Research Institute Technical Report, 1989a.

Merrill, M.D. and Li, Z. An Instructional Design Expert System. *Journal of Computer-Based Instruction*, 1989b, *16*(3), 95-101.

Merrill, M.D., Li, Z., and Jones, M.K. First Generation Instructional Design, Second Generation Instructional Design. *Educational Technology*, January and February 1990, *30* (1, 2).

Part II
Intelligent CAI

Part II
Section One

Introduction to
Intelligent CAI

Computer-Aided Instruction: Toward a New Direction

John M. Morris

Writing a decade ago, John Kemeny (1972) foresaw the possibility of "a new man-computer partnership to provide the means which, combined with sufficient concern by men for their fellowmen and for future generations, can hopefully bring about a new golden age for mankind." As president of Dartmouth College, Kemeny was in a position to require all students to study BASIC, the computer language that he had designed. Clearly, he believed that instruction in computer programming could play an essential role in education.

At about the same time, Anthony Oettinger (1969) was exposing some of the problems that schools were having in attempting to use modern technology without a clear assessment of its role. He nevertheless wrote glowingly of the potential value of a computer-aided instruction (CAI) system, which could provide a "private tool for the learner, animated blackboard for the lecturer, or anything in between . . ."

Patrick Suppes (1966), perhaps the best-known early advocate of CAI, described its potential in these terms: "One can predict that in a few more years millions of school children will have access to what Philip of Macedon's son Alexander enjoyed as a royal prerogative: the personal services of a tutor as well-informed and responsive as Aristotle."

Several major problems stood in the path of the brave new world that Kemeny, Oettinger, and Suppes foresaw:

- The cost of equipment appeared to be far too high for elementary school systems to consider.
- More significantly, the cost of course development was too high, unless it could be spread over a much larger group of students than was likely to be available.

John M. Morris is Senior Associate, Measurement Concept Corporation, Rome, New York.

- Although courses prepared by some of the leaders in CAI had impressive results, there were complaints about the courses prepared by less gifted teachers: they could easily be dull textbook surrogates or flashcard holders that added nothing to education but enormous expense.
- Packaged courses were inflexible: scientific discoveries, historical events, changing emphases, and more recent scholarship rapidly rendered the courses obsolete.
- There was no effective way for the individual teacher to customize available courses to match his or her own approach or teaching environment. As a result, even when computer-assisted courses were available, the teacher might be forced to accept them on an as-is basis, or to abandon CAI methods rather than suffer with a marginal package. What was needed was some method of introducing minor changes while leaving the more expensive overall approach and most contents intact.

The dramatic drop in the cost of computer equipment has begun to bring an answer to some of these problems. Small but versatile minicomputers and cheap microcomputers have made it possible for some elementary schools to provide a desktop computer for every member of a class. With computers in thousands of homes and classrooms, it has become possible to prepare courseware that has a wide enough audience to pay the cost of its development. The field has become both competitive and lucrative enough to make it attractive to very talented instructors, which should mean courseware of better quality. Finally, more flexible and powerful systems have made it possible to prepare and revise courses quickly, at a reasonable cost.

The existence of a wider audience has not been ignored by potential courseware developers. At a relatively small conference on computers in elementary education in Syracuse, New York, for example, more than 20 CAI vendors were present, including traditional textbook publishers, equipment manufacturers, game developers (who see CAI as a profitable sideline for their computer games), and many new groups specializing in CAI. The next few years will see a shakeout in the industry as teachers and students gain experience in the use of different types of courseware and become more selective in their choices.

One disturbing question has been the general effects of computer instruction on the children themselves. Coupled with the widespread debate concerning the possible harmful effects of computer games on children, the question of the effects of computer learning on personality and behavior remains completely open.

In contrast with the bright promises of some of the CAI pioneers, there have been serious doubts concerning the value of computer training for children. Joseph Weizenbaum, one of the best-known and best-qualified of these critics, believes that an insistence upon "instrumental reason"—that is, reasoning which does not raise questions concerning social and ethical goals—characterizes the thoughtless dependence on computer methods. "When instrumental reason is the sole guide to action, the acts it justifies are robbed of their inherent meanings and thus exist in an ethical vacuum," Weizenbaum (1976) notes.

In a similar vein, Hubert Dreyfus (1972) wrote: "Computers can only deal with facts, but man—the source of facts—is not a fact or set of facts, but a being who creates himself and the world of facts in the process of living in the world."

Unfortunately, neither Weizenbaum nor Dreyfus provides empirical support for these particular claims, but they should not be taken any less seriously for that reason. Perhaps the clearest picture of their position would be given by experiments of a decade ago in which baby monkeys were raised by surrogate "mothers" made of rags and wires. These surrogates provided the babies with all their needs, except one: the chance to observe what it was like to be an adult monkey. When the babies survived, they appeared to be seriously psychotic. Similarly, it might be that a child trained largely by computer would lose precisely the ingredient that a good teacher must provide: a model of what it is like to be an ethical human being. This ethical element is far more important, in the long run, than most of the other things the child might learn—like the names of the states or a method for finding square roots.

On a more mundane level, critics like Oettinger have suggested that CAI could be boring and ineffective, as well as expensive. Only a limited range of courses was thought to be amenable to computer methods, courses like mathematics and computer programming. Courses in the arts and in the humanities might not fit the drill-and-test model used by the first CAI programs. Moreover, the practice of substituting a computer "language" for foreign languages in the primary and secondary schools, as well as in the colleges, would be depriving the child of access to a rich cultural heritage at an age when language acquisition is easiest.

Newer approaches attempt to meet criticisms like these. Learning to program a computer-controlled mechanical turtle, for example, can mean opening up a wide range of problem-solving skills that can be applied to other areas of the curriculum. Learning to program the turtle is a great deal more than a simple exercise in programming (see Papert, 1980).

CAI Has Changed: The Role of Artificial Intelligence Research

The type of instruction offered by CAI courses has changed. The computer is no longer an expensive flashcard holder or surrogate textbook but an active participant in the learning process. Since much of this new direction has been inspired by work in Artificial Intelligence (AI), it will be important to call attention to AI as an example of a new direction in CAI.

AI has come out of the laboratory and into the factory, school, home, and office. Learning systems and knowledge-based systems, as well as systems for machine-supported inference, are increasingly being proposed as central to the development of "fifth generation" computers (Yasaki, 1982). As these systems are applied to CAI, the goal is development of a learning system in which the child is the teacher and the machine is the learner. This approach reverses the traditional model, in which the computer is a pre-programmed teaching machine, which cannot be modified by the learner. "The revolutionary effects of the technology in education are tied to the nature of the computer itself . . . if a computer is viewed not as a source of information but as a problem-solving device . . ." (Fiske, 1982).

The computer can be seen as providing enrichment, rather than the desiccation that Weizenbaum feared. Launching a new program for the Sloan Foundation, for support of technological education in the liberal arts curriculum, Stephen White (1981) writes: "The computer stands in an odd relationship to applied mathematics and technological literacy. Looked at from one point of view, the computer *is* applied mathematics; looked at from another point of view, it is a glorious technological achievement. It represents in itself the close relationship between analytic skills and technology: the best way to discover what a computer can do is to know how it works; the best way to discover how it works is to know what it can do. It lies at the crossover between the two modes of thought, enriching and enriched by both."

As it happens, while AI research has produced some very interesting systems, they also appear to be very expensive, hand-constructed systems that cannot be applied to a broad range of subject matter (Barr and Feigenbaum, 1982). What is needed is a bridge between the sophisticated, expensive approach used by AI research, with its emphasis on the active participation of the learner, and the easily written and easily modified approaches of contemporary course-writing systems.

Our own research is intended to develop a system that will provide such a bridge. CAST, Computer Assisted Self Teaching, is intended to play the role of intermediary between the simple drill-and-test approach of many current CAI systems and the more elaborate techniques used by researchers in Artificial Intelligence. CAST makes it possible for a teacher to write very simple, straightforward courseware, but also to add computational facilities, colorful displays, and audible outputs when they would enhance or support the educational goals.

It is based on the PILOT language, which was recently singled out (Kearsley, 1982) as the one author language that was simple enough for a non-programmer to use. It takes only a few minutes to learn the basic commands and to write simple scripts for courses. Instructors and other course writers are able to write scripts during their first lesson in CAST. Nevertheless, the syntax of the CAST language permits indefinite expansion of its repertoire to include split-screen, graphics, and other advanced functions.

The simplicity and flexibility of the language mean that an instructor can make changes in a script whenever they are needed. This approach also means that a researcher can rapidly prepare several versions of a script for testing various approaches to the course material.

CAST is really a research tool for the development and testing of new techniques in CAI, as well as an author language. For example, I have been writing a series of scripts for CAST that will teach CAST itself, using the system to test and run the students' trial scripts. In other words, the student is writing scripts in CAST from the beginning, submitting these to the interpreter, and obtaining results—all within the context of a CAST script. One of the CAST's useful features is its ability to call on itself, giving the student the chance to learn by actually writing scripts.

For that matter, CAST could call on compilers for FORTRAN, BASIC, PASCAL, or any other language available on the host system, in order to teach students these languages. An educator could develop programs to teach logic or calculus, or any other subject for which a simulation program was available. CAST has a window to the UNIX operating system, through which it can call on all the features of UNIX. This means that CAST can be used as a framework for writing courses in programming, mathematics, engineering, physics, chemistry, or other topics, using any available software to perform computations or to simulate

experiments in exactly the way that AI programs do. If a program for language translation were available, CAST could use it as the basis for teaching a foreign language. In short, CAST is a tool for developing systems with the sophistication of artificial intelligence teaching systems, but without the work required to develop those systems from scratch.

While the basic CAST syntax is simple enough for anyone to learn, the full power of a programming language and of the UNIX operating system will be there when it is needed.

One of the things that a research worker might try is to let children write their own courses in CAST, on the theory that teaching something is one of the best ways of learning it. A young person might, for example, develop a course in "How to Drive a Car Without Smashing It—and Yourself." This could be a very effective way for the course writer to learn the rules of safe driving. What seems most important in this approach is that it calls upon the child as an active participant in learning, rather than a passive sponge.

For someone using CAST as a research tool, one particularly useful facility is its ability to maintain student records and to record results of instruction sessions. This means that the research worker can develop full protocols for each student, to locate bugs in the courses, as well as to record the student's progress, or lack of it.

The communications resources of the UNIX environment make it possible to provide on-line facilities to other researchers, and to students who want to take any of the available courses. CAST is installed and in use in a nearby college, for interactive use on their time-sharing computer system. There is no reason in principle why students there could not arrange to take their courses from terminals in their homes. The possibility that a community-oriented technical college like this could offer courses to students in their homes is only one of the exciting possibilities that this approach offers.

Conclusion

In my discussion of the effects of computer instruction, I included some rather fearful comments from people like Weizenbaum and Dreyfus. Essentially, their criticisms suggest that using the computer can destroy the richness of full existence as a human being, by substituting symbol manipulation for real human sensations and emotions. This is a serious charge, but there has been little real research to determine the effect that interaction with a computer has on the personality of the student. For this purpose, CAST provides a research environment that could be used to answer these questions. It is available on-line to teachers and research workers who simply want to try it out, and to those who have a definite research program on which to work.

I believe that the outcome of research into the effects of the computer on children will show that an approach which emphasizes active thought and participation in the learning process has a positive effect on the learner's sense of accomplishment and feelings of personal worth. If this is correct, then the partnership between human and computer will enhance our lives in a way that fulfills the prophecies and hopes of the pioneers. ☐

References

Barr, A., and Feigenbaum, E.A. *The Handbook of Artificial Intelligence.* Los Altos: William Kaufmann, Inc., 1982, Vol. II, 223-294.

Dreyfus, H.L. *What Computers Can't Do: A Critique of Artificial Reason.* New York: Harper & Row, 1972, 202-203.

Fiske, E. Computers Alter Life of Pupils and Teachers. *The New York Times,* April 4, 1982, *1,* p. 42.

Kearsley, G. Authoring Systems in Computer Based Education. *Communications of the ACM,* July 1982, p. 430.

Kemeny, J.G. *Man and the Computer.* New York: Scribners, 1972.

Oettinger, A.G. *Run, Computer, Run: The Mythology of Educational Innovation.* Cambridge: Harvard University Press, 1969, p. 214.

Papert, S. *Mindstorms.* New York: Basic Books, 1980, 135-140.

Suppes, P. The Uses of Computers in Education. *Scientific American,* September 1966, p. 207.

Weizenbaum, J. *Computer Power and Human Reason: From Judgment to Calculation.* San Francisco: Freeman, 1976, p. 276.

White, S. *The New Liberal Arts.* New York: Alfred P. Sloan Foundation, 1981.

Yasaki, E.K. Tokyo Looks to the '90s. *Datamation,* January 1982, 110-115.

Intelligent Computer-Assisted Instruction: An Explanation and Overview

Franklin C. Roberts and Ok-choon Park

In the last few years, artificial intelligence (AI) has emerged from the research labs to become a central component in many areas of high-technology development: computer vision, speech generation, robotics, and expert problem-solving systems are but a few of the many ways in which artificial intelligence has been applied to solving problems in high-technology areas. Artificial intelligence is defined as the attempt to get computers to perform tasks that if performed by a human being, intelligence would be required to perform the task.

In addition to the application areas mentioned above, AI has been applied in the field of education as well, with the result often referred to as intelligent tutoring systems or intelligent computer-assisted instruction (ICAI). ICAI systems have taken on many forms, but essentially they have separated the major components of instructional systems in a way which allows both the student and the program a flexibility in the learning environment more closely resembling what actually occurs when student and teacher sit down one-on-one and attempt to teach and learn together. This article is an attempt to briefly review the structure of ICAI systems, give some examples of such systems, and discuss their relative strengths and weaknesses.

Three Components of ICAI Systems

ICAI systems apply principles of artificial intelligence in the representation of domain knowledge, natural language dialogues, and methods of inference. The operational functions of an ICAI system are determined by three main components or modules. These modules represent the three main components of any instructional system, namely the content to be taught, the inherent teaching or instructional strategy, and a mechanism for understanding what the student does and does not know. In ICAI systems, these modules are referred to as the expertise, student, and tutoring modules (Clancey, Barnett, and Cohen, 1982). Due to the size and complexity of most ICAI programs, not all of the three components are fully developed in every system. Most systems focus on the development of a single part of what would constitute a fully usable system (Clancey, 1979). The ultimate goal of ICAI, however, is to have a system which has powerful models in each of these three components, and to have these components work together to produce the most effective learning environment possible. Each of these modules is elaborated on below.

1. *Expertise module.* An expertise, or problem-solving module, consists of the domain knowledge that the system is imparting to the student. This knowledge includes both the content to be taught and how to use that knowledge to solve related problems. The latter of these is referred to as procedural knowledge, and represents the procedures used by "experts" in solving problems of this type. The expertise module is charged with the task of generating questions and evaluating the correctness of a student's problem solution. The knowledge of subject matter may be represented by one or more of the following methods: (a) semantic nets in a huge, static database that incorporate all the facts to be taught; (b) procedural experts that correspond to subskills that a student must learn in order to acquire the complete skill being taught; (c) production rules that are used to construct modular representations of skills and problem-solving methods; and (d) multiple representations that combine the semantic nets of facts and the procedures of functional behaviors of the facts (Clancey *et al.*, 1982).

2. *Student module.* The student module is a method of representing the student's understanding of the material to be taught. This module is used to make hypotheses about the student's misconceptions and suboptimal performance strategies so that the system can point them out, indicate why they are wrong, and suggest corrections. Modeling the student knowledge uses (a) simple pattern recognition applied to the student's response history and (b) flags in the subject-matter semantic net (or the rule base) representing areas that the student has mastered. Major information sources for maintaining the student module are (a) student problem-solving behavior (implicit), (b) direct questions asked of the student (explicit), (c) assumptions based on the student's experience (historical), and (d) assumptions based on some measure of the difficulty of the subject material (structural).

Franklin C. Roberts and Ok-choon Park are Senior Researchers in Education Systems Research and Development, Control Data Corporation, Minneapolis, Minnesota.

3. *Tutoring module.* A tutoring module is a set of specifications of how the system should present materials to the student. The tutoring module integrates knowledge about natural language dialogues, teaching methods, and subject materials. This module communicates with the student in selecting problems for him or her to solve, monitoring and criticizing his or her performance, providing assistance upon request, and selecting remedial materials. The strategy in the tutoring module is based on one of the following methods: (a) a diagnostic or debugging approach in which the system debugs the student's misunderstanding by posing tasks and evaluating his or her response; (b) the Socratic method, which involves questioning the student in a way that will encourage him or her to reason about what he or she knows and thereby modify his or her conceptions; or (c) a coaching method in which the student is engaged in some activity like a computer game to encourage skill acquisition and general problem-solving ability. (See Clancey *et al.*, 1982, for a comprehensive description of the above three components.)

Development of ICAI Systems

Carbonell's (1970) SCHOLAR system for teaching South American geography served as an impetus for the development of ICAI systems. SCHOLAR utilizes a complex but well-defined information structure in the form of a network of facts, concepts, and procedures as a database. The elements of this network are units of information defining words and events in the form of multi-level tree lists. In SCHOLAR, the Socratic style of tutoring dialogue is used. The system first attempts to diagnose the student's misconceptions and then presents materials that will force the student to see his or her own error (Collins, Warnock, and Passafiume, 1975). SCHOLAR's inference strategies, for answering student questions and evaluating student answers, are independent of the content of the semantic net and applicable in different domains.

SCHOLAR is extended by the WHY program (Stevens and Collins, 1977). WHY tutors students in the causes of rainfall, a complex geophysical process that is a function of many interrelated factors. WHY implements the Socratic tutorial heuristics that describe the global strategies used by human tutors to guide the dialogue.

O'Shea developed a system at the University of Leeds in England referred to as a self-improving quadratic tutor (O'Shea, 1979). This system has two principal components: one is an adaptive teaching program which is expressed in a set of production rules, and the other is the self-improving component which makes experimental changes in the production rules of the teaching program. The system is designed to conduct experiments on the teaching strategy by altering the production rules. Data are kept on the effectiveness of the changes, and those modifications which result in improved student performance are incorporated into the set of production rules. This work is particularly interesting in its adaptive nature and has not been investigated to any great extent. Another self-adapting ICAI system of note is Kimball's self-improving tutor for symbolic integration. A description of this system can be found in Kimball (1973) and Sleeman and Brown (1982).

Brown, Burton, and Bell (1975) developed the SOPHIE system, which is an attempt to create a "reactive" learning environment in which the student acquires problem-solving skills by trying out his or her own ideas rather than by receiving instruction from the system. SOPHIE incorporates a model of the knowledge domain along with heuristic strategies for answering a student's questions, provides critiques of his or her current learning paths, and generates alternative paths (Brown and Burton, 1978a). SOPHIE allows the student to have a one-to-one relationship with a computer-based expert who helps the student come up with his or her own ideas, experiment with these ideas, and, when necessary, debug them.

The principles of SOPHIE have been applied to constructing a diagnostic model (BUGGY) in learning basic mathematical problem-solving skills (Brown and Burton, 1978b) and for developing a computer-coaching model in a discovery learning environment (Burton and Brown, 1979). The BUGGY program provides a mechanism for explaining why a student is making an arithmetic mistake, as opposed to simply identifying the mistake. BUGGY allows teachers to practice diagnosing the underlying causes of students' errors by presenting examples of systematic, incorrect behavior.

The coaching model is used to identify diagnostic strategies required to infer a student's misunderstandings from the observed behaviors. It is also used as a tutoring strategy for directing the tutor to say the right thing at the right time (Burton and Brown, 1979). WEST is a coaching program designed to teach the appropriate manipulation of arithmetic expressions in a computer gaming environment (Burton and Brown, 1979). Another coaching program is Goldstein and Carr's (1977) WUMPUS. WUMPUS is designed to foster the student's (game player's) ability to make proper logical and probabilistic inferences from the given information.

Clancey's (1979) GUIDON, another program for teaching diagnostic (medical) problem-solving, is different from other ICAI programs in terms of the mixed-initiative dialogue. GUIDON uses the prolonged and structured teaching interactions that go beyond responding to the student's last move (as in WEST and WUMPUS) and repetitive questioning and answering (as in SCHOLAR and WHY). In GUIDON, the tutoring rules are organized into discourse procedures and the subject materials (medical diagnostic rules) are hierarchically grouped into a separate system, called MYCIN. MYCIN is a computer-based consultation system for the diagnosis and therapy of infectious diseases.

Suppes and his associates also applied artificial intelligence techniques in the development of a proof checker (EXCHECK) capable of understanding the validity of a student's mathematical proof (Blaine and Smith, 1977). EXCHECK has no student module, but its inference procedures in the expertise module allow it to make assumptions about a student's reasoning and track his or her solutions, thus providing a "reactive environment" similar to that of SOPHIE. Clancey *et al.* (1982) thoroughly reviewed eight representative ICAI systems: SCHOLAR, WHY, SOPHIE, WEST, WUMPUS, GUIDON, BUGGY, and EXCHECK.

Another application of artificial intelligence techniques for computer-based education is to create a new educational environment through full control of the learning experience by the student (Papert, 1980). Papert's LOGO is a special language designed for this purpose. Taylor (1980) calls this approach "use of computer as a tutee" to distinguish it from other approaches in which the computer is used as a "tutor." However, this approach is not considered as an ICAI system in this article because of its different educational perspective and operational procedures.

ICAI Systems: Potentials and Limitations

Intelligent CAI systems represent the state-of-the-art in what "could be" in computer-based instruction (CBI). The structure of these systems offers a model for CBI systems of the future; and, as such, they have the potential of offering fertile research opportunities in exploring how students learn and how we might be more effective in teaching them. At the same time, the rhetoric surrounding this work often leaves the reader with the impression that ICAI systems that can intelligently teach any subject on any terminal are "just around the corner," and *this is clearly not the case.* In some limited circumstances, ICAI systems can be used to deliver instruction today; the biggest potential impact, however, is in their potential for offering insights into the various components in the teaching-learning process. Some of the more prominent advantages and disadvantages of these

systems and the work on which they are built are offered below.

Advantages and Potentials of ICAI Systems

Instructional research in the classroom has a great many limitations, but probably the most significant of these is the difficulty in isolating instructional strategies that can be replicated with other teachers and different students over various subject areas. Traditional CBI has offered a research environment which can overcome some of these obstacles, but even there the distinction between content, teaching strategy, and student characteristics often becomes blurred. Perhaps the biggest benefit that ICAI systems have to offer is the ability to unambiguously isolate each of the four components of ICAI systems: (1) student characteristics (through the student model), (2) the instructional strategy used (via the tutoring module), (3) the subject matter to be taught (through the knowledge representation system), and (4) the nature of communication between student and teacher (as manifested in the natural language system). Each of these four areas represents major efforts being conducted in traditional instructional and classroom research. More cooperation between the AI and educational communities might offer both sides some benefits.

A second potential offered by ICAI systems is concerned with a major shift now occurring in the CBI field—namely, the change from programming languages to authoring systems. In the programming language environment, the author writes lines of code which intermix information about the content, the student, and the instructional strategy being used. The authoring language environment typically isolates these components and offers the author higher-level alternatives in manipulating the various components. The similarities between the structure of authoring systems and ICAI systems is probably not coincidental, and as authoring systems continue to make headway in the CBI field, work in ICAI can offer valuable insights into alternative ways in which authoring systems might be built.

A third advantage of ICAI comes as a spin-off in investigating how people learn. An excellent example of this is in the work accomplished in building the BUGGY system. Historically, teachers have generally believed that most of the errors students commit in arithmetic were random aberrations of the correct method of solution. While there was always the belief that some systematic errors probably did occur, the huge number of possible error patterns made the task virtually impossible for any classroom teacher. In the development of BUGGY, the researchers considered all possible student solution paths, both correct and incorrect, for solving arithmetic problems. The correct path was then compared to the path the student actually took, and they found that nearly 80 percent of all student errors were systematic in nature. The result of this is that by carefully choosing example items for students to solve, evidence can be built up which shows the misconceptions which students have. As a result, instruction can be specifically remedial for correcting a student's misconception, or "bug" as it is called. The larger benefit here is that through complex, probabilistic reasoning (often called fuzzy reasoning in AI), many other relationships in the teaching/learning process may also be made more clear to us.

The fourth and final benefit of ICAI systems presented here is in the areas in which they can be implemented today. The best example of this is the GUIDON system, and it is happening in conjunction with an area of AI known as expert systems. Expert systems are an application of AI techniques which simulate the problem-solving of experts in such areas as chemical analysis, medical diagnosis, and computer fault diagnosis. Given the relevant information, these systems can often solve problems as effectively as experts in the field. In addition, once the problem is solved, they can explain the reasoning they used to arrive at their conclusion. This has prompted many of the AI researchers in expert systems to proclaim that it is "just a small step to take this ability to explain and make it into a teaching system." Well, the step is a large one, but some significant strides have been made, and those made with the GUIDON system are exemplary.

GUIDON is an expert teaching system used in conjunction with the expert problem-solving system called MYCIN, a medical program for diagnosing myocardial infarctions. What really makes this work significant, however, is in the evolution of MYCIN and other expert problem-solving systems like it. After MYCIN was proven to be effective in diagnosing myocardial infarctions, the researchers investigated whether the problem-solving logic used in MYCIN might not also be useful in solving other kinds of similar problems. The medical knowledge was extracted from the system, leaving an empty version of MYCIN's problem-solving logic called EMYCIN (for essential, or empty MYCIN). Other content domains were then entered into EMYCIN and it was found that (with certain restrictions) EMYCIN was just as effective in solving these new problems. Even more impressive is the fact that GUIDON was found to be a useful teaching system with these new content areas as well. With the advent of these "generic" expert systems that only need to have new content domains entered, the ten

to 50 person-years generally associated with expert systems development has dropped to one to three years, and their use has correspondingly increased. This will likely be the most productive area of ICAI development throughout the next decade.

Problems and Limitations of ICAI Systems

In considering the state-of-the-art of artificial intelligence as it relates to CBI, it is important to keep in mind a distinction between "what might be" and "what is." Many of the write-ups in the literature discuss a prototype system, the problems encountered in that system, and the recommendations for how those problems might be solved. This is very different from describing a system that has actually solved those problems. Another misleading notion can be found in the names given to many of the components of ICAI systems. The expert teaching models, for instance, are considerably less than models of expert teaching; they are usually just a set of rules used for teaching the content in question. Whether they are the best models or expert models is another question.

However, most of the problems and limitations inherent in existing ICAI systems will most likely be resolved at some time in the future. The key question is not if, but when, will these problems be resolved? Before trying to answer this question, we offer a brief review of some of the more prominent limitations of current ICAI systems.

One of the most prevalent limitations in ICAI systems is in the nature of the student-computer dialogues. While most ICAI systems recommend a natural language dialogue between student and computer, most existing systems are considerably more narrow than most natural environments. Understanding natural language is an extremely complex task, and one which is being heavily researched in the AI community. In the meantime, existing systems must require the students to use a subset of the language, often with some syntax rules that must also be followed. Of course, when the computer does not understand a student's utterance, a parroting response, such as "What do you mean by . . .," can always be issued recursively until an understandable response is provided. However, until the natural language problem is solved, this will be a limiting factor in the use and development of ICAI systems.

A second limitation can be found in the inherent assumption that we can understand what a student knows by comparing the student model to the corresponding expertise model. The problem here is that we do not know very much about the differences in how people reason, and the expertise model may not be appropriate for all students; this may be even more true when considering the cognitive developmental stages that pre-adult students must go through. However, while this is a limitation for existing systems, it can also be seen as a research opportunity in the development of future systems.

A third limitation is in the extreme labor-intensive nature of ICAI systems development. The amount of time and effort required to build an ICAI system which teaches even a small amount of content is still enormous, often on the order of many person-years. While generic expert systems hold a potential for significantly reducing this development time, the current state-of-the-art almost precludes any ICAI development except for research purposes.

A fourth limitation has been in the content domains chosen for implementation. Most ICAI systems have been restricted to the highly-structured content areas like mathematics, electronics, and games. While Carbonell's geography lesson shows that this need not be the case, the wide applicability of ICAI systems and models needs to be verified in other content domains as well.

A final issue which will limit the near-term usage of ICAI systems is in the inherent hardware and software requirements. Most ICAI systems require very powerful LISP processing machines. There are some desktop computers available now that will handle these requirements very well; however, their cost is generally prohibitive for the individual consumer (50K-100K). In addition, current AI research is moving toward machines which can perform parallel processing, and this will probably increase the hardware costs, at least in the foreseeable future. However, computer hardware costs have a long-standing tradition of dropping dramatically, and accordingly, this problem may only be a temporary one.

Summary

In summary, intelligent computer-assisted instruction is the attempt to provide a natural (computer-based) environment for the student which simulates what occurs between a student and tutor in a one-on-one situation. ICAI systems are modular in nature, with the common components being a student module, a tutoring module, and an expertise or problem-solving module. Each of these modules interacts with the others, and the result is communicated to the student through a natural language, mixed initiative dialogue.

While ICAI systems represent the state-of-the-art in computer-based instruction, their impact on instructional delivery is not likely to be widespread in the near-term. They offer an ideal laboratory environment for investigating many of the components in any instructional system, and can also be

used as structural models for the recent advent in authoring systems. They have also provided some insights into how people learn by providing an immediate, powerful analysis of student response patterns. While these advantages are promising, there are limits to be overcome as well. The natural language environments that currently exist are fairly rigid, and work in natural language understanding will have to be furthered before this problem can be overcome. In addition, the student and teaching models rely heavily on models of learning which are still being developed. Other limiting factors include the huge amounts of development time required to build an ICAI system, the costly hardware requirements, and the narrow range of content domains for which ICAI systems have been built.

A common question asked in this context is: When will ICAI systems become readily available in the marketplace? Unfortunately, this is not a simple question to answer. Clearly, we have already seen some influence from the work being done in ICAI in the development of authoring systems, if not directly, at least in the similarity of their structures. With the current proliferation in the use of expert systems in business, industry, and government, we may see actual ICAI systems like GUIDON implemented on a widespread scale in the next five to ten years. Much of the work in natural language might also be implementable in non-AI environments in ways which could facilitate a student's ability to ask questions of his or her computer-tutor. But given the work that remains to be done, the small amount of work that is occurring in ICAI, and the long-term development time that is required in many of these systems, the authors' opinion is that widespread use of true ICAI systems will undoubtedly occur, but not for 15 to 20 years.   □

References

Blaine, L., and Smith, R.L., Jr. Intelligent CAI: The Role of the Curriculum in Suggesting Computational Models of Reasoning. *In Proceedings of the 1977 ACM Annual Conference*, October 1977, Seattle, 241-246.

Brown, J.S., and Burton, R.R. A Paradigmatic Example of an Artificially Intelligent Instructional System. *International Journal of Man-Machine Studies*, 1978a, *10*, 323-339.

Brown, J.S., and Burton, R.R. Diagnostic Models for Procedural Bugs in Basic Mathematical Skills. *Cognitive Science*, 1978b, *2*, 155-192.

Brown, J.S., Burton, R.R., and Bell, A.G. SOPHIE: A Step Toward Creating a Reactive Learning Environment. *International Journal of Man-Machine Studies*, 1975, *7*, 675-696.

Burton, R.R., and Brown, J.S. An Investigation of Computer Coaching for Informal Learning Activities. *International Journal of Man-Machine Studies*, 1979, *11*, 5-24.

Carbonell, J. AI in CAI: An Artificial Intelligence Approach to Computer-Assisted Instruction. *IEEE Transactions on Man-Machine Systems*, 1970, *11*, 190-202.

Clancey, W.J. Tutorial Rules for Guiding a Case Method Dialogue. *International Journal of Man-Machine Studies*, 1979, *11*, 25-50.

Clancey, W.J., Barnett, J.S., and Cohen, P.R. Applications-Oriented AI Research: Education. In A. Barr, and E. Feigenbaum (Eds.), *The Handbook of Artificial Intelligence: Volume II*. Los Altos, CA: William Kaufmann, 1982.

Collins, A., Warnock, E.H., and Passafiume, J.J. Analysis and Synthesis of Tutorial Dialogues. *Psychology of Learning and Motivation*, 1975, *9*, 49-87.

Goldstein, I., and Carr, B. The Computer as Coach: An Athletic Paradigm for Intellectual Education. Paper presented at the annual conference of the Association for Computing Machinery, Seattle, October 1977.

Kimball, R. Self-Optimizing Computer-Assisted Tutoring: Theory and Practice. *Institute of Mathematical Studies in the Social Sciences, Psychology and Education Series, Technical Report No. 206*, June 25, 1973.

O'Shea, T. A Self-Improving Quadratic Tutor. *International Journal of Man-Machine Studies*, 1979, *11*, 97-124.

Papert, S. *Mind Storms: Children, Computers, and Powerful Ideas*. New York: Basic Books, 1980.

Sleeman, D., and Brown, J.S. *Intelligent Tutoring Systems*. New York: Academic Press, 1982.

Stevens, A.L., and Collins, A. The Goal Structure of a Socratic Tutor. Paper presented at the annual conference of the Association for Computing Machinery, Seattle, October 1977.

Taylor, R.P. *The Computer in the School: Tutor, Tool, Tutee*. New York: Columbia University, Teachers College Press, 1980.

Part II
Section Two

Aspects of
Intelligent CAI

Conventional CBI Versus Intelligent CAI: Suggestions for the Development of Future Systems

Ok-choon Park and Robert J. Seidel

The goal of intelligent computer-assisted instruction (ICAI) is to apply artificial intelligence (AI) techniques to the development of highly individualized and powerful computer-based instructional (CBI) systems. Following Carbonell's (1970) SCHOLAR, about two dozen ICAI programs were produced. Although the practical value of the current ICAI systems, in terms of instructional effectiveness and efficiency, has yet to be evaluated, their functional capability has demonstrated clearly that AI techniques have provided a powerful means for the development of highly adaptive CBI systems. In fact, the ICAI movement is the single most salient collective effort in extending the range of CBI for the last one and one-half decades. The movement has much promise and much can be expected from it in the future (Suppes, 1984).

Since ICAI has evolved from the field of computer science, but not from instructional psychology or technology, most ICAI programs have not incorporated those common instructional theories and design principles which have been proved valuable in practice and are widely accepted by instructional developers and teachers.

Concurrently, few AI techniques have been applied in the educational technology community to the development of CBI programs. This is mainly due to the lack of technical resources and skills necessary for the development of sophisticated and labor-intensive ICAI programs.

ICAI is an attempt to advance the current state of CBI by the application of AI technology. However, ICAI is fundamentally different from traditional CBI in terms of the basic philosophies underlying the structures and development processes of the systems. In this article, we attempt to discuss the important differences for the researchers/developers of both CBI and ICAI to better understand the respective current state and needs of computer-delivered instructional systems developed by the other scientific community. The purpose of this article is to stimulate combined and cooperative efforts between researchers/developers in AI (including ICAI) and instruction (including CBI) for the development of future computer-delivered instructional systems.

Development Goals

Traditional CBI has been developed by educational researchers and training developers to solve their practical problems by applying computer technology. Educators and trainers are mostly interested in the improvement of instructional effectiveness and efficiency by applying various types of computer software techniques and instructional strategies in the development of CBI lessons and CBI management systems.

In contrast, ICAI has been initiated basically by computer scientists to explore the capability of AI techniques in the process of learning and teaching. Therefore, the focus of ICAI projects was on the technical aspects of the system (e.g., knowledge representation techniques, natural language dialogues, inferencing mechanism, etc.) rather than on the instructional features. The initial interest, at least, of ICAI researchers was in the manipulation of specific AI techniques in order to observe how they work in the instructional process rather than to improve instructional effectiveness and efficiency of the systems.

Once the functional capabilities of AI techniques are successfully tested in the learning and teaching process, future efforts for the development of computer-delivered instructional systems should determine how and what kinds of AI techniques should be applied for the development of instructionally effective and efficient systems in the given situation.

Theoretical Bases

Many CBI systems have been criticized as being developed in a theoretical vacuum (Kearsley and Seidel, 1985). However, most CBI programs have incorporated some principles of learning and instruction in one form or another. For example, the early forms of CBI were strongly influenced by Skinnerian behaviorism. Although a programmed instructional paradigm is still popular among CBI developers, it has been evolved by adopting a "systems approach" to instructional development (e.g., Gagne and Briggs, 1979). A systems approach allows CBI authors to incorporate various instructional principles and research findings in the design

Ok-choon Park and Robert J. Seidel are with the U.S. Army Research Institute for the Behavioral and Social Sciences, Alexandria, Virginia.

and development process. However, the application of the systems approach to CBI development is limited by the developer's knowledge in the field of learning and instruction and the system's (hardware and software) capability.

Along with the exploration of AI techniques in the instructional process, however, many ICAI projects have sought to better understand cognitive processes involved in learning and teaching specific tasks. For example, "overlay" (Carr and Goldstein, 1977) and "buggy" (Brown and Burton, 1978) methods are designed to make inferences about the student's cognitive structure and process involved in learning the given task. Some of the knowledge representation methods (e.g., semantic networks) are also developed on the basis of cognitive models of human memory and cognition (Quillian, 1968). Thus, many ICAI researchers designed and built their systems on the theoretical notions of cognitive science that have grown out of information processing theory in cognitive psychology (Hayes-Roth and Thorndike, 1985).

If instruction is a prescriptive science and the prescriptions should be derived from the descriptive (and diagnostic) theories of learning psychology (including cognitive science), the theoretical approaches taken in the conventional CBI and ICAI need to be incorporated in the process of development of future computer-delivered instructional systems. Most conventional CBI programs are focused on the prescriptive features of instruction without sufficient consideration of descriptive and diagnostic processes of instruction. In contrast, most ICAI programs mainly emphasize the descriptive learning process and diagnostic procedures, with little attention to the prescriptive process of instruction.

System Structures and Functions

In most CBI systems, all of the instructional components (i.e., subject content, student information, and instructional strategy) are stored and implemented in a single structure. Although some systems (Seidel, 1971) have separate modules to store the instructional components independently, their operational procedures (including instructional presentations) are still determined by pre-entered specific pieces of information and by

A major portion of this paper is included in a section of the authors' chapter, "ICAI: Old Wine in New Bottles or New Vintage." In G.P. Kearsley (Ed.), *Artificial Intelligence and Instruction: Applications and Methods*. Reading, MA: Addison-Wesley, in press.

pre-defined algorithmic procedures. This style of CBI is called "ad hoc, frame-oriented" CAI (Carbonell, 1970). In the frame-oriented structure, the student has little or no initiative in the instructional process.

Most ICAI programs are basically organized into a modular structure consisting of three main components of instruction: a knowledge base, student modeling module, and instructional strategy (or teaching expertise) module. In its nature, ICAI is generative in that it processes knowledge stored in the system to ask questions and respond to the student. Many ICAI systems have abilities to carry on natural language dialogues with the student. The natural language dialogue ability allows "mixed initiatives" between the student and computer with questions and answers from both sides. That is, ICAI systems use instantaneous inferential processes to diagnose the student's learning needs and prescribe instructional treatments. The flexible modular structure, inferential capability and mixed-initiative capability of ICAI are very desirable features for the development of powerful CBI systems in the future.

Instructional Approaches

Because conventional CBI has been developed as an instructional delivery system, the basic instructional approaches used in CBI are not much different from the commonly practiced approaches in schools and training environments. An exception is the application of the computer's interactive and recordkeeping capability for individualized instruction. In schools and training environments, teachers and trainers should successfully communicate their knowledge to the students to achieve instructional objectives within given constraints (e.g., time). Thus, most instructional methods take a teacher-centered expository form, which requires the student first to understand the teacher's instruction, and then to practice given questions for the reinforcement of his or her understandings. This teacher-centered expository approach was strongly influenced by Skinnerian behaviorism. However, specific methods applied in the expository approach are not limited to behavioristic principles. Actually, many different types of instructional strategies have been applied in CBI depending upon the purpose of the instruction (Hunter, Kastner, Rubin, and Seidel, 1975) as well as the characteristics of students and subject matter contents. Furthermore, many CBI developers try to incorporate cognitive principles and strategies in their development process, as the concern for teaching cognitive tasks grows and many instructional psychologists' theoretical perspectives shift from behaviorism to cognitive psychology.

In contrast, many ICAI researchers adopted John Dewey's philosophy, "learning-by-doing," as the basic instructional approach in the system (Dewey, 1910; Sleeman and Brown, 1982). In this approach, the student is required to engage actively in the instructional process to formulate and test his or her own ideas and to witness the consequences resulting from the system's reactions to his or her behaviors (Brown, Burton, and deKleer, 1982). Brown, Burton, and Bell (1975) argue that this approach elicits optimal learning and refer to the conditions for this approach as the "reactive learning environment." Thus, in most ICAI systems, instructional methods take a student-centered discovery form, and tutorial dialogues are basically determined by the student's conceptual understandings and learning behaviors. The student-centered, guided-discovery approach is represented by two specific tutorial methods: Socratic and coaching. The Socratic method provides the student with questions guiding him or her through the process of debugging his or her own misconceptions (Carbonell, 1970; Stevens, Collins, and Goldin, 1979); the coaching method provides the student with an environment (e.g., computer games) in which he or she can enjoy and learn as a consequence of fun (Burton and Brown, 1982; Goldstein, 1982). Actually, the provision of "reactive learning environment" has been historically used in the development of curriculum models by early child educators following Piagetian theory (Piaget, 1954; Piaget and Inhelder, 1964).

Methods of Structuring Knowledge

In CBI, task analysis is a common method used to identify tasks and sub-tasks to be taught and content elements required to learn the tasks. Two common methods of task analysis are an algorithmic approach and a hierarchical approach. A combination of the two methods may be used for a complex psycho-motor skill or a cognitive problem-solving task (Gagne, 1985; Dick and Carey, 1978).

In ICAI systems, methods for structuring knowledge to be taught are determined from the AI knowledge representation technique, which is selected by the developer to organize the knowledge into a data structure. Whereas task analysis used by CBI developers is a systematic method to identify all necessary sub-tasks and content elements required to learn the final task, AI knowledge representation methods are techniques to organize knowledge (including the sub-tasks and content elements) into a data structure for the manipulation in the computer system. Representative knowledge representation methods include (a) semantic methods, (b) production systems, (c) procedural representations, (d) scripts-frames, and (e)

logic (see Chapter III, Barr and Feigenbaum, 1981).

Although task analysis is not an inherent element of the knowledge representation techniques, a few ICAI researchers have applied the common task analysis methods or proposed new methods in the development of the knowledge base (or expertise module). The GOMS model proposed by Card, Moran, and Newell (1983) seems to be an indication of some AI researchers' realization of the importance of task analysis in the development of the knowledge base. The GOMS model is a task analysis procedure to identify four components of the learner's cognitive structure: (a) a set of Goals, (b) a set of Operators, (c) a set of Methods for achieving the goals, and (d) a set of Selection rules for choosing among competing achievement methods for goals. The use of both task analysis procedures and AI knowledge representation techniques will facilitate the design and development process of future ICAI systems. Task analysis methods will be used to identify knowledge components necessary to learn the given task, while AI knowledge representation techniques will be applied to organize and intelligently manipulate the identified knowledge components into a computer data structure.

Methods of Student Modeling

The early forms of CBI took programmed instructional paradigms, and most instructional strategies, including sequence, were determined from binary judgments on the student's responses (correct or incorrect). However, following Atkinson's (1972, 1976) mathematical model for selecting optimal instructional presentation items, a number of quantitative procedures have been applied to model the student's learning and to select instructional treatments on the basis of the quantitative information. For example, Suppes, Fletcher, and Zanotti (1975, 1976) used a regression analysis method for predicting the student's learning achievement and for selecting optimal instructional treatments. Hansen, Ross, and Rakow (1977) also developed a regression model for adaptive instruction in CBI. Tennyson and his associates (Rothen and Tennyson, 1978; Park and Tennyson, 1980) applied a Bayesian probability theorem for the development of an adaptive CBI system. In the quantitative model, the student learning is characterized in a probabilistic term. (For a review of quantitative models of adaptive instruction, see Park and Tennyson, 1983; Tennyson and Park, 1984.)

Development of a powerful student model has been a main research issue for many ICAI projects (e.g., BUGGY, LMS, ALGEBRA, etc.). The student modeling method used in ICAI is basically qualitative. In a qualitative model, the student learning is assessed from the analysis of his or her response (or response pattern); the modeling is a process of making inferences about the student's conceptions and misconceptions. Two representative methods used to model the student's learning in ICAI are: (a) the overlay method which compares the student's performance to a computer-based expert's behavior on the same task (Carr and Goldstein, 1977), and (b) the bug identification method which represents domain knowledge as rules and potential misconceptions and errors as variants of the rules (Brown and Burton, 1978; Sleeman, 1982).

Although the qualitative model relies on the system's subjective judgment of the student's response (frequently, a single response more than a response pattern) rather than an objective criterion, the effort to combine the two approaches (quantitative and qualitative) in the student modeling process has not yet been proposed. Also, future ICAI developers should consider including important learner variables (e.g., intellectual ability measures, cognitive styles, etc.) in the modeling process of the student learning behavior and in the instructional prescription process.

Instructional Formats

The early CBI programs were mostly developed to supplement regular instructional process, and the most common CBI format was drill-and-practice. However, the format has been diversified as CBI has become a main instructional delivery system. Common CBI formats include tutorial, drill and practice, games, and simulations. Games are divided into two types: intrinsic games, in which learning the game rules and skills constitutes the main instructional objectives; extrinsic games, in which the games are used as auxiliary devices for facilitating learning and maintaining motivation (cf., Malone, 1981). Most simulations are divided into three types: physical, situational, and process simulations (see Alessi and Trollip, 1985). Although the CBI formats are somewhat arbitrarily classified for practical convenience, the classification indicates the variety of CBI applications.

In contrast, most ICAI systems are basically classified into two types of instructional formats: tutorial and games. A tutorial in ICAI is somewhat different from a tutorial in CBI in that ICAI tutorial is basically a series of question-response processes, while CBI tutorial emphasizes the system's expository presentation of instruction. Although some questions may follow the expository presentation in CBI, the questions are to assure or reinforce the student s understanding of the presentation. In ICAI, however, the question

and response process is to make inferences about the student's conceptual understanding of the given problem and to determine the instructional process to be immediately followed. The purposes of using games are also different. In CBI, games are used to teach the gaming rules and skills (in intrinsic games) or to maintain the student's motivation (in extrinsic games). In contrast, the primary purpose of using games in ICAI is to provide a "reactive learning environment" in which the student explores his or her own interest (e.g., WEST, WUSOR). ICAI games seem to be similar to extrinsic games in CBI because the subject content to be taught is independent of the gaming structure and rules. However, providing a reactive learning environment is quite different from using games as simple motivational devices because the student is expected to develop a higher level of knowledge (e.g., problem-solving strategies) than that directly required in the given subject content by exploring and testing his or her own interest and ideas in the gaming process. Regardless of which of the above approaches is followed, the basic nature of instructional formats and the design of micro-level instructional strategies (e.g., specific question and feedback strategies) to be implemented in the instruction should be determined on the basis of the purpose of the instruction, task and learner characteristics, and other situational variables (e.g., time to learn and resources constraints).

Subject Matter Areas

CBI has been widely used in virtually all different kinds of subject matter areas, from highly-structured math and science to relatively ill-structured language and even arts. However, most applications of ICAI have been limited to relatively well-structured subject areas such as mathematics (e.g., WEST, WUSOR, BUGGY, LMS), computer programming (e.g., BIP, PROUST, SPADE), medical diagnosis (e.g., GUIDON), electronics (e.g., SOPHIE), etc. The limited application of ICAI to relatively well-structured subject areas is partially ascribed to the ICAI authors' primary purpose of their projects. As we discussed earlier, their initial goal was to explore the capability of AI technology in the instructional process rather than to develop usable instructional systems. Thus, most ICAI researchers seemed to have first chosen AI techniques to explore in the systems and then selected subject matter areas which were most appropriate for the manipulation of the selected AI techniques (Fletcher, 1984). However, more ICAI programs will be developed to solve real-world problems, as more ICAI researchers/developers are involved in the development of education and training programs, and as more educators and trainers are interested in the application of AI technology.

System Development Process

As we discussed earlier, the development of most CBI programs has taken a kind of systems approach which requires some or all of the following processes: analysis, design, development, formative evaluation, implementation, summative evaluation, and maintenance. Typical members of the development team include an instructional designer, a subject matter expert, and developer(s) with computer programming skills. When an authoring system is used, roles of the development team members may be different, depending upon the capability of the authoring system. Most authoring systems provide computer-coding capability without requiring programming from the developers; some systems have built-in facilities to help the developer analytically organize the subject content, and select and design instructional strategies.

Because few ICAI projects have been systematically or chronologically documented, the development process of ICAI systems cannot be described in a generalizable procedure. However, the different goal of ICAI researchers from that of CBI developers indicates that their development procedures also are different. For example, GUIDON was simply extended from MYCIN to test the feasibility of a rule-based expert system in teaching; SCHOLAR, and WHY focused on tutorial dialogues for handling unanticipated student questions and generating instructional materials for the student; BUGGY, ALGEBRA, and LMS were designed to analyze student errors and to model his or her learning behaviors.

Some ICAI projects required the extensive involvement of domain knowledge experts (e.g., GUIDON). For this case, a main responsibility of ICAI developers was to extract necessary knowledge components from the expert and to codify them into the system. However, most ICAI systems were apparently developed by ICAI researchers alone without much involvement of instructional designers (or psychologists) and subject matter experts. Because instructional issues were not the primary concern of the ICAI researchers, it was obvious that instructional psychologists were not included in the development teams. Furthermore, ICAI researchers apparently chose subject matter areas with which they were mostly familiar and comfortable to test their research curiosities with the minimum involvement of other people. Thus, the ICAI development process was determined by the individual researcher's goals, characteristics of the domain knowledge selected for the research, and their skills; and, as a result, the development process seems to be very variable among projects.

The developers of future ICAI systems are strongly encouraged to adopt systems approaches widely used in the instructional technology community. The systems approach may not only facilitate the design and development process, but also improve the quality of instructional programs. Also, the development of future ICAI systems should have more involvements of instructional psychologists, educators, and subject matter experts.

System Validation

In CBI, the success of the program is determined by the degree of its instructional effectiveness and efficiency. The degree of the program's sophistication or capability to handle special processes is not an important criterion to evaluate the system. To assure the program's effectiveness and efficiency, the CBI development process is monitored with different evaluation methods such as subject matter expert review, one-on-one try-out, pilot test, etc.

In contrast, the success of an ICAI program is mostly determined from its capability to handle specific features or processes involved in instruction (e.g., inferencing mechanism, bug analysis procedure, natural language dialogue capability, etc.). Apparently, no systematic evaluation procedures (formative or summative) have been used in ICAI to assure the quality of the program during the development process or to validate its success after development. Because of the unique interest and purpose of ICAI researchers, a program seemed to be considered "successful" only if it "runs" as it was designed. As the purpose of the development of ICAI programs is changed from research exploration to practical application, however, future ICAI programs are expected to focus more on the instructional effectiveness and efficiency. Also, systematic evaluation procedures should be applied for validating the development process and effectiveness of the programs.

Hardware and Software

During the 1960s and 1970s, special computer systems such as PLATO, IBM 1500, TICCIT, and recently WICAT and IVIS (DEC) were developed mainly for CBI. These systems have their own CBI authoring languages: TUTOR (PLATO), Coursewriter (IBM 1500), and TAL (TICCIT). Although the special systems, except IBM 1500, are still widely used, most of current CBI programs are developed and implemented by using microcomputers. Most microcomputers have been developed for general uses, including education. That is, main hardware for CBI consist of a few special kinds of mainframe-based systems (e.g., PLATO and TICCIT) and recently developed microcomputers. Software used for the development of CBI programs consists principally of four different levels: general purpose computer languages (e.g., BASIC, PASCAL, C, FORTRAN, etc.), system-specific authoring languages (e.g., TUTOR, COURSEWRITER, TAL, etc.), system-independent CBI authoring languages (e.g., PILOT, PLANIT, etc.), and authoring systems (or aids) which provide facilities to develop CBI lessons without programming skills (e.g., Hazeltine's ADAPT) (Kearsley, 1983). A well-developed authoring system may provide the author with additional capabilities to design instructional strategies and to organize subject contents into structured formats.

In contrast, most ICAI programs have been developed and delivered by using special hardware systems designed for AI works, such as Symbolics, Xerox D Machines, TI Explorer, Lamda, etc. Software as well is limited to a few specific languages such as LISP and PROLOG because of the unique capabilities of the languages to handle complex tasks involved in AI efforts (for example, computing with symbolic expressions rather than numbers, representing data as linked-list structures in the machine and as multi-level lists on paper, etc.). Simplified versions of LISP and PROLOG have recently become available on a few microcomputers. Also, efforts to develop ICAI authoring programs are currently being undertaken. However, the current use of hardware and software for the development of ICAI programs is still limited to a few specific types. To promote the application of AI techniques by various types of users in education and training, more ICAI programs should be developed and delivered by using microcomputers.

Conclusion

As revealed in our comparison between conventional CBI and ICAI, the most important contribution made in the development of ICAI systems is not in the form of an intellectual breakthrough in the field of learning and instruction, but rather in the development of powerful computer systems that are able to effectively capture human beings' learning and teaching processes (Suppes, 1984). Thus, many ICAI systems have apparently contributed to a better understanding of cognitive processes involved in learning specific skills and knowledge. ICAI systems clearly demonstrated the state-of-the-art levels that CBI could attain in terms of the functional capability in future development. However, the extent of their practical value as instructional systems is yet limited, mainly because insufficient attention has been given to important instructional issues in the development process.

AI technology has provided us with a powerful tool for exploring and advancing our knowledge of how to learn and teach. However, the development of effective and efficient instructional systems strongly requires combined and cooperative efforts from researchers and developers in both AI and instructional psychology. Winston (1984) emphasized the importance of this cooperative effort by describing current progress of AI as an "age of partnerships, a period when researchers in AI began to admit that there were other researchers, particularly linguists and psychologists, with whom people in AI can form important liaisons." In order for this cooperation to occur, they must understand and communicate with each other and to that end we can hopefully make significant progress in our knowledge of "how to teach" and can develop powerful adaptive instructional systems. □

References

Alessi, S.M., and Trollip, S.R. *Computer-Based Instruction: Methods and Development.* Englewood Cliffs, NJ: Prentice-Hall, 1985.

Atkinson, R.C. Ingredients for a Theory of Instruction. *American Psychologist*, 1972, *27*, 921-931.

Atkinson, R.C. Adaptive Instructional Systems: Some Attempts to Optimize the Learning Process. In D. Klahr (Ed.), *Cognition and Instruction*. New York: John Wiley, 1976.

Barr, A., and Feigenbaum, E.A. *The Handbook of Artificial Intelligence, Vol. 1.* Los Altos, CA: William Kaufman, 1981.

Brown, J.S., and Burton, R.R. Diagnostic Models for Procedural Bugs in Basic Mathematical Skills. *Cognitive Science*, 1978, *2*, 155-192.

Brown, J.S., Burton, R.R., and Bell, A.G. SOPHIE. A Step Towards a Reactive Learning Environment. *International Journal of Man Machine Studies*, 1975, *7*, 675-696.

Brown, J.S., Burton, R.R., and deKleer, J. Pedagogical, Natural Language and Knowledge Engineering in SOPHIE I, II and III. In D. Sleeman and J.S. Brown (Eds.), *Intelligent Tutoring Systems*. New York: Academic Press, 1982.

Burton, R.R., and Brown, J.S. An Investigation of Computer Coaching for Informal Learning Activities. In D. Sleeman and J.S. Brown (Eds.), *Intelligent Tutoring Systems*. New York: Academic Press, 1982.

Carbonell, J.R. AI in CAI: An Artificial Intelligence Approach to Computer-Assisted Instruction. *IEEE Transactions on Man-Machine Systems*, 1970, *11*, 190-202.

Card, S,K., Moran, T.P., and Newell, A. *The Psychology of Human-Computer Interaction.* Hillsdale, NJ: Lawrence Erlbaum Associates, 1983.

Carr, B., and Goldstein, I.P. *Overlays: A Theory of Modeling for Computer-Aided Instruction.* Artificial Intelligence Laboratory Memo 406 (Logo Memo 40). Massachusetts Institute of Technology, 1977.

Dewey, J. *How We Think*. Boston, MA: Heath, 1910.

Dick, W., and Carey, L. *The Systematic Design of Instruction*. Glenview: Ill: Scott, Foresman and Company, 1978.

Fletcher, J.D. Intelligent Instructional Systems in Training. In S.A. Andriole (Ed.), *Applications in Artificial Intelligence*. Princeton, NJ: Petrocelli, 1984.

Gagne, R.M. *The Conditions of Learning* (4th edition). New York: Holt, Rinehart, and Winston, 1985.

Gagne, R.M., and Briggs, L.J. *Principles of Instructional Design* (2nd Edition). New York: Holt, Rinehart, and Winston, 1979.

Goldstein, I.P. The Genetic Graph: A Representation for the Evolution of Procedural Knowledge. In D. Sleeman and J.S. Brown (Eds.), *Intelligent Tutoring Systems*. New York: Academic Press, 1982.

Hansen, D.N., Ross, S.M., and Rakow, E. *Adaptive Models for Computer-Based Training Systems*. Annual report to Navy Personnel Research and Development Center. Memphis, TN: Memphis State University, 1977.

Hayes-Roth, B., and Thorndike, P.W. Paradigms for Intelligent Systems. *Educational Psychologist*, 1985, *20*, 231-241.

Hunter, B., Kastner, C.S., Rubin, M.L., and Seidel, R.J. *Learning Alternatives in U.S. Education: Where Student and Computer Meet*. Englewood Cliffs, NJ: Educational Technology Publications, 1975.

Kearsley, G.P. *Computer-Based Training: A Guide to Selection and Implementation*. Menlo Park, CA: Addison-Wesley, 1983.

Kearsley, G.P., and Seidel, R.J. Automation in Training and Education. *Human Factors*, 1985, *27*, 61-74.

Malone, T.W. Toward a Theory of Intrinsically Motivating Instruction. *Cognitive Science*, 1981, *5*, 130-145.

Park, O., and Tennyson, R.D. Adaptive Design Strategies for Selecting Number and Presentation Order of Examples in Coordinate Concept Acquisition. *Journal of Educational Psychology*, 1980, *72*, 362-370.

Park, O., and Tennyson, R.D. Computer-Based Instructional Systems for Adaptive Education: A Review. *Contemporary Education Review*, 1983, *2*, 121-135.

Piaget, J. *The Construction of Reality in the Child*. New York: Basic Books, 1954.

Piaget, J., and Inhelder, B. *The Early Growth of Logic in the Child*. New York: Harper and Row, 1964.

Quillian, M.R. Semantic Memory. In M. Minsky (Ed.), *Semantic Information Processing*. Cambridge, MA: MIT Press, 1968.

Rothen, W., and Tennyson, R.D. Application of Bayes' Theory in Designing Computer-Based Adaptive Instructional Strategies. *Educational Psychologist*, 1978, *12*, 317-323.

Seidel, R.J. *Current Status of Computer-Administered Instruction Work Under Project IMPACT*. Professional paper 18-72, Alexandria, VA: Human Resources Research Organization, 1971.

Sleeman, D. Assessing Aspects of Competence in Basic Algebra. In D. Sleeman and J.S. Brown (Eds.), *Intelligent Tutoring Systems*. New York: Academic Press, 1982.

Sleeman, D., and Brown, J.S. *Intelligent Tutoring Systems*. New York: Academic Press, 1982.

Stevens, A.L., Collins, A., and Goldin, S. Misconceptions in Students' Understanding. *International Journal of Man-Machine Studies*, 1979, *11*, 145-156.

Suppes, P. Observations About the Application of Artificial Intelligence Research to Education. In D.F. Walker and R.D. Hess (Eds.), *Instructional Software*. Belmont, CA: Wadsworth, 1984.

Suppes, P., Fletcher, J.D., and Zanotti, M. Performance Models of American Indian Students on Computer-Assisted Instruction in Elementary Mathematics. *Instructional Science*, 1975, *4*, 303-313.

Suppes, P., Fletcher, J.D., and Zanotti, M. Models of Individual Trajectories in Computer-Assisted Instruction for Deaf Students. *Journal of Educational Psychology*, 1976, *68*, 117-127.

Tennyson, R.D., and Park, O. Computer-Based Adaptive Instructional Systems: A Review of Empirically Based Models. *Machine-Mediated Learning*, 1984, *1*, 129-153.

Winston, P.H. Perspective. In P.H. Winston and K.A. Pendergast (Eds.), *The AI Business: Commercial Uses of Artificial Intelligence*. Cambridge, MA: MIT Press, 1984.

Functional Characteristics of Intelligent Computer-Assisted Instruction: Intelligent Features

Ok-choon Park

Many ICAI systems are claimed as powerful instructional systems although they often have very few functions to perform the instructional process. In contrast, some instructional developers describe their conventional CBI program as "intelligent systems," although the programs do not have any or very few intelligent features that AI researchers have developed and tested in ICAI systems. After examining functional components of an ICAI system required to be qualified as an instructional system, in this article, six intelligent features of ICAI systems are discussed to provide directions for the research and development of future ICAI systems and for the evaluation of the intelligent dimensions of existing ICAI and conventional CBI systems. Finally, a multi-disciplinary co-operative effort for the development of an ICAI system is recommended in a schematic form.

Intelligent computer assisted instruction (ICAI) is a type of computer-based instruction (CBI) that has evolved with the application of artificial intelligence (AI) methods and techniques. AI is a field of computer science that seeks to develop computer systems which represent and use knowledge to perform complex reasoning tasks: tasks typically requiring intelligence if performed by a human being (Barr and Feigenbaum, 1982).

The effort to develop computer systems emulating intelligent human problem-solving and thinking processes, started with the seminal work of Newell and Simon (1963), has resulted in the emergence of several machine intelligence paradigms (Hayes-Roth and Thorndyke, 1985): (a) the cognitive model paradigm addressing the task of representing human information processing as a collection of computer programs; (b) the expert advisor paradigm referring to the use of AI programs to achieve input-output characteristics of a skilled human specialist providing consultation in a narrow but knowledge-rich area of expertise; (c) the intelligent interface, pertaining to the system's ability to communicate with the user according to his/her needs and convenience; and (d) the intelligent instructor paradigm, which resembles what actually occurs when teacher and student sit down one-on-one and attempt to teach and learn together (Roberts and Park, 1983). In addition, the development of autonomous systems like intelligent robots has been an important field in AI.

Although Hayes-Roth and Thorndyke identify ICAI as an independent research and development paradigm in AI, the development of an ICAI system requires an integrated application of all four paradigms listed above. The modeling of human cognition, the representation of the expert's problem solving process, and intelligent system-user interface constitute only subsets of the functional capabilities required in the teaching and learning process of an ICAI system. Thus, the functional capabilities of ICAI systems are unique and much more complicated than those of other intelligent systems. The development of an ICAI system requires a systematic approach to integrate various types of expertise into a system.

The purpose of this article is (1) to examine the functional characteristics of ICAI, focusing on its intelligent features; and (2) to discuss the requirements of a multi-disciplinary cooperative effort for its development. I think that the systematic description of the functional characteristics of ICAI is important for providing directions for the research and development of future systems and for the evaluation of the intelligent dimensions of existing systems. Specific AI methods and techniques (e.g., search, knowledge representation, inferencing, machine learning, natural language dialogue, etc.) have been studied and used to develop intelligent computer systems; however, a review of AI methods and techniques is beyond the scope of this article.

A Typical Model of ICAI

To describe the functional characteristics of ICAI systems, I first present a typical ICAI model which describes the important components and their structural relationships. ICAI systems have been developed on many different structural forms. However, the operational functions of an ICAI system are determined by four major components or modules: (a) the expertise module, (b) the student model module, (c) the

Ok-choon Park is a Senior Research Psychologist, Training Research Laboratory, the U.S. Army Research Institute, Alexandria, Virginia. The opinions expressed in this article are those of the author and do not express or imply the views of the U.S. Army Research Institute, the U.S. Army, or the Department of Defense.

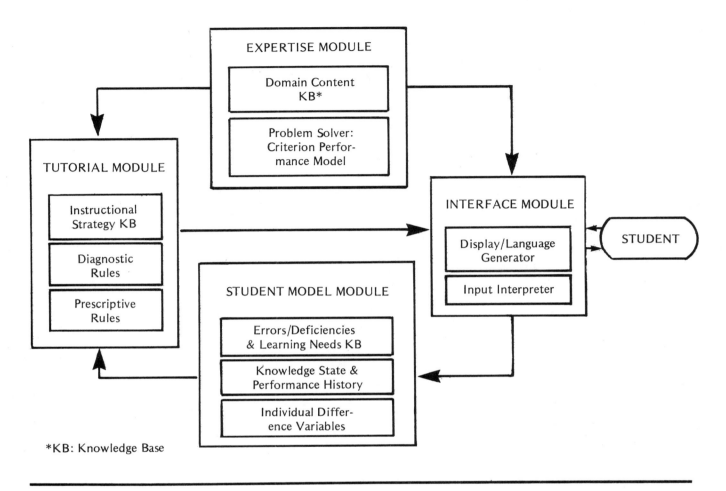

Figure 1

A Schematic Representation of ICAI System

EXPERTISE MODULE

Domain Content KB*

Problem Solver: Criterion Performance Model

TUTORIAL MODULE

Instructional Strategy KB

Diagnostic Rules

Prescriptive Rules

INTERFACE MODULE

Display/Language Generator

Input Interpreter

STUDENT

STUDENT MODEL MODULE

Errors/Deficiencies & Learning Needs KB

Knowledge State & Performance History

Individual Difference Variables

*KB: Knowledge Base

tutorial module, and (d) the interface module (see Figure 1).

The **expertise module** consists of two sub-components: the domain knowledge base and the criterion-performance model. The domain knowledge base contains content elements necessary for the student to learn the domain knowledge and procedures for using the knowledge in solving problems in the domain area. The criterion-performance model is a computer-based expert that solves the same problem given to the student so that the system can evaluate the student's performance.

The **student model** consists of three subcomponents: (a) the student knowledge base and performance history, (b) learning deficiencies and learning needs catalogues, and (c) a data base of individual difference variables. The student knowledge base and performance history represent the stu-

dent's most recent performance level and reasoning strategies that he/she has used in the learning process. The learning deficiencies and learning needs catalog represents the student's misconceptions and suboptimal performance strategies that he/she may use to solve problems in the domain area. A data base containing the student's important individual difference variables can be included as a subcomponent in the student-model module (Park, 1983a).

The **tutorial module** consists of three subcomponents: (a) an instructional knowledge base containing various types of instructional strategies (Park, 1983b), including domain independent and domain-specific strategies, (b) a diagnostic rule base for making inference about the student's misconceptions and learning needs, and (c) a prescriptive rule base for selecting best instructional treatments on the basis of his/her learning needs.

The **interface module** consists of two subcomponents: the display and/or language generator and the student's input interpreter.

As Figure 1 shows, information in the student-model module is continuously updated as interactions between the student and system occur. The tutorial module diagnoses the student's learning needs on the basis of the information in the student-model module and the computer-based expert's solution (or performance) in the expertise module on the same problem given to the student. The tutorial module also specifies the instructional prescriptions to present to the student by selecting specific content elements from the domain knowledge base in the expertise module and specific instructional strategies (e.g., presentation formats and procedures) from the instructional strategy knowledge base in the tutorial module. The interface module generates the instructional presentation displays by integrating the content elements (selected from the domain knowledge base) into instructional formats (selected from the instructional strategy knowledge base) as specified in the prescriptive rules. Specific instructional issues that should be considered for the development of ICAI modules are described elsewhere (see Park, Perez, and Siedel, 1987; Park and Siedel, 1987).

Functional Characteristics of ICAI

The primary purpose of ICAI is to apply AI methods and techniques to the development of a powerful adaptive instructional system (Park, in press). Thus, it is necessary to identify the required components and functions of an instructional system before discussing its intelligent features. As Figure 1 shows, a complete ICAI system should have functions which represent the four components of an instructional system: an expertise module, student-model module, tutorial module, and interface module. However, the figure does not necessarily indicate that the system should have all of the four modules to perform the functions. The functions representing the four components may be integrated and performed within a single-module structure. Because of the complexity and size of a complete ICAI system, many existing systems have focused on the development of a single module which constitutes a fully usable system (Barr and Feigenbaum, 1982). However, some existing ICAI systems do not have the functions for representing one or more instructional components. For example, PROUST (Johnson and Soloway, 1987), BUGGY (Brown and Burton, 1978), LMS (Sleeman, 1982), and STEAMER (Hollan, Hutchins, and Weitzman, 1984) do not have functions to provide direct instruction. In my view, an ICAI system should have functions for representing all four instructional components (i.e., representation of domain knowledge, modeling of student learning behavior, providing instruction, and interactive interface) to be qualified as an instructional system, regardless of its structure (single module or multiple modules). However, it should be noted that the multiple modular system has advantages in developing, modifying, and maintaining the system. For example, decomposing an instructional system first into its functional components permits greater precision in building the module(s).

Many existing ICAI systems developed by AI researchers are identified as instructional systems although they do not have functions to represent one or more instructional components described above. In contrast, some instructional researchers and educational technologists describe their conventional CBI programs as "intelligent systems," although the systems do not have any or very few intelligent features that AI researchers have developed and tested in ICAI systems. I think that psychological and methodological approaches to deal with instructional problems are different issues from the concerns with the system's intelligent features to determine the system's functional capability and flexibility for implementing the approaches. In previous studies (Park, Perez, and Seidel, 1987; Park and Seidel, 1987), I discussed the similarities and differences of psychological and methodological approaches taken by ICAI developers and conventional CBI developers. In this article, I discuss the intelligent features of the ICAI system in terms of its functional characteristics and capabilities.

Generative Function of Instructional Presentation

In conventional CBI, the system's capability to adapt instructional processes to the individual student's learning needs is very limited because every instructional event and interaction to occur between the system and student need to be specified in advance in programming algorithms. To overcome this limitation inherent in conventional CBI, a notion of generative CAI was proposed in the late 1960s (see Uttal, Rogers, Hieronymous, and Pasich, 1969). Generative CAI has the capability to generate new presentations from the combinations of different elements in a large database (see Koffman and Blount, 1975). However, the generative capability is limited to simple drill-and-practice type of questions in arithmetic and language vocabulary learning tasks. Also, the adaptive capability to the individual student's learning needs is minimal because the questions are randomly selected within a given range of difficulty level. AI methods and programming techniques for handling complex processes involved in the machine knowledge representation and inference (e.g., computing with symbolic expressions rather than numbers and representing data as linked-list structures) have provided a means to vastly improve the generative function of instructional presentations in an ICAI system. This generative function has been demonstrated in many existing ICAI systems.

Mixed Initiative Function of Instruction

In conventional CBI, every possible interaction is specified in advance in programming algorithms. Consequently, the system initiates every instructional activity, and the student is just passively involved in the decision process. However, AI methods and programming techniques used to develop the computer's natural language dialogue capability (e.g., pattern matching and parsing techniques) have been applied to develop ICAI systems in which the student is allowed to interrupt the instructional process, ask questions, and provide comments and other inputs. The system's understanding of natural language is a very complex task, and one which is being heavily researched in the AI community. Although most existing ICAI systems' natural language dialogue capability is considerably more narrow than live tutoring environments, the mixed initiative capability, which allows both the system and student to initiate instructional activities, is an important "intelligent" feature to approach the live one-on-one tutoring process.

The notion of "mixed initiative" originally proposed by Carbonell (1970) is different from the menu-based learner-control options in conventional CBI. While the student's initiative in the menu-based learner-control option is limited to selecting one of the given alternatives in the menu, the student's option in the mixed initiative environment is wide open to the extent that the system understands the natural language. Furthermore, the student's option in the menu-based system can be selected only by providing a special command after completing or stopping the main instructional process, while the mixed initiative environment includes the student's initiative as a principal part of the instructional process.

Modeling Function of the Student Learning Process

The main purpose of modeling the student's learning process is to assess the current state of his/her knowledge and skills on the given task, to identify his/her misconceptions, learning problems and needs, and to provide the most reliable diagnostic information for the prescription of instructional treatments. In CBI programs developed on the basis of Skinner's (1958) linear instructional paradigm, there is no concept of student modeling and every student receives the same instructional presentations with the same sequence. The branch-

ing method based on Crowder's (1957) intrinsic instructional program determines the interactive sequence between the student and system solely from his/her on-task response to a given question. In this paradigm, the diagnostic information regarding the student's performance is limited to a single response to the immediately preceding question, and the required response type is a simple "correct/incorrect" or a multiple choice answer. Although a notion of "response-sensitive strategy" has been proposed and tested to provide learning theory-based interactive sequences (see, Park and Tennyson, 1980, 1986; Tennyson, Park and Christensen, 1985), the basic parameter used to determine the system-student interactions in these studies has continued to be limited to the student's immediate, prior, single response to a "true/false" or multiple choice type of question.

The student modeling function of ICAI goes beyond the limitation of the conventional branching method. The "overlay" method (Carr and Goldstein, 1977) shows what the student has learned and attempted to learn; the "buggy" method (Brown and Burton, 1978) identifies the specific problems and misconceptions the student has and the cause of the problems/misconceptions; the "path-tracing" method (Anderson, Boyle, and Reiser, 1985) traces the student's learning process along an ideal model of the learning process, and diagnoses the kind of problems/misconceptions the student has at a particular stage of the learning process. The diagnostic decision is made on the student's learning history rather than his/her single, immediate past response (for a review of student modeling types and techniques, see Van-Lehn, 1986).

Qualitative Decision-Making Function of Instruction

There are some conventional CBI systems that make instructional decisions (diagnosis and prescription) on the basis of the student's learning history data rather than his/her single last response to a given question. These systems are developed using sophisticated mathematical probability models (see Atkinson, 1976; Hansen, Ross, and Rakow, 1977; Park and Tennyson, 1980; Rothen and Tennyson, 1978; Suppes, Fletcher, and Zanotti, 1976). However, the instructional decision-making procedure in ICAI is different from the mathematical model-based procedures in conventional CBI systems. The diagnostic and prescriptive procedures in the mathematical approach are selected on the basis of quantitative information characterized in probability terms (for a review of quantitative CBI adaptive models, see Park and Tennyson, 1983; Tennyson and Park, 1984). In contrast, the decisions in ICAI are made on the basis of qualitative information (Clancey, 1986) obtained in the process of the system's inference about the student's current learning state and misconceptions/learning problems (see next section on "Function of Inference"). Most ICAI systems are directly concerned with qualitative issues such as classification of elements, causal networks, procedural networks, and models that relate structure to functions. They are not concerned with explaining functional relationships of the components based on quantitative predictions. They may base their simulations on quantitative models as did SOPHIE and STEAMER, but their explanations to students are strictly in qualitative terms (Fletcher, in press). Representing psychological learning processes and internal knowledge state into mathematical probability is extremely difficult, if possible at all. In addition, the human expert teacher's decision process is intuitive rather than probabilistic. Therefore, the qualitative decision-making function of ICAI is a significant advance for the development of systems that resemble a human expert teacher.

Function of Inference

The inferencing function is the heart of AI-based software systems, including ICAI and expert systems, because the degree of the system's intelligence is basically determined by its reasoning capability to draw inferences. The system's capability to draw the same inferences from similar user (student) intentions and meanings reflected in different syntactic and semantic representations (even with different level of certainty information) is one of the unique and most promising ICAI characteristics. When the ICAI system interprets the student's inputs, diagnoses his/her misconceptions and learning needs, and generates instructional presentations, it draws inferences on the basis of available information at that time which is usually insufficient, inconclusive, and incomplete. The system may calculate the certainty factor of its inferences according to heuristic methods representing common sense, judgmental knowledge. The certainty factor may be used to determine the execution priority of alternative decisions derived from the inference.

The inferencing function is generally performed using a goal-directed backward (top-down) chaining mechanism. In backward chaining, the system initially has sets of IF-THEN rules related to the interpretation of the student's inputs (e.g., response, comments, etc.), diagnostic procedures, and instructional prescriptions, including the selection of knowledge elements and presentation formats and procedures. The system attempts to find information that satisfies the antecedent condition of a specific rule using a parsing technique to handle the insufficient and incomplete nature of the information. If information satisfying the rule cannot be found, the system attempts to seek another rule. If the system fails to find a satisfactory rule, the system may ask a question to the student to obtain the requisite information, or the system may select a generic default rule which is designed to handle information that does not satisfy any of the rules. Another common mechanism that can be used to perform the inferencing function of the system is the data-driven forward chaining. In forward chaining, the input data initially determines which rule can be satisfied. From this rule, a new intermediate conclusion may be produced that may satisfy higher-order rules (see Barr and Feigenbaum, 1981).

Self-Improving Function

Another important intelligent characteristic of ICAI is the capability to monitor, evaluate, and improve its own teaching performance. In conventional CBI, if the input information is the same, the system's decision is always the same, regardless of how powerfully adaptable it is to individual student's learning needs. However, a system with self-critical and self-improving functions can be developed using the AI techniques investigated by machine learning researchers. The system can observe its own teaching performance, make explicit experimental changes in its teaching strategies, and evaluate such changes after teaching more students or teaching the same student more materials. The effectiveness of the diagnostic and prescriptive rules may be assessed against prespecified criteria. If the rules do not perform to the criterion level, the system may generate possible changes in the rules on the basis of the information in the student model. The change may be a simple selection of another existing rule as an alternative, modification of the conditional and action parameters in the rule, or generation of a new rule by establishing new conditional and action parameters. Because the rules should be amenable to automatic manipulation in the context of the self-improving process, the system needs to operate an "amender" which identifies the rules to be changed and edits functions which execute the changes (see O'Shea, 1982). It is expected that research on machine learning (Self, 1986; Mikaulski, 1983) will significantly contribute to the development of self-improving ICAI systems.

Many existing ICAI systems have the capability to implement one or more of the intelligent characteristics described above, although the technical procedure and functional flexibility of the imple-

Figure 2

Requirements of Cooperative Effort

ICAI Modules	Expertise Requirements			
	Domain Expert	Expert Instructor	Instructional Psychologist	AI Expert
Expertise Module	X	X		X
Student-Model Module	X	X	X	X
Tutorial Module		X	X	X
Interface Module		X	X	X

mentation vary among the systems. However, few existing systems, if any, have the capability to implement all of the intelligent characteristics. Development of an ICAI system which can implement all of the characteristics to a satisfactory level may be a formidable task in the near future, but it is an important challenge with which AI researchers, instructional psychologists, and developers should be able to cope. Meantime, the ICAI characteristics described above may be used to evaluate the intelligent features of existing and future ICAI and conventional CBI systems.

Requirements of Cooperative Efforts

The development of an ICAI system requires expertise in the following areas: the given subject domain, instructional psychology and design, teaching of the given domain, and computer science (particularly, AI). The cooperative effort among the experts is necessary to develop each of the ICAI modules (see Figure 1). The subject domain expert provides a performance (or problem-solving) model of the given task to evaluate the student's performance and reasoning strategies. The instructional psychologist/designer provides information necessary for developing an instructional strategy knowledge base and diagnostic and prescriptive rules. Information provided by the domain expert and instructional psychologist needs to be supplemented by an expert instructor of the given domain. The expert instructor may provide the prerequisite knowledge the student must learn in order to achieve the criterion performance. It is a common problem that a subject domain expert has difficulties in decomposing his/her internally compiled body of knowledge into teachable sequential parts. The expert instructor of the given domain may provide information for developing the task-dependent instructional strategies and the task-specific diagnostic and prescriptive rules. The AI expert integrates all of the information provided by the domain expert, instructional psychologist/designer, and expert instructor of the domain into an executable ICAI structure using AI methods and other computer programming techniques.

Figure 2 illustrates the necessary expertise for the development of each of the four ICAI modules. That is, development of each of the four ICAI modules requires a cooperative effort among the experts as follows: (a) the expertise module—a subject domain expert, expert instructor of the given domain, and AI expert; (b) the student-model module—a subject domain expert, expert instructor, instructional psychologist/designer, and AI expert;

(c) the tutorial module—an expert instructor, instructional psychologist/designer, and AI expert; (d) the interface module—an expert instructor, instructional psychologist/designer, and AI expert. These experts are expected to work together to build a complete, functionally powerful and instructionally effective ICAI system, as represented in Figure 1.

Because of the requirement of a unique computing process in AI works, ICAI systems have been developed and delivered thus far using special hardware systems and programming languages. However, the rapid development of computer technology will soon allow most kinds of computers, including personal microcomputers, to have the capability of handling computing processes required in AI development. The different versions of AI programming languages, such as LISP and PROLOG, are already available in many personal computers. In the meantime, it is expected that AI researchers and cognitive scientists will further advance the current AI technology, such as natural language dialogues, inference processes for capturing human reasoning, machine learning, etc.

In conclusion, AI technology has provided us with a powerful tool for exploring and advancing our knowledge of how to learn and teach. However, the problem of "how to learn and how to teach" will not be solved by simply increasing the functional power of the computer as an instructional delivery system. We must first identify and analyze the different types of expertise and their structural and functional relationships required for the development of an ICAI system (Seidel, Park, and Perez, in press). Then, we should integrate the multi-disciplinary expertise into an ICAI structure (as proposed in Figure 1), in which we can implement the six intelligent functions described in this article. Again, the development of an ideal ICAI system requires an interdisciplinary team effort, including inputs from subject domain experts, instructional psychologists/design experts, expert instructors of the given domain areas, and computer scientists, particularly AI experts (as illustrated in Figure 2). □

References

Anderson, J.R., Boyle, C.F., and Reiser, B.J. Intelligent Tutoring Systems. *Science*, 1985, *228*, 456-462.

Atkinson, R.C. Adaptive Instructional Systems: Some Attempts to Optimize the Learning Process. In D. Klahr (Ed.), *Cognition and Instruction*. New York: John Wiley and Sons, 1976.

Barr, A., and Feigenbaum, E.A. *The Handbook of Artificial Intelligence*. Vol. 1. Los Altos, CA: William Kaufman, 1981.

Brown, J.S., and Burton, R.R. Diagnostic Models for Procedural Bugs in Basic Mathematical Skills. *Cognitive Science*, 1978, *2*, 155-192.

Carbonell, J.R. AI in CAI: An Artificial Intelligence Approach to Computer-Assisted Instruction. *IEEE Transactions on Man-Machine Systems*, 1970, *11*, 190-202.

Carr, B., and Goldstein, I.P. Overlays: A Theory of Modeling for Computer-Aided Instruction. *Artificial Intelligence Laboratory Memo 406*, Massachusetts Institute of Technology, 1977.

Clancey, W.J. Qualitative Student Models. In J.F. Traub, G.J. Grosz, B.W. Lampson, and N.J. Nilsson (Eds.). *Annual Review of Computer Science, Vol. 1*. Palo Alto, CA: Annual Reviews, Inc., 1986.

Crowder, N.W. Automatic Tutoring by Means of Intrinsic Programming. In E.H. Galanter (Ed.), *Automatic Teaching: The State of Art*. New York: John Wiley and Sons, 1959.

Fletcher, J.D. Intelligent Training System in the Military. In. G.W. Hopple and S.J. Andriole (Eds.), *Defense Applications of Artificial Intelligence: Progress and Prospects*. Lexington, MA: Lexington Books/D.C. Heath and Company, in press.

Hansen, D.N., Ross, S.M., and Rakow, E. Adaptive Models for Computer-Based Training Systems. *Annual Report to Navy Personnel Research and Development Center*. Memphis, TN: Memphis State University, 1977.

Hayes-Roth, B., and Thorndyke, P.W. Paradigms for Intelligent Systems. *Educational Psychologist*, 1985, *20*, 231-241.

Hollan, J.D., Hutchins, E.L., and Weitzman, L. STEAMER: An Interactive Inspectable Simulation-Based Training System. *Artificial Intelligence Magazine*, 1984, *5*, 15-27.

Johnson, W.L., and Soloway, E. PROUST: An Automatic Debugger for Pascal Programs. In G.P. Kearsley (Ed.), *Artificial Intelligence: Applications and Methodology*. Redding, MA: Addison-Wesley, 1987.

Koffman, E.B., and Blount, S.E. Artificial Intelligence and Automatic Programming in CAI. *Artificial Intelligence*, 1975, *6*, 215-234.

Michaulski, R.S. A Theory and Methodology of Inductive Learning. *Artificial Intelligence*, 1983, *20*, 111-161.

Newell, A., and Simon, H.A. GPS: A Program that Simulates Human Thought. In E.A. Feigenbaum and J.A. Feldman (Eds.), *Computers and Thought*. New York: McGraw-Hill, 1963.

O'Shea, T. A Self-Improving Quadratic Tutor. In D. Sleeman and Brown (Eds.), *Intelligent Tutoring Systems*. New York: Academic Press, 1982.

Park, O. Adaptive CBI Model: Aptitude-Matched and Response-Sensitive Approaches. *Journal of Computer-Based Instruction*, 1983a, *9*, 245-255.

Park, O. Instructional Strategies: A Hypothetical Taxonomy. *Control Data Corporation Technical Report TR-1983-3*. Minneapolis, MN: Control Data Corporation, 1983b.

Park, O., Perez, R.S., and Seidel, F.J. Intelligent CAI: Old Wine in New Bottles or a New Vintage? In G.P. Kearsley (Ed.), *Artificial Intelligence: Applications and Methodology*. Reading, MA: Addison-Wesley, 1987.

Park, O., and Seidel, R.J. Conventional CBI Versus Intelligent VAI: Suggestions for the Development of Future Systems. *Educational Technology*, May 1987, *27*(5), 15-21.

Park, O., and Tennyson, R.D. Adaptive Design Strategies for Selecting Sequence Number and Presentation Order of Examples in Coordinate Concept Acquisition. *Journal of Educational Psychology*, 1980, *72*, 362-370.

Park, O., and Tennyson, R.D. Computer-Based Instructional Systems for Adaptive Education: A Review. *Contemporary Education Review*, 1983, *2*, 121-135.

Park, O., and Tennyson, R.D. Computer-Based Response-Sensitive Design Strategies for Selecting Presentation Form and Sequence of Examples in Learning Coordinate Concepts. *Journal of Educational Psychology*, 1986, *78*, 153-158.

Reiser, B.J., Anderson, J.R., and Farrell, R.G. Dynamic Student Modeling in an Intelligent Tutor for LISP Programming. *Proceedings of IJCAI-85*. Los Angeles, CA: IJCAI, 1985.

Roberts, F.C., and Park, O. Intelligent Computer-Assisted Instruction: An Explanation and Overview. *Educational Technology*, January 1983, *23*(1), 7-12.

Rothen, W., and Tennyson, R.D. Application of Bayes' Theory in Designing Computer-Based Adaptive Instructional Strategies. *Educational Psychologist*, 1978, *12*, 317-323.

Seidel, R.J., Park, O., and Perez, R.S. Expertise of ICAI: Development Requirements. *Instructional Science*, in press.

Self, J. The Application of Machine Learning to Student Modeling. *Instructional Science*, 1986, *14*, 327-338.

Skinner, B.F. Teaching Machines. *Science*, 1958, *128*, 969-977.

Sleeman, D.H. Assessing Aspects of Competence in Basic Algebra. In D.H. Sleeman and J.S. Brown (Eds.), *Intelligent Tutoring Systems*. New York: Academic Press, 1982.

Suppes, P., Fletcher, J.D., and Zanotti, M. Models of Individual Trajectories in Computer-Assisted Instruction for Deaf Students. *Journal of Educational Psychology*, 1976, *68*, 117-127.

Tennyson, R.D., and Park, O. Computer-Based Adaptive Instructional Systems: A Review of Empirically Based Models. *Machine-Mediated Learning*, 1984, *1*, 129-153.

Tennyson, R.D., Park, O., and Christensen, D.L. Display Time Interval and Response-Sensitive Sequencing as Instructional Design Variables in Concept-Learning Using Computer-Based Instruction. *Journal of Educational Psychology*, 1985, *77*, 481-491.

Uttal, W.R., Rogers, M., Hieronymous, R., and Pasich, T. *Generative Computer-Assisted Instruction in Analytic Geometry*. Newburyport, MA: Entelek, Inc., 1969.

VanLehn, K. Student Modeling in Intelligent Teaching Systems. *Research Planning Forum for Intelligent Tutoring Systems*. San Antonio, TX: Air Force Human Resources Laboratory, 1986.

Adaptive Instructional Simulations to Improve Learning of Cognitive Strategies

Klaus Breuer and Halyna Hajovy

The past decade has seen a rapid increase in the application of computer technology in education. Promising uses have included drill and practice routines (Salisbury, in press), intelligent tutoring programs (Sleeman and Brown, 1982), expert systems (Collins and Stevens, 1983), and simulations (Breuer, 1985). However, the fragmented treatment of the various applications has severely limited the integration of computing technology into the mainstream of educational environments (Kearsley and Seidel, 1985). For example, drill and practice programs are viewed as supplemental instructional activities reserved for remediation (Alessi and Trollip, 1985), while intelligent tutoring programs are at best demonstration programs adopted from training situations.

Likewise, simulations, while using the highly powerful computer tools of on-line interactions and iterative processing capabilities, have been restricted to modelling specific situations and/or phenomena in the acquisition of skills in unguided discovery approaches (Wedekind, 1982). More recently, research work in adaptive instructional systems has shown the potential of intelligent computer-based management systems that integrate the various applications to account for the range in learning conditions (Tennyson and Park, 1984).

At the present time, most of the research on adaptive instructional systems has focused on the assessment and learning of intellectual skills (see Tennyson and Park, 1987). Examples of this work are seen in the adaptive programs of Ross and Rakow (in press), Scandura (1984), Seidel (1975), and Tennyson (1984). These programs possess highly developed monitoring systems which individually assess and instruct learners in the acquisition of conceptual and procedural knowledge. The purpose of this article is to suggest, from the findings of our initial research, that the adaptive approach in instruction can be extended for use in simulations.

Whereas the current adaptive approach to instructional systems is to improve knowledge acquisition (i.e., encoding) and storage (coding) by monitoring and adjusting instruction according to moment-to-moment learning needs, we propose monitoring and adjusting simulation-based instruction to improve memory retrieval processes for cognitive strategy learning (i.e., creativity, productive thinking, and problem formation). Simulation seems to be an appropriate instructional strategy for this higher order learning process because of its ability to provide extensive practice in decision-making and because of its integrative effect in the retrieval process (Gagne, 1985).

Although simulations seem to be an appropriate means for the learning of cognitive strategies, there are a number of basic learning and instructional problems which need consideration before integrating them into an adaptive instructional system. The first is to consider the difference between learning a given task and the learning of cognitive strategies. Typically, simulations have been used for the learning of specific task related skills (see Table 1); thus, they offer no direct instructional objective for cognitive strategy learning. Evaluations of such demonstration and training simulation programs emphasize that for complex tasks, the simulations are most often inadequate because the learners lack the necessary knowledge before entering the program. Also, once in the simulation there is no means to provide remediation or help in recalling necessary knowledge. In situations where learning cognitive strategies is the objective, one inadequacy is the failure to integrate the simulation into a curriculum; thus, the simulation is an isolated piece of self-directed instruction.

In summary, we propose that adaptive instructional simulations offer a means to improve the learning of both content (in a well defined curriculum) and cognitive strategies. The view in the former condition is the elaboration and/or additive learning of information with the latter condition being the acquisition of cognitive structural complexity.

Adaptive Instructional Simulations

For an evaluation of the impact of computer-based instructional simulations on cognitive processes, we refer to Table 1, where educational uses of simulations are considered in reference to conditions of instruction.

The overview on the instructional applications

Klaus Breuer is with the University of Paderborn, West Germany. Halyna Hajovy is with Tennyson and Associates, Inc., St. Paul, Minnesota.

Table 1

Educational Uses of Simulations

Conditions of Instruction	Uses of Simulations (computer-based models of dynamic systems)			
	demonstration	training	modelling	environmental representation
learning activities	observation of system changes	application of procedures	variation of variables and interrelationships	problem-oriented decision-making
learning objective	knowledge of structures and dynamics of complex systems	internalization of defined procedures	strategies of scientific encounter	knowledge and skills refinement and development of heuristics

of simulations in Table 1 provides a means to distinguish between learning objectives and the various educational approaches. In Table 1 we show that higher order cognitive processing is not within the scope of simulation applications for either the demonstration or training approaches. Rather, it is aimed at in the approaches of modelling and environmental representation. Modelling focuses the learning on scientific encounter as, for example, in expert decision-making. The environmental representation approach can be applied to any subject matter domain which allows for an operationally defined contextual model, and requires the cognitive process of integrating and creating knowledge.

In such a context, the necessary problem-oriented retrieval and processing of knowledge and skills results in both content learning and conceptual process learning. That is, existing concepts or skills are revised and enhanced in application, and strategies for the appropriate selection and application of concepts and/or skills are developed. To avoid mere trial and error approaches by students, the process of learning is monitored and guided by the adaptive simulation. An essential component of this simulated guidance process is the employment of cooperative learning group interactions, in which the decision-making processes are monitored to ensure both content acquisition and conceptual complexity development (Johnson and Johnson, 1982; Breuer, 1985).

The purpose of this article is to introduce the variables and conditions necessary to implement adaptive simulations into a curricular and instructional learning environment that would provide intelligent monitoring of individual student learning at the cognitive strategy level of cognition. As such, we are proposing the concept of adaptive simulations at two levels of instructional decision-making as follows:

- Assessment of individual differences in reference to variables of student cognition and memory. The purpose of level one, using methods of artificial intelligence, is an assessment of student knowledge (i.e., student model) in respect to the information to be learned (i.e., knowledge base). On this basis the necessary conditions of instruction would be specified. In those situations where the student would be assessed at the cognitive strategy level of learning, the conditions of instruction would specify a simulation mode of learning.

- Within the simulation mode, on level two, the system would adapt instruction according to moment-to-moment learning needs. The adaptive variables would deal primarily with (a) providing necessary knowledge and (b) checking for possible development of misconceptions.

To illustrate the variables and conditions of adaptive simulations using artificial intelligence methods, we will use the Minnesota Adaptive Instructional System (MAIS) presented in Tennyson's article in this issue. The MAIS is based on two levels of a learning environment: (a) the curricular, termed macro; and (b) the instructional, termed micro (Tennyson and Park, 1987). Briefly, the macro level provides an assessment of each student according to the variables of cognition, affect, and memory. In the memory variable (i.e., student model), knowledge is assessed by AI methods to determine each student's current state of necessary knowledge (i.e., background, associative, and prerequisite) and prior knowledge (including misconceptions) in reference to the information to be learned. The cognition and affect variables provide additional individual difference information for the student model. By combining the three assessment variables with a student model, the macro level decision-making parameters of the expert tutor model (i.e., inference engine) can specify the conditions of instruction for effective learning at the micro level according to the Gagne (1985) hierarchy of learning conditions (i.e., verbal information, intellectual skills, and cognitive strategies).

To illustrate the integration of the adaptive simulation method in the MAIS, consider first the student who is assessed at the macro level to have the necessary knowledge for a given learning task. This student would be assigned at the micro level to a specific simulation adjusted to his or her individual prerequisites and then monitored during the simulation for any further learning needs. Now consider the student who is assessed not to have sufficient necessary knowledge. In this situation, the student would be assigned to one of the other levels of learning and receive appropriate adaptive instruction on the necessary knowledge before entering the simulation condition of instruction.

The instructional approach presented here is taken from a research program that is empirically testing instructional design variables directly associated with the improvement of learning through adaptive simulations. The initial research efforts have extended from the programmatic investigations of Breuer (in press) which show the effectiveness of computer-based simulations in the improvement of cognitive complexity. Next, we briefly summarize the instructional design process for developing simulations at the highest order of cognitive processing (see Table 1).

Design Strategy

The first step in the design of an adaptive simulation is the development of a curriculum plan that includes learning objectives for cognitive strategies. The curriculum analysis should include a content analysis to outline the information base and a task analysis for the definition of associated necessary skills. Both of these analyses provide the basis for the student assessment on the three types of necessary prerequisite knowledge (i.e., background, associative, and prerequisite). With reference to the students' cognitive abilities, the assessment must include a measure of the student's levels of cognitive complexity. Matching of conceptual level in the cooperative groups would be based on this assessment process.

Step two is the development of the macro and micro expert tutor model into which the adaptive simulation variables are integrated. The Tennyson article lists the instructional variables from which appropriate simulation strategies can be prescribed. In addition to the Tennyson instructional variables, we propose that cognitive strategy learning is improved in cooperative learning environments. The purpose of the computer in such small-group situations is twofold: (a) to monitor student decision-making, and (b) to ensure that students have adequate knowledge as well as to check for misconceptions. The former condition provides the opportunity for cognitive strategy development while the latter monitors content usage and acquisition.

The measurement of student cognition is part of the macro level assessment process for the student model. Within the student model, student conceptual complexity is measured for placement in homogeneous groups for simulation instruction. Although much research on cooperative learning has shown to be effective in problem-solving situations, the research by Breuer shows that conceptual complexity improvement comes when students at the same level work together to make decisions rather than in heterogeneous groups where students at lower levels can only observe outcomes from higher ability students.

Another important design concept in the curriculum planning process is the development of situations that require decisions which are basically on a range from poor to good, rather than right or wrong. In this way, the consequences of decision-making are relative, and require not only the retrieval of knowledge stored in memory, but the creation of new knowledge as well. In this way, the student develops conceptual complexity as well as acquiring more domain-specific knowledge. The expert tutor model needs to monitor student decisions to make sure the created knowledge is within the parameters of the knowledge base to control for, in most cases, possible misconceptions.

Summary

The adaptive instructional strategy briefly proposed here is an entirely new application of simulation uses in the improvement of learning for creativity, productive thinking, and problem formation and solving. We are proposing that simulations be both adaptive to individual differences and learning needs as well as be an integral component of a specific curriculum. In this way, instruction can promote the interrelationship between content and the learning process. The results should be the acquisition of domain-specific knowledge and the development of cognitive strategies. □

References

Alessi, S.M., and Trollip, S.R. *Computer-Based Instruction: Methods and Development*. Englewood Cliffs, NJ: Prentice-Hall, 1985.

Breuer, K. Computer Simulations and Cognitive Development. In K.A. Duncan and D. Harris (Eds.), *The Proceedings of the World Conference on Computers in Education 1985 WCCE/85*. Amsterdam, The Netherlands: North Holland, 1985.

Breuer, K. Voraussetzungen und Zielvorstellungen fur das computerunterstutzte Lehren und Lernen. *Unterrichtswissenschaft*, in press.

Collins, A., and Stevens, A.L. A Cognitive Theory of Inquiry Teaching. In C.M. Reigeluth (Ed.), *Instructional Design Theories and Models: An Overview of Their Current Status*. Hillsdale, NJ: Erlbaum, 1983.

Gagne, R.M. *Conditions of Learning (4th Ed.)*. New York: Holt, Rinehart, and Winston, 1985.

Johnson, D.W., and Johnson, F.P. *Joining Together: Group Theory and Group Skills*. Englewood Cliffs, NJ: Prentice-Hall, 1982.

Kearsley, G., and Seidel, R.J. Automation in Training and Education. *Human Factors*, 1985, *27*(1), 61-74.

Ross, S.M., and Rakow, E.A. Adapting Instruction to Learner Performance. In D.H. Jonassen (Ed.), *Instructional Designs for Microcomputer Courseware*. Hillsdale, NJ: Erlbaum, in press.

Salisbury, D.A. Effective Drill and Practice Strategies. In D.H. Jonassen (Ed.), *Instructional Designs for Microcomputer Courseware*. Hillsdale, NJ: Erlbaum, in press.

Scandura, J.M. Cognitive Instructional Psychology: System Requirements and Research Methodology. *Journal of Computer-Based Instruction*, 1984, *11*, 14-21.

Seidel, R.J. *Learner Control of Instructional Sequencing Within an Adaptive Tutorial CAI Environment*. HUMMRO Technical Report, *75-5*, 1975, 1-50.

Sleeman, D., and Brown, J.S. *Intelligent Tutoring Systems*. New York: Academic Press, 1982.

Tennyson, R.D. Application of Artificial Intelligence Methods to Computer-Based Instructional Design: The Minnesota Adaptive Instructional System. *Journal of Instructional Development*, 1984, *7*(3), 17-22.

Tennyson, R.D., and Park, O. Computer-Based Adaptive Instructional Systems: A Review of Empirically-Based Models. *Machine-Mediated Learning*, 1984, *1*, 129-153.

Tennyson, R.D., and Park, O. Artificial Intelligence and Computer-Assisted Learning. In R. Gagne (Ed.), *Instructional Technology: Foundations*. Hillsdale, NJ: Erlbaum, 1987.

Wedekind, J.P.E. Computer-Aided Model Building and CAL. *Computers and Education*, 1982, *6*, 145-151.

MAIS: An Educational Alternative of ICAI

Robert D. Tennyson

The past 15 years have seen an increasing growth in the use of computer technology in education and training. However, improvements in learning as a result of using this technology have not yet been realized (Clark, 1985). A major obstacle in the lack of learning improvements is the failure of instructional designers to successfully integrate learning theories with the unique attributes of computer technology (Petkovich and Tennyson, 1984, 1985). Typically, computer-based instructional design strategies have been univariate in applying learning theories; relying mainly on the use of methodologies found in non-technology-assisted learning systems instead of fully employing the computer's capabilities. The conventional instructional strategies for computer-assisted instruction (CAI) include drill and practice, tutorials, games, and simulations (Alessi and Trollip, 1985). In terms of employing computer capabilities, the uses of graphics in games and simulations are well developed but with minimal direct influence in improving learning. However, the capabilities of computer hardware and software design make it possible to develop learning environments that can integrate a range of instructional strategies currently known to improve learning as well as making it possible to add new strategies.

Demonstration programs in education using artificial intelligence/expert systems methods have shown that the computer's more powerful attributes can be applied to instruction (Tennyson and Park, in press). These few prototype ICAI systems, (e.g., SOPHIE, SCHOLAR, WUMPUS, and others), however, continue to limit themselves to the use of one instructional strategy or learning variable within their tutor models. The focus of the developers for the ICAI prototypes has been on how to more fully employ the power of the computer by applying intelligent software programming

techniques. However, even with extending the use of such computer attributes, a major ICAI limitation is still the unidimensional approach to learning and, therefore, the use of one instructional strategy regardless of the learning need and individual differences (e.g., the Socratic method used in many ICAI programs). In summary, the educational applications of computers have not in large part been fully realized because of both the apparent narrow use of learning theories and instructional strategies and the failure to fully exploit the power of the computer (see also Seidel, 1978).

Conventional ICAI

Most current development efforts in ICAI have come from a computer science orientation. The focus of computer science research in ICAI has followed an expert systems approach in the field of artificial intelligence. The practice in ICAI design has been to develop methods that would enhance the components of an expert system environment in which the main components are a knowledge base (an expert's knowledge of a domain of information) and an executive system (composed of production rules for searching through the knowledge base to help solve problems). Added to the ICAI/expert system approach has been the student model (knowledge that a given student has in memory in reference to the content of the instructional program) and an executive system (i.e., tutor model) tailored to a specific instructional strategy.

The research paradigm in computer science is concerned with the development of appropriate software and, sometimes, hardware tools to design operational computer-based systems. The movement in artificial intelligence has been with designing tools that would allow the design of systems with the ability to solve problems that would normally resemble human thinking. However, in educational and psychological research, the experimental process requires the testing of variables in an empirical environment. And, in instructional research, the focus is on testing variables that can be shown to improve learning. The research methods that we have used in our research program on ICAI variables have come from the educational research paradigm, not the computer science paradigm. Thus, our concern has been not in software tool development as in the conventional ICAI research paradigm, but in investigating variables and conditions that can be empirically tested as showing improvements in learning.

The research objective, as focused in my research program for the Minnesota Adaptive Instructional System (i.e., the MAIS), is to empirically investigate generalizable instructional variables which are

Robert D. Tennyson is Professor of Educational Psychology, University of Minnesota, Minneapolis, Minnesota.

clearly defined within an educational psychology perspective. My goal, along with my colleagues, is to significantly contribute to instructional theory and practice such that instructional system developers will have appropriate variables by which to design and implement good instruction.

Conventional ICAI and the MAIS

In summary, the MAIS research and development program differs from the current efforts in ICAI prototypes development in the following ways:

- The student assessment process includes, in addition to a student model, a cognitive model and affective model. Resulting is a *learner model* based on a holistic approach to student assessment rather than just an at-the-moment assessment approach found in conventional ICAI.
- Expands the instructional variables and computer-based enhancements of the instructional level expert tutor model. Whereas conventional practice in ICAI is to employ one instructional strategy within the tutor model, we employ an expert tutor model capable of prescribing meta-instructional strategies based on both moment-to-moment individual needs and differences and longitudinal, curricular needs and refinements.
- Employment of an expert tutor model at the curricular (macro) level that complements the instructional (micro) level expert tutor model. The responsibility of the curricular expert tutor model is to establish diagnostic scenarios for prescribing the conditions of instruction to be used at the micro level. This activity is enhanced by employing the concept of competing perspectives (Schank and Childers, 1984). Currently, no ICAI program uses a curricular component or the AI design concept of rules representing different perspectives.
- Places the knowledge base at the curricular level rather than the current ICAI practice of having it at the instructional level. The purpose here is twofold: (a) to allow for more possible variations in instructional strategies, and (b) to provide for possible developmental growth in students throughout a curriculum (Fischer, 1980).
- By including a curricular level expert tutor model, it is possible to use an iterative updating system to enhance the adaptive variables within the instructional level expert tutor model.
- Employment of a learner model at the cur-

ricular level that allows for a cumulative history of student learning throughout the instruction. This information provides increasingly better data by which to adapt the instruction the longer the student is learning.

- The expert tutor model concept of the MAIS more closely meets the standard educational definition that a tutorial method implies a relationship agreement between a given student and the teacher, not an instructional strategy as commonly defined in conventional ICAI literature (e.g., the Socratic method is an instructional strategy that is one of possible instructional strategies to use in a tutorial relationship). In terms of our research program, the expert tutor model resembles the attributes of an experienced teacher, not a software tool.
- Another fundamental difference in our educational approach is the analysis method employed to structure the knowledge base. In conventional ICAI methods, the knowledge base is developed using the expert systems approach of knowledge engineering. In contrast, we employ methods more directly related to cognitive psychology, especially as applied to memory and developmental theories.

MAIS Research Program

The goal of our programmatic research for the MAIS has been to investigate instructional variables and conditions that improve learning through the use of adaptive instructional strategies. To accomplish this research goal, we have extended the research focus of the MAIS in two important ways.

- First, by initiating research in the integration of individual difference variables within the concept of the student model. This was done by extending the learner assessment process to include a cognitive model (e.g., intelligence, aptitude, achievement) and an affective model (e.g., motivation, perseverance, personality) along with the student model. The elaborated learner model is integrated at the curricular level with the knowledge base to provide the means for iteratively updating the adaptive instructional strategies at the instructional level. An important task in this regard has been the design of an expert tutor model capable of developing for each student different perspectives on the prescribed instruction.
- Second, by testing instructional variables associated with the learning conditions of verbal information and cognitive strategies (Gagne, 1985).

In our early investigations (reviewed in Tennyson, Christensen, and Park, 1984), the MAIS research program tested nine instructional variables directly related to the learning of intellectual skills (i.e., concept and rule learning) (see also Tennyson and Christensen, in press). Our more recent work, for example, is looking at the use of adaptive simulation variables to improve both content acquisition and development of cognitive strategies (see Breuer's article in this special issue). Implied in this research effort is the continued development of the MAIS expert tutor model at the instructional level. With the integration of the curricular expert tutor model, we are able to extend the formal heuristic methods of the inference engine of the MAIS to the more advanced methods of inference-making offered by informal heuristic methods (Fisher, 1986).

Our current research effort focuses on the study of instructional variables and conditions on a longitudinal basis, so as to further develop the MAIS to include the additional management requirements for the curricular level. Thus, the MAIS provides us with the opportunity to study the integration of the curricular component with the instructional component. The iterative relationship between the two components provides a means for refining both the curricular and the instructional needs per individual student. The basic theoretical model of the expanded MAIS is presented in Tennyson and Park (in press).

MAIS: Adaptive Instruction

We distinguish here between individualized instruction and self-instructional teaching. The former refers to how students are assessed and assigned instruction while the latter is a method of instruction. An integral condition of the research-based intelligent management system of the MAIS is that it adapts to individual learner needs based on assessments occurring externally and internally to the instruction. Typically, assessments are made prior to and/or after the instruction. Our research findings show that student assessment during learning is a powerful method of adapting instruction to the student's moment-to-moment learning needs (Park and Tennyson, 1980). Furthermore, the system employs an iterative method of intelligence such that the management decisions will become increasingly refined the longer the student is in the learning environment. This form of iterative updating of the decision-making process is in direct contrast to most current ICAI methods of reactive decision-making.

Another important feature of the research-based MAIS is that it employs a cognitive psychology approach to the selection of instructional strategies (Tennyson and Cocchiarella, 1986). Basically, the MAIS deals with the concepts of learning, memory, and cognition within the framework of the curricular and instructional levels of education and training. That is, the MAIS defines instructional variables and conditions that predictably improve (a) the acquisition of information, (b) the storage and retrieval of knowledge, and (c) the creative and productive thinking processes. The potential of the computer in terms of its power and speed for variable manipulations and calculations makes it possible to construct an AI instructional system capable of handling the complexity presented by the application of an instructional theory that accounts for learning, memory, and cognition.

Design of the MAIS

The MAIS is designed around the three concepts of learning, memory, and cognition within the conditions of curriculum and instruction. Figure 1 presents a graphic representation of the current version of the MAIS. Within the curricular or macro level, we define variables that relate directly to the concepts of memory and cognition, while at the instructional or micro level, we define variables that relate to the concept of learning. The variables within the macro component establish the conditions of instruction while the micro component adapts the instruction to meet moment-to-moment individual student learning needs. Both components interact in an iterative fashion such that the initial conditions of instruction established by the expert tutor model in the macro adapts at the micro level according to learner progress and needs in learning.

The basic research goal of the MAIS project has been to approach intelligent management systems from a curricular level instead of the conventional, instruction-only level. Typical designs for computer-based management systems have rarely expanded the function of management beyond that of student record keeping and have operated with branching routines composed of finite-sets of possible remediations and options.

A primary purpose of the MAIS research program has been to investigate individual difference variables that would contribute to the initial conditions of instruction within the specifications of a given curriculum. A second purpose has been to investigate variables and conditions by which adaptive instructional systems can iteratively update the conditions of instruction as the individual student progresses through the curriculum. The term "dynamic" is used to describe this relationship between the macro- and micro-level expert

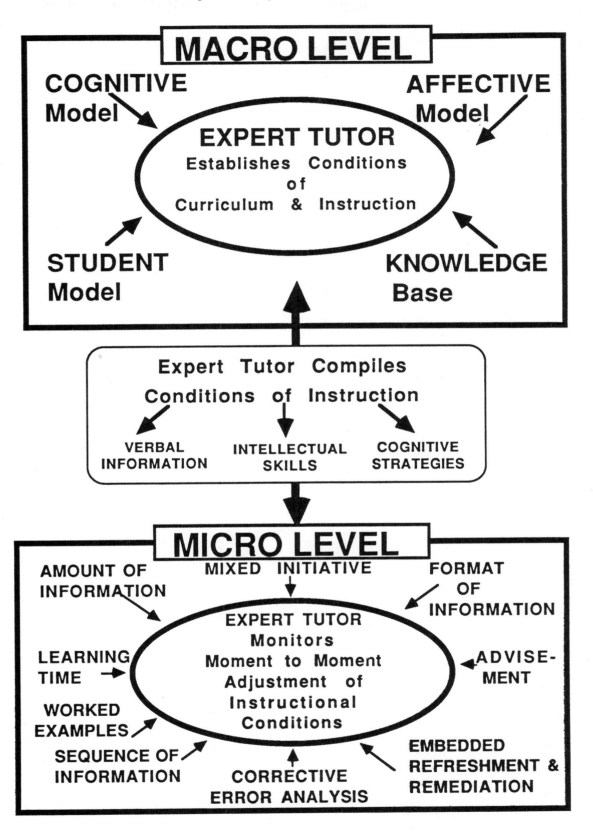

tutor models such that as a learner progresses through instruction, appropriate information can be continuously sent back to the macro-level to constantly refine the decision making for the succeeding conditions of instruction: In other words, the MAIS employs variables that learn how to improve instructional decision making.

Macro-Level

Figure 1 shows the five main variables of the macro-level component. Three of these variables—cognitive model, affective model, and student model—represent areas of individual differences within the context of a learner model. Research findings have shown that each of these variables has differing effects on learning and, therefore, needs constant adjustment based on the fourth variable, the curricular knowledge base. The fifth variable, expert tutor model, is the decision-making component of the system. The function of the expert tutor model is to establish the conditions of instruction within the context of the curriculum. The macro-level expert tutor model compiles the initial parameters of instruction, with the micro-level expert tutor model making necessary adjustments at the moment of learning.

Micro-Level

The instructional level of the MAIS deals directly with student learning at the verbal information, intellectual skills, and cognitive strategies conditions of learning. From the nine instructional variables shown in Figure 1, an instructional strategy is compiled from the macro-level expert tutor model. The instructional conditions appropriate for cognitive strategies learning are discussed in the Breuer and Hajovy article in this special issue. Verbal information learning is a special condition of the intellectual skills condition; therefore, I will not elaborate here on the unique conditions required for the learning of declarative knowledge. The unique conditions basically deal with issues of placement and pacing of item repetition.

Briefly, the nine instructional variables that form the possible meta-instructional strategies are as follows (see Figure 1):

• **Worked Examples.** The learning of complex concepts and rules can be improved if the student understands the underlying principle(s) of the information to be learned. Learning conceptual knowledge is the purpose of expository instruction where best examples are presented to show attributes or procedures and the context of the application of the concept's or rule's underlining principles. The computer enhances this form of expository instruction by requiring the student to use input devices to pace the elaboration materials rather than just presenting directly the solution.

• **Amount of Information.** To improve the efficiency of instruction, the MAIS employs a conditional probability statistic to determine when a student reaches mastery. This variable continuously monitors student progress in learning so as to provide sufficient information for attainment of concept mastery. In cognitive psychology terms, this variable focuses on procedural knowledge development.

• **Sequence of Information.** In the learning of coordinated concepts and rules, many errors of misconception can be prevented by the way the information is sequenced. The sequence heuristic of the MAIS is based on the psychological principles of under- and overgeneralization, not a random or branching format favored by conventional ICAI and CAI programs. The sequence heuristic also improves development of a schematic structure in memory so that conditional knowledge is developed.

• **Format of Information.** An important principle of good teaching is to engage students as soon as possible in the process of decision-making or problem-solving. For each student, however, this point in time differs because of the level of knowledge understanding required to solve problems. The purpose of this variable is to monitor the learning need for additional expository information to ensure adequate conceptual knowledge formation. Thus, if a student shows during problem-solving situations the need for additional conceptual (or principle) understanding, additional expository instruction can be presented.

• **Learning Time.** An important characteristic of an expert tutor is the ability to monitor student learning in reference to efficient use of time. That is, the tutor knows when to interact with the student so as to provide assistance. For example, when first trying to solve a problem, the student indicates by not responding that he or she needs help; the tutor offers assistance instead of trying to force the student to make a solution and therefore a possible error. The purpose of this variable is to be a more active rather than the passive computer-based tutor typical of conventional ICAI and CAI. This variable is primarily concerned with the formation of conceptual knowledge as contrasted with procedural knowledge development.

• **Corrective Error Analysis.** Helping the student to understand a mistake is the purpose of this variable. Too often instructional help is not directly related to the learner's specific problem, thus the student is given excessive information which might even mask or hide the learning problem. This is especially the case in learning more complex concepts and rules. In most situations the form of analysis is content specific; however, the important concern is to design a system that can identify possible specific errors rather than the typical CAI method of feedback and branching.

- **Mixed Initiative.** A major shortcoming of technology-based instructional systems is their ability to allow for student questions. With this variable, it is possible for the student to query the MAIS. For example, if the student does not understand a given procedure or needs an elaboration of some given attribute, they can ask the system. The MAIS then forms a dialogue with the student to understand the student's question. This is another way to help in the formation of conceptual knowledge.

- **Advisement.** An underlying principle of the MAIS is that the student is making progress in learning towards mastery. Because the student is also involved in various forms of decision-making and is putting forth effort in learning, the student needs to be continuously informed of progress. To accomplish the goal of informing students of their progress and to even inform them of need, the MAIS advises students of both their current progress and the necessary instruction to reach mastery. Because this is an adaptive system, changing from moment-to-moment, advisement is provided concurrently with the instructional activities.

- **Embedded refreshment and remediation.** Learning within a domain of information usually implies making connections between concepts and rules. Most often the learning of connections, and therefore the schematic structure of the domain, is made by the student in memory. However, when the learning of new information requires the connection to prerequisite knowledge and the students cannot retrieve that knowledge, they need help. The purpose of this variable is to sense this need and provide the appropriate help. If the need is only for help in making the connection (i.e., the student knows the prerequisite knowledge), information on the prerequisite knowledge is presented in an expository form at that point. The term embedded refreshment is used to describe this process of helping the student recall the specific prerequisite knowledge at the moment they need to make the connection. If, however, the student needs more than just recall, but needs relearning, remediation is provided.

The expert tutor model at the micro-level adapts continuously the meta-instructional strategy compiled by the macro-level expert tutor model. Student learning outcomes are iteratively re-turned to the macro-level to further enhance the instruction for preceeding instruction.

Summary

Our concern in the MAIS research program is not to just develop a prototype system (as in the conventional ICAI research methods of tool making), but to empirically investigate the relationships between the variables of the learner model and how that relationship, along with the integration with the curricular knowledge base, enhances the instructional strategy decision-making at the micro-level. In other words, in contrast to conventional ICAI research, which seeks to test software intelligence techniques, we seek to investigate *variables that can intelligently improve learning.*

We are continuing to investigate a research-based intelligent learning system that can on one hand provide an evaluation of each student (i.e., a highly information-rich learner model) and, on the other, can be directly associated with the instructional prescription process. We are doing this within the framework of AI methods that will assist in the improvement of the system's inferential ability by adding the concept of system "discovery." That is, the proposed system will not only assess students prior to and continuously during learning, but will also improve its inferential ability by itself learning.

In summary, the MAIS research and development program focuses on the study of intelligent learning systems from an educational research paradigm, with variables and hypotheses directly related to the improvement of learning through the use of adaptive instructional methods. To accomplish this goal, we integrate, where appropriate, variables and conditions from a wide range of disciplines and fields of study, including cognitive psychology, developmental psychology, computer science, management information sciences, as well as numerous fields in educational psychology (e.g., evaluation and measurement, reading, and instructional technology and design).

Currently, we know a lot about human learning and, in specific situations, we can actually show how a given variable or condition of instruction can significantly improve certain types of learning. However, the large number of instructional variables and strategies cited in the literature show that learning is a complex phenomenon, requiring more than the generalizable application of one or two strategies. Our research demonstrates that with computer technology, it is now possible to make use of the wide range of instructional variables to develop meta-instructional strategies to improve learning within specific needs. Through the use of AI methods, sophisticated management systems can be developed to make use of the known means to improve learning in cost-effective systems. Our basic research program will extend the work currently being done on the MAIS such that a total, technology-assisted learning system can be designed and tested. It will provide the knowledge base by which current educational and training systems can be adapted and future systems can be designed. □

References

Alessi, S., and Trollip, S. *Designing Computer-Based Instruction*. Englewood Cliffs, NJ: Prentice-Hall, 1985.

Clark, R.E. Evidence for Confounding in Computer-Based Instruction Studies: Analyzing the Meta-Analysis. *Educational Communication and Technology Journal*, 1985, *33*, 249-262.

Fischer, K.W. A Theory of Cognitive Development: The Control and Construction of Hierarchies of Skills. *Psychological Review*, 1980, *87*, 477-531.

Fisher, E.M. Building AI Beyond Closed Doors. *Datamation*, August 1, 1986.

Gagne, R.M. *Conditions of Learning* (4th Ed.) New York: Holt, Rinehart, and Winston, 1985.

Park, O., and Tennyson, R.D. Adaptive Design Strategies for Selecting Number and Presentation Order of Examples in Coordinate Concept Acquisition. *Journal of Educational Psychology*, 1980, *72*, 362-370.

Petkovich, M.D., and Tennyson, R.D. Clark's "Learning from Media": A Critique. *Educational Communication and Technology Journal*, 1984, *32*, 233-241.

Petkovich, M.D., and Tennyson, R.D. A Few More Thoughts on Clark's "Learning from Media." *Educational Communication and Technology Journal*, 1985, *33*, 146.

Schank, R.C., and Childers, P. *The Cognitive Computer*. Reading, MA: Addison-Wesley, 1984.

Seidel, R.J. Learner Control of Instructional Sequencing Within an Adaptive Tutorial CAI Environment. *Instructional Science*, 1978, *7*, 37-80.

Tennyson, R.D., and Christensen, D.L. MAIS: An Intelligent Learning System. In D. Jonassen (Ed.), *Instructional Designs for Microcomputer Courseware*. Hillsdale, NJ: Erlbaum, in press.

Tennyson, R.D., and Cocchiarella, M.J. An Empirically Based Instructional Design Theory for Teaching Concepts. *Review of Educational Research*, 1986, *56*, 40-71.

Tennyson, R.D., and Park, O. Artificial Intelligence and Computer-Based Learning. In R.M. Gagne (Ed.), *Instructional Technology: Foundations*, Hillsdale, NJ: Erlbaum, 1987.

Tennyson, R.D., Park, O., and Christensen, D.L. Display Time Interval and Response-Sensitive Sequencing as Instructional Design Variables in Concept-Learning Using Computer-Based Instruction. *Journal of Educational Psychology*, 1985, *77*, 481-491.

The Role of Tutorial and Experiential Models in Intelligent Tutoring Systems

M. David Merrill
Contributing Editor

Most current instruction is standup lecture supplemented by printed materials such as technical manuals and text books. We have yet to implement on a wide scale any technological advance in instruction including language laboratories, instructional television, teaching machines, or computer-assisted instruction. *Why?*

Each of these technological advances has promised radical change and order of magnitude improvement in learning. None of them have delivered. The zealots among the advocates for ICAI (Intelligent Computer Assisted Instruction) or ITS (Intelligent Tutoring Systems) are once again promising order of magnitude improvement in learning and citing "conventional CAI (computer-assisted instruction)" as ineffective. Frequently straw man examples of CAI are described to show how ineffectively CAI uses the power of the computer. The examples frequently chosen are the worse case drill and practice type instruction that those with any CAI expertise would also eschew. The advocates of this advanced method of instruction have managed so far to avoid collecting any hard data demonstrating the effectiveness of ITS compared with conventional CAI or any other instructional method. It is highly likely that when this data is collected it, like effectiveness data for the technological innovations of the past, will also show NSD (no significant differences) in student learning performance (Clark, 1983).

In the final analysis, however, comparative studies are meaningless anyway. They focus our attention on the wrong variables. Comparing CAI with live teachers suggests that the computer itself makes some difference in learning. When all other variables are controlled, such as content organization and instructional strategy, there will

M. David Merrill is Professor, Instructional Technology Department, Utah State University, Logan, Utah.

always be no differences. The real question is whether the computer allows us to implement instructional strategies that would be difficult or impossible to implement with live teachers. If so then we may demonstrate that the more easily implemented instructional strategy or content representation leads to an improvement in learning rather than the fact that it was implemented via a computer.

In a parallel way the comparison of ITS and CAI is a meaningless comparison. Some of the instructional procedures advocated by intelligent CAI can be approximated via conventional CAI. For example, mixed initiative dialogues are cited as one of the goals of ITS. Putting aside the question of natural language processing, which many ITS investigators have now acknowledged may be unnecessary, it is possible to approximate a mixed initiative dialogue using conventional CAI that may be more flexible than some of the mixed dialogues possible via more intelligent implementations. A recent demonstration of an intelligent system illustrated how the student can ask the system to define a technical term or provide an example of the term. This is limited student initiated dialogue. In the mid 1970s my colleagues and I designed the TICCIT system (Merrill, Schneider, and Fletcher, 1980). It had a learner control "higher order language" consisting of queries or directions that the student could give to the system at any time. These included the following: Show me a map, objective, rule, example, practice item, easier example, harder example, easier practice item, harder practice item, provide help for the rule, help for the example, help for the practice item, tell me how I'm doing, tell me what I should do next. This is a significant number of requests that the student could make of the system at any time. The system would respond by providing the information requested, often dynamically generating the information based on the request of this specific student and his/her previous requests. Is this a mixed initiative dialogue? Is this an intelligent system?

Some ITS systems include coaches (for example, WUMPUS and WEST; see Sleeman and Brown, 1982). The TICCIT system includes an ADVISOR. The TICCIT advisor monitors the performance of the student while interacting with the system. It keeps track not only of right/wrong answers but which learner control requests the student has made and which parts of the available material the student has seen. Is this a student model? The advisor provided two modes of guidance, solicited and unsolicited. Unsolicited advice consists of messages warning the student about the consequence of the choices being made and advising, but seldom

Figure 1

The Branching Programmed Instruction Model

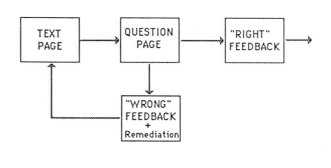

Figure 2

The Tutorial Model

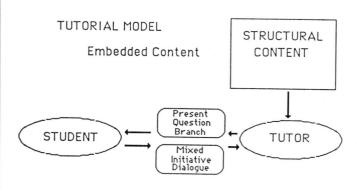

compelling, the student to take alternative actions. Solicited advice indicates what options are available, what the student has seen, and also what the student should do next. Is this a coach? Is this an intelligent tutoring system or conventional CAI?

Too much attention has been focused on the wrong question. Software intelligence is not a variable. Instructional strategy and not software intelligence will cause any differences in learning outcome that may exist. The use of sophisticated programming techniques will not automatically guarantee more effective instructional strategies or more adequate content representations. Many of the so-called intelligent tutoring systems implement ineffective instructional strategies. The only possible advantage of intelligent programming techniques is that they may enable us to implement instructional strategies that are not easily implemented using other instructional delivery systems. This requires that we know what those instructional strategies are and not merely assume that because our system is "intelligent" it is therefore automatically better.

The Tutorial as an Instructional Model

Much of traditional CAI is based on the **Branching Programmed Instruction Model** illustrated in Figure 1. The instructional strategy consists of the following events: (1) Present a page of text (which may include graphics) for the student to study. (2) Ask a question. (3) If the student's answer is correct, provide feedback saying you are correct and if the student's response is incorrect provide feed-

back plus remedial material (which is sometimes omitted). (4) Repeat this cycle. This model is often called "tutorial" CAI.

Tutorial CAI is often equated with the Socratic model. Many people believe that the Socratic model represents the ideal educational interaction. The Socratic method consists of asking questions to draw out of the student the understanding of the phenomena being discussed. A Socratic procedure attempts to correct student errors by showing how his reasoning is faulty, where he has misconceptions and where his understanding is incomplete. Collins and Stevens (1983) have presented a set of rules governing the use of this method. However, most tutorial CAI programs fail to follow these rules of inquiry. In most tutorial CAI the student is first presented information, usually as a paragraph of text, perhaps accompanied by graphic information, and then asked questions (often one question) about this text. It is this programmed instruction model that is often cited as inadequate by the advocates of ITS.

Many ITS programs are also firmly rooted in the philosophy of Socratic tutorials. The goal seems to be to duplicate Mark Hopkins on the other end of the log. Figure 2 illustrates the tutorial model as it is envisioned by the Socratic method and as it is implemented by many CAI and ITS systems. The computer program selects information from the subject matter content and presents it to the student via text/graphic frames or helps the student to see the relationships in the content via question frames (inquiry teaching) or tests the student's understanding via question frames. In a mixed initiative dialogue the student is able to direct the sequence of these presentations to some extent but the critical variable is still the extraction of parts of the content and embedding these content fragments in presentations or questions for the student.

Figure 2 indicates that the subject matter content in this model is usually "structural" or static in nature as opposed to "behavioral" or experiential. Structural content is subject matter as it is represented in a book. Principles are extracted and recorded, experiments are described or illustrated. Students may be allowed to branch from place to place but the information presented at any of these locations was previously selected and organized by the tutor (or the designer). On the other hand, "behavioral" or experiential content is responsive. It enables the student to change parameters and see the consequences. It simulates real events and procedures where input from the student results in a change in the phenomena simulated.

Is the tutorial the ideal teaching strategy? Is the tutorial the universal teaching strategy? The answer to both questions is NO. Socrates and Mark Hopkins are both highly overrated. There are many things that cannot be taught very well via tutorial dialogues. It is difficult via a tutorial to teach the procedures for operating a piece of machinery, for trouble shooting a circuit, for drawing a circuit diagram or for designing a house. In fact any instructional outcome which involves learning a procedure or understanding a process is difficult to teach through only a tutorial.

Should tutorials be used at all? YES, but that use should be limited. Tutorials are best in two circumstances. First, to focus a student's attention while interacting with a more experiential representation of some phenomena. A tutorial dialogue may help a student focus his attention and see relationships for which mere exploration is insufficient. Second, to help a student overcome misconceptions or misunderstandings after having explored some experiential environment. This is a remedial or clarifying role. However, when it comes to primary instruction tutorial conversations are seldom sufficient.

In the ITS community we overuse the word tutorial and tutor. We have come to equate all teaching functions with tutoring. We have made instruction and tutoring synonymous. These terms are not synonyms. Tutoring is a special instructional technique. A critical characteristic of tutoring is the selection and presentation of fragmented, embedded subject matter. Whether the tutoring system is based on "intelligent" programs or more conventional programming techniques is far less important to the instructional outcomes. The widespread adoption of the term "Intelligent Tutoring Systems" is unfortunate.

An Experiential Instruction Model

A computer is not a single medium but a multimedia device. Rather than a single metaphor (tutoring) it is possible to think of many metaphors to represent the various interactions that are possible. In addition to a participant in a conversation where there is give and take, the computer can be a laboratory where the student can manipulate devices, change data, observe reactions and test hypotheses. The computer can be a blueprint or a circuit diagram which the student can design or change. The computer is a drawing table where the student can illustrate his/her ideas and have them critiqued. The computer is a word processor which enables the student to edit material and have this editing monitored. The computer is a calculator, a control panel, a machine, or any of a hundred devices to be manipulated. To limit the metaphor for instruction to the computer as tutor is to limit the nature of the instruction.

The computer is more than a tutor. The computer can be not only the tutor but also the subject matter. Almost any phenomena can be simulated and the student can be given control over this simulation to explore, experiment, predict, and interact with the subject matter itself. The computer can also be an expert to demonstrate the correct way to perform a procedure or to show the correct way to set up an experiment. The computer can be a coach or advisor to watch over the student's shoulder while he performs experiments, designs apparatus, solves problems. When the student is in trouble the computer can intervene to help the student with the problem, provide missing information or guide the student down a different path. Seeing the computer merely as a tutor is to limit our view. The computer can be many things simultaneously, and the most effective instruction is that instruction that enables the student to interact directly with the subject matter (simulated by the computer), watch an expert perform a task (simulated by the computer), engage in a Socratic dialogue about our exploration with some subject matter, or receive coaching as he attempts to perform some complex cognitive task. To limit the student's interaction with the computer to only one or some subset of these possibilities fails to take advantage of the tremendous flexibility of this tool.

Figure 3 represents a simple experiential model of instruction. It differs from the tutorial model in that the student interacts directly with some be-

Figure 3

A Simple Experiential Model

havioral representation of subject matter. A behavioral representation is one which provides some controllable microworld with which the student can manipulate and observe. A behavioral representation provides a simulation of some process or procedure which enables the student to interact in such a way that the consequences of the student's actions are reflected in the reactions of the system.

The most common form of transaction with such a controllable microworld is to allow the student to explore and discover the relationships involved. Often such exploration is the only transaction provided as illustrated in Figure 3. However, exploration is only one type of transaction with an experiential representation of subject matter. According to Webster, one definition for a transaction is, "a communicative action or activity involving two parties or two things reciprocally affecting or influencing each other." A transaction is the mutual, dynamic, real-time give and take which is possible through a computer. An instructional transaction is a dynamic interaction between the program and the student in which there is an interchange of information (see Merrill, 1985, 1986, 1988).

Figure 4 illustrates an experiential model of instruction which includes a variety of transactions. While exploration is appropriate in some situations it is often not sufficient to enable the student to learn the necessary procedures or to understand all of the relationships included in the experiential simulation. Figure 4 indicates that if the experiential representation involves a process of exploration, then other possible transactions may include demonstration, explanation, prediction, and error detection.

Demonstrations can be very structured or very general. A demonstration may pose a problem and show the student the consequence of certain parameter values. A demonstration may merely show how the system works or illustrate some specific principles within the system.

An explanation is the ability to answer the question, "Why does this work?" The system explains or shows the underlying principles on which the simulation is based.

Prediction is a transaction which poses problems for the student and requires the student to form and test hypotheses about possible outcomes. While exploration allows the student to form and test his/her own predictions about the system, a prediction transaction structures and/or sequences this hypothesis testing activity.

Error detection or trouble shooting introduces inconsistent principles or errors into the experiential representation and requires the student to find and/or correct these errors.

Transactions form the interface of the student with the experiential representation of the subject matter. The student is often able to learn more from some form of structured transactions than from open ended learner controlled exploration.

Figure 5 adds an advisor function to the experiential model. The advisor function is similar to the "Coach" in some ITS systems. An advisor monitors the student's exploratory behavior and provides guidance about what the student should try next in order to maximize the relationships learned. In Figure 5, with multiple transactions included, the advisor may also serve to select or suggest what transaction should be used next and when it is advantageous to change to a new type of transaction with the content representation.

Adding a student model and an expert model, as in Figure 6, expands the system to include all of the components frequently mentioned as necessary for an ITS system. The student model provides the necessary information for the advisor to guide the student's interaction with the system in an individualized way. The expert enables the system to judge the student's performance against a mastery model or enables the system to demonstrate expert performance to the student.

Figure 4

Experiential Model with Multiple Transactions

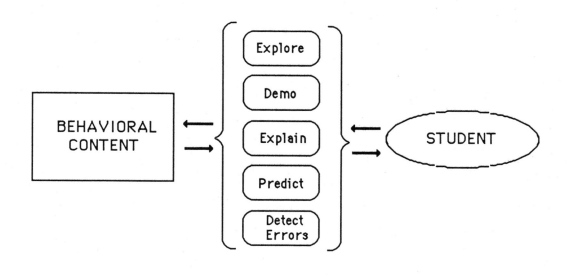

Figure 5

Experiential Model with Advisor

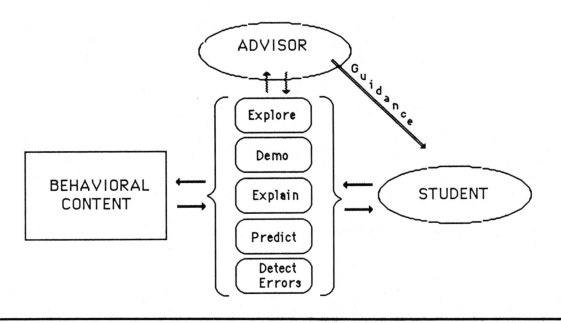

Figure 6

ITS Experiential Model with Advisor

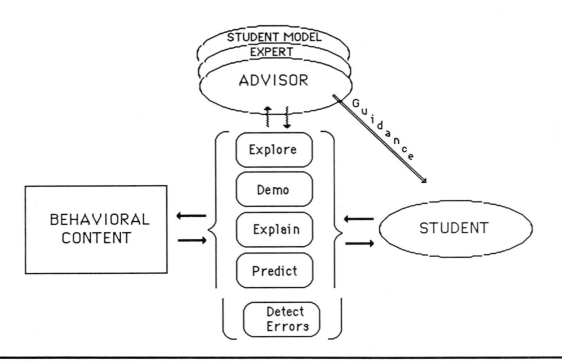

Figure 6

ITS Experiential Model with Advisor

It is also possible to expand the system to include an expert system as a job aid for the student to use in interacting with the experiential representation (not shown). In this case there could be two separate expert systems, one which is a job aid to be used by the student in interacting with the content and the other a model of the optimal or desired interaction with the system.

Finally, Figure 7 combines a tutorial system with an experiential system. This would enable the advisor to direct or guide the student to engage in a tutorial conversation for the purpose of focusing attention on critical relationships in the experiential representation or for the purpose of helping the student overcome misconceptions which may have arisen from interacting with the system. In this case the advisor can also serve as a tutor engaging the student in mixed initiative conversation about his/her interactions with the experiential representation of the subject matter.

Summary

We have considered some of the conceptual underpinnings of ITS. We have suggested that intelligence *per se* is not a variable of importance to instructional outcomes but merely a designation of the sophistication of the programming involved in implementing an instructional system. If an intelligent system implements an ineffective instructional strategy, then the instructional outcome will be no better than if this instructional strategy were implemented via conventional CAI, a live teacher, or some other delivery system. The learning outcome is a function of the representation of the content and the instructional strategies involved, rather than whether or not the system is "intelligent."

We have suggested that a more critical variable is tutorial versus experiential interactions. Tutorial interactions have a role primarily to direct attention or to overcome misconceptions. We have represented a continuum of instructional models. Useful implementations of each of these models in this continuum could improve instruction, not because they are "intelligent" but because effective instructional strategies may be more easily implemented with systems having these characteristics than is possible with other instructional delivery systems.

Expert Systems and Intelligent CAI

Figure 7

ITS Experiential/Tutorial/Advisor Model

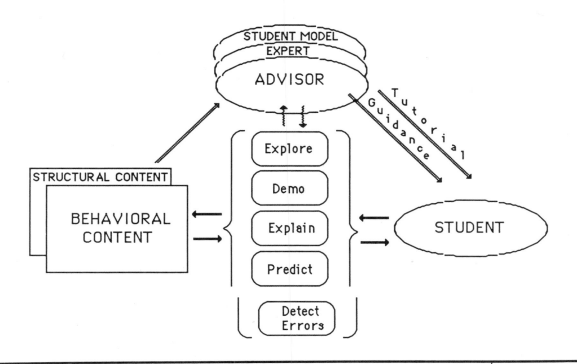

In the final analysis let's focus our attention on the real variables involved rather on the form of our implementation. Some remarkable strides have been made in developing sophisticated programming techniques that may make it possible to implement more effective instructional strategies. However, we must be careful not to assume that intelligent programming techniques *per se* will result in more effective learning. Our attention should concentrate on the intelligent use of computers in instruction, whether or not they involve intelligent programming techniques. □

References

Clark, R.C. Reconsidering Research on Learning from Media. *Review of Educational Research, 53*(4), 1983, 415-459.

Collins, A., and Stevens, A.L. A Cognitive Theory of Inquiry Teaching. In Charles M. Reigeluth, *Instructional Design Theories and Models: An Overview of their Current Status*. Hillsdale, NJ: Lawrence Erlbaum Associates, 1983.

Merrill, M.D. Where Is the Authoring in Authoring Systems? *Journal of Computer Based Instruction*, 1985, *12*(4), 90-96.

Merrill, M.D. Prescriptions for an Authoring System? *Journal of Computer Based Instruction*, 1987, *14*(1).

Merrill, M.D. Chapter 3, Applying Component Display Theory to the Design of Courseware. In D.H. Jonassen, *Instructional Designs for Microcomputer Courseware*. Hillsdale, NJ: Lawrence Erlbaum Associates, 1988.

Merrill, M.D., Schneider, E.W., and Fletcher, K.A. *TICCIT*. Instructional Design Library (Vol. 40). Englewood Cliffs, NJ: Educational Technology Publications, 1980.

Sleeman, E., and Brown, J.S. *Intelligent Tutoring Systems*. New York: Academic Press, 1982.

Part II
Section Three

Perspective and
Critique

Individualizing Instruction Through Intelligent Computer-Assisted Instruction: A Perspective

Jung-Shing Yang

Individualized instruction has long been extolled as the ideal instruction to fulfill the dream of democratic education. However, while most educators recognize that individualized instruction is tailored to accommodate a particular learner's interests, abilities, and learning styles, they are inclined to confuse *individual* instruction with *individualized* instruction.

Individual instruction treats one student at a time. The nature of the instruction, however, may not be tailored to fit the unique condition of the particular learner. Furthermore, individualized instruction need not be individual instruction. Group interaction can be a format for some individualized instruction, provided that the instructional materials and learning activities are appropriate to the specific needs of the learners in the group.

While it is generally believed that computer-assisted instruction (CAI) can individualize instruction, most marketed CAI courses are examples of individual instruction rather than individualized instruction. The CAI courseware is delivered mostly in a "one student to one computer" base. There is, then, no doubt of its being individual instruction. However, if the CAI courseware does not have an adaptive function to tailor the instruction to the unique needs of each learner, it is not and cannot be individualized instruction.

Based on the distinction between individual and individualized instruction, the following sections will further explore a way leading future CAI toward genuine individualized instruction.

Parameters of Individualized Instruction

Bergan and Dunn (1976) suggest six attributes of individualized instruction:

Jung-Shing Yang is a graduate student at the University of Southern California, Los Angeles.

1. A broad array of educational objectives and extensive alternative content.
2. A variety of instructional procedures, settings, and contexts.
3. An extensive cross-indexing of these curricular objectives, materials, methods, and learning contexts.
4. An extensive data base regarding the individual student's interests, abilities, aspirations, optimum learning styles, long-range goals, and ambitions.
5. An extensive cumulative record on each student regarding his past academic accomplishments and academic records.
6. A file of information regarding the constraints being imposed upon the planning for and by the student resulting from parental wishes, state and local requirements, and restrictions imposed upon the system by virtue of supply, logistics, and administrative considerations.

While these six attributes provide a static description of individualized instruction, five parameters of dynamically describing the progress of an individualized instruction have been identified and discussed by Merrill (1984) and Tennyson (Tennyson, Christensen, and Park, 1984), as follows:

1. **Individualization of instructional amount.**

Instructional amount refers to how much instruction a learner receives. It can be further classified into two sub-categories:

a. **Topics:** A learner selects topics from the content list of a course according to his or her interests. A properly designed course should have an extensive range of topics to permit a learner to skip some uninteresting or inappropriate material.

b. **Displays:** Learners receive various information and/or exercises in a topic according to their abilities. The number of displays a learner receives in a topic may differ from others in quality (different difficulty levels) and/or quantity (different amount of explanations or practices).

2. **Individualization of display time.**

Display time refers to the speed of learning or pacing. It is externally paced if a display turns to a new "page" when a fixed time span has elapsed. If the speed of external pacing is the same for all learners, there is no individualization of display time. However, if the speed of external pacing is varied based on the ability of a learner, there is an individualized adaptation. In most CAI courseware, turning to a new display happens only after a learner has hit a key to continue, and therefore the display time is self-paced.

3. **Individualization of instructional sequence.**

Individualized instruction must allow a learner to reorganize the sequence of instructional materials to fit his or her previous experiences, learning styles, and cognitive structures.

4. Individualization of personal attention.

Personal attention refers to the feedback and reinforcement a learner receives during the instructional procedures.

5. Individualization of internal learning activities.

Individualized instruction not only manipulates the instructional materials, but also interacts with a learner's internal learning activities. While effective individualized instruction must harmonize with a learner's mental processing skills, a learner's internal learning activities can also be influenced to a certain degree by external information.

Research on Individualized Instruction

Studies on CAI are used here to examine the possible effects of various parameters of individualized instruction.

Instructional Amount

Educators have long been aware that various learners—based on their aptitudes, prior experiences, and motivations—may need different amounts of instruction to master a lesson. For example, less experienced learners in a subject field need detailed instruction to remediate their learning deficiency. On the other hand, too much instruction bores the high-aptitude learners and decreases their learning achievement as well as wasting their learning time. Therefore, in order to improve the effectiveness and efficiency of learning, an adaptation of instructional amount is needed for various learners.

The individualization of instructional amount in CAI can vary from no adaptation to full adaptation. While most CAI courseware requires learners to take the same amount of instruction, some courseware does vary the instructional amount by a pre-task assessment. Tennyson (Tennyson et al., 1984) calls the pre-task adaptive strategy a "partial-adaptive" strategy. He asserts that "Students' learning needs fluctuate in two important ways during instruction. First, different abilities may be required at different stages of a given task. . . . Second, abilities may change as students continue to work on a given task" (Park and Tennyson, 1980, p. 362). It seems clear that no matter how sophisticated a pre-task adaptive strategy is, it is unlikely to exactly predict the progress of a learner on the instruction. Therefore, an on-task adaptive strategy which continuously modifies the instructional amount based on the assessment of a learner's progress may more appropriately individualize the instruction. Tennyson then claims that a "full-adaptive" strategy should include both pre-task and on-task information.

There are two ways of dynamically adjusting the amount of instruction based on on-task information: a program control system and a learner control system. Tennyson and his colleagues, after reviewing a series of their studies, conclude that adaptive CAI is more effective than the non-adaptive CAI; that adaptive control based on on-task information is more effective than adaptive control based on pre-task information; and that learner control with advisement is more effective than program control, while program control is more effective than learner control without advisement (Tennyson et al., 1984).

Ross (1984) after examining his several studies on adaptive strategy indicates that varying instructional amount improves learning achievement, and program control systems are superior to learner control systems. However, we need to note that the learner control referred to in Ross's studies is a control without any feedback or diagnostic information generated to the learner.

Merrill, on the other hand, believes that, provided sufficient information, learners are able to select the optimum amount of instruction they need to master lessons. After conducting several studies to examine this belief, he (1980) concludes that students who control the amount of instruction do score as well as, if no better than, those who receive maximum instruction, but significantly better than those who receive minimum instruction. Therefore, using learner control to individualize instruction, if it is not more effective in achievement, surely is more efficient in regard to instructional amounts offered.

In general, these cited studies show that individualizing the amount of instruction has a potential for generating effective learning. Particular promise is seen in a dynamically adjusted adaptive strategy based on on-task information and a learner-controlled system with advisement. However, Gay (1985) allowed a learner control group to control instructional delivery, including instructional amount, while a program control group received fixed instruction. He finds that while high prior conceptual understanding subjects in the learner control condition performed equally well on a posttest but were more efficient in the use of instructional material and time than subjects in the program control condition, low prior conceptual understanding subjects in the learner control condition had significantly lower posttest scores than those in the program control condition. His study suggests a moderate effect of prior knowledge on the adaptation of instructional amount.

In practice, educators have found that some types of learners, especially beginning and slow learners, just cannot afford to skip some instructional materials. They may pass the competence test at the end of the instruction, but in the long run, skipping certain instruction may inhibit their future learning. Also in certain well structured courses, allowing students to control the instructional amount may skip some important information and therefore decreases the learning achievement. The effects of varying instructional amount on different types of learners or courses should be further explored.

Display Time

People are aware of the differences in processing time for the storing and retrieving of information. It is generally recognized that each learner has his particular learning speed, and the speed may vary in subjects, environments, and times. The individualization of learning speed is critical to both the efficiency and the effectiveness of learning. In a sense, without sufficient time for processing information, slow learners gain little from quick pacing. In contrast, quick learners are bored with slow pacing of instruction, resulting in a decrease in achievement and a waste of time.

In designing the learning speed of a CAI courseware, there are two strategies: external pacing and self-pacing. External pacing can also be fixed or individualized to various learners.

After reviewing a number of studies on pacing, O'Neal in Merrill's paper (1984) reports mixed results. However, he points out that "[with some training] self-paced learners may be considerably more efficient than externally-paced learners" (p. 235). He also finds that slow learners perform better in externally slow-paced instruction than in self-paced instruction.

While most instructional designers intuitively believe that self-pacing is a critical factor in the success of individualized instruction, Reiser (1984) finds that "students tend to proscrastinate when they are given the opportunities to pace themselves through a course" (p. 41). Belland *et al.* (1985) also report that external pacing allowing a reasonable amount of time for reading and mental processing of information is more efficient and effective than self-pacing. However, learning performance is significantly decreased by allowing only the reading time and eliminating the cognitive processing time in external pacing condition.

It seems that while self-pacing ideally can vary the learning speed to fit a learner's need, it is usually misused by low-motivated learners. On the other hand, a fixed external pacing may force learners to keep up with page-turning and maintains their attention, but it does not fit the learning speeds of various learners. Two issues are involved: the difference between learners' comfortable learning speed and effective learning speed, and the effects of external pacing with individualization.

Kolers *et al.* in a study (1981) found that "Systems in which, by program control, text was presented at rates 10 percent or 20 percent faster than the preferred scrolling rate should lead to more efficient performance, but might create some problems of user acceptance" (p. 517).

The second issue is based on the consideration that if courseware is used in a group featuring significantly varied students, a fixed external pacing is not appropriate. Adjusted external pacing based on a learner's ability may be able to complement the deficiencies of both self-pacing and external pacing without individualization. However, to date, we don't have much research to address this issue.

Though studies have indicated that instructional time is a valuable independent variable in the research on individualized instruction, most of the details remain unexplored.

Instructional Sequence

The necessity of individualizing the instructional sequence is based on a belief that if the structure of instruction is closely related to the structure of a learner's knowledge, then learning achievement will be improved significantly.

According to Merrill (1984), the control of instructional sequence can be divided into two categories. The "content control" alters the sequence of units or topics in a course. The "display control" alters the sequence of instructional materials in a unit. In content control, O'Neal reports in Merrill's paper (1984) that allowing students to reorganize the sequence of units or topics is at least as effective as presenting fixed sequences, and its learning time is considerably less.

In display control, Merrill (1984) reviewed his five studies and found no consistent evidence of a superiority of display control over the no-display control. However, further analysis revealed that "performance is superior when a rule-example-practice order is followed" (p. 236).

Jonassen (1985) indicates that if the goal of instruction is classification, the deductive sequence, in which the rule is followed by examples, is effective. If we want a learner to transfer rules to novel situations, the inductive sequence, in which examples are presented before the rule, should be used. In practical education, most "effective" instruction is usually designed in a rule-example-practice order, because the achievement test is mostly purposed to examine classification skills. It is not a surprise to find that those students who follow the deductive sequence perform better in achievement tests than those students who adopt other sequences. However, the superiority of deductive sequence on posttest does not mean it is a better learning strategy, but rather that the test is unable to measure other impacts of altering instructional sequence. This may explain why Merrill's studies cannot find consistent evidence regarding the control of instructional sequence.

While Merrill emphasizes the learner control of instructional sequence, Tennyson builds a program-controlled instructional sequence. In a study (Park and Tennyson, 1980) he reports that "students in the response-sensitive [a branching based on learners' history] group not only performed better, but also needed less on-task learning time and fewer examples than the response-insensitive [a branching based on single response of a learner] group" (p. 362).

One issue related to controlling instructional sequence is whether students are capable of reorganizing the instruction to fit their abilities or cognitive styles. If a student doesn't have the ability, or he/she is totally unfamiliar with the subject topics, letting a learner control the instructional sequence may result in a disaster. A program-controlled system seems effective in such situations. However, the effects of these strategies need to be examined with various students as well as in various subjects. Also, the measurement instrument should be more well considered to examine the real impacts of altering instructional sequence.

Personal Attention

Page (1958) points out that giving appropriate attention will positively influence learning achievement. CAI courseware is extolled for providing the function of personal attention. However, the feedback and reinforcement in most CAI courseware is uniform to all learners. In daily lives, we have been aware that incentives which work for one learner may be meaningless for others. Therefore, in order to achieve the best motivation of a learner, it is important to vary within-task feedback and reinforcement on an individual basis.

Ross (1984) reports that strong effects are achieved with greater discrimination of incentive values. Gaynor (1981) finds that "although not significant, immediate feedback yielded seemingly better results than the EOS [end-of-session] feedback with the low mastery group while the EOS feedback appears to have been more effective with the high mastery group" (p. 131). Cohen (1985) reviews studies on feedback and concludes that it is important to take the intended learner into account in order to decide when, how much, and what type of feedback should be presented. In general, she suggests that "too much feedback, or feedback messages that are too long and time-consuming can slow down the pace of instruction and cause a confident student to feel impatient and frustrated" (p. 35). On the other hand, they are necessary for a beginner.

Although we have lots of studies on number, type, and presented time of feedback and reinforcement, questions such as how to apply these findings to meet characteristics of learners, and how to design a dynamically adjusted adaptive strategy to individualize attention, still remain untouched.

Internal Learning Activities

While theories of instructional psychology have recently shifted from behavioral orientation to cognitive orientation (Resnick, 1981), more and more educators recognize the importance of internal processing by a learner. McEwing and Roth (1985) remarked that "this feeling of being able to deal with an important new area of knowledge and of self-satisfaction enables the student to manipulate the learning environment effectively and cope with problems which arise in the learning process" (p. 30). Therefore, if an instruction can be tailored to meet the ability of a learner, the feeling of being capable of learning successfully may modify the learner's internal process such as motivation and how much effort is needed in learning.

However, before one understands the mental operations of a learner, it is difficult to tailor the instruction to match the internal processing of a learner. It is even more difficult to provide advisement to a learner in order to influence his or her mental activities. Studies on behavioral objectives have suggested that learning can be positively affected by a student's being aware of what needs to be learned. Tennyson suggests that advisement based on a continued evaluation of a learner's progress may influence his or her internal processing and thus improve learning. His studies (Tennyson and Buttrey, 1980; Tennyson, 1980, 1981; and Johansen and Tennyson, 1983) reveal that the advisement strategy has more significant effects than the no-advisement strategy on learning achievement.

Ross, in his review (1984), cited two studies examining whether the knowledge structure of a learner influences the learning results. In these studies, one group was given instruction adapted to the learners' background, and the other group was given instruction using examples from an unfamiliar field. The result showed that the instruction adapted to the learners' internal structure was more effective than its counterpart.

Merrill has categorized the control of internal learning activities into "conscious cognition" and "meta-cognition" (Merrill, 1980). The former refers to "the way a student processes the information presented by a given display"; and the latter refers to "the 'how to study' model which the student uses to guide his/her interaction with the instructional system being used" (pp. 89-90). In the TICCIT system, he built in two function keys: key "help" helps a learner process the instruction, and key "advice" gives the statistics of the learners' progress and suggests what to do.

Merrill believes that tailoring instruction to fit the internal processing of a learner is possible through a learner control system. He also believes that providing strategy training to learners can modify their internal processing and thus increase learning results. Several studies have been conducted to examine his beliefs; however, the results are vague and do not support his assumptions (Merrill, 1984). He explains that perhaps "the directions we used [in these studies] were inadequate to change a life-long habit" (p. 237). Nevertheless, examining the inconsistent results of Merrill's and Tennyson's studies suggests some moderator variables may exist between the external information and internal process. More theories and examinations are needed.

Traditional CAI as Individualized Instruction

Historically, the development of CAI is not initiated by a particular instructional problem; rather it is developed first, then educators try to find out what problems it can solve. That is why at its beginning stage, CAI was only used to make possible the automation of instruction (Gagne and Dick, 1983). More recently, computers have been used as a device to represent cognitive theories. This may be the result of a shifting of emphasis from the comparison of computer hardware with human beings to the comparison of various strategies embedded in computers.

Although thousands of CAI courseware programs are available on the market, the quality is doubtful. It seems doubtful also that most instructors and courseware designers clearly know what CAI can do to improve instruction.

Most educators distinguish CAI from CMI. For them, CAI and CMI are two different concepts, and also two different types of software. The former is used as instruction to teach something to students, while the latter is used as a tool to collect and calculate information about students. Though most CAI courseware does have a built-in management system, its managerial func-

tion is quite simple and limited. The management system only records the performance of learners, and makes its branching based on a singular response. The design of such a management system is only for the convenience of teachers rather than to assist students in managing their learning activities.

From the viewpoint of individualizing instruction, it is true that most existing CAI courseware programs are relatively "dumb." Without a sophisticated managerial function to provide sufficient information about the progress of a learner, most CAI programs are limited in their abilities to select appropriate types of information, to prescribe the amount of instruction, to reorganize the order of materials, and to advise the learner. This kind of CAI courseware is quite awkward in providing learners a specialization of instruction to meet their unique conditions.

Bergan and Dunn's discussion of individualized instruction defines at least two features, extensive instructional materials and managerial information. While traditional CAI is capable of varying instruction to a certain degree, it is not "intelligent" enough to appropriately tailor instruction to match the needs of individual learners, nor is traditional CAI capable of containing extensive information to allow the tailoring possible.

ICAI: The Future CAI as Individualized Instruction

According to Gable and Page (1980), the evolution of teaching programs consists of four stages. The lowest level of teaching programs consists of a series of sequenced "frames." Proceeding to the next frame requires understanding of the previous frame. The second level of teaching programs is represented by the form of "scrambled textbooks." A student responds to a question and, based on the response, the next instruction is chosen. The third level is called "adaptive." The branches in this level are based on the history of responses rather than on a single response. The so-called adaptive system is designed to "understand" learners and, therefore, to make a smart decision on selecting a next instruction. The fourth level is called "generative." Generative systems are designed to "understand" the material, and then provide information and problems in different forms. The instructional material is generated through an algorithm which consists of a sentence generating system and numerous rules of a subject knowledge.

Most of the current CAI courseware falls into the second stage. They are the computer version of the scrambled textbooks. However, following the improvement of computer technology and programming skills, especially the development of artificial intelligence, teaching programs are moving to the development of the third or even the fourth stage.

In other words, CAI courseware is moving from "dumb" to "intelligent," because it can understand the student as well as the material (through an adaptive strategy and artificial intelligence skills). "Intelligent" CAI (ICAI) is thus named to represent the new development.

Roberts and Park (1983) believe that "ICAI systems apply principles of artificial intelligence in the representation of domain knowledge, natural language dialogues, and methods of inference." (p. 7) The ICAI system so defined includes a knowledge base and an inquiring system, but it does not focus on the learner and thus may not be appropriate for education.

Suppes (1979) suggests seven basic features of an ICAI program from an educational viewpoint:

"1. . . . . [The ICAI] represents an application of information processing models in psychology.

2. The student has an internal model of any skill he is using to perform a task.

3. The analysis of errors made by the student leads to insight into the bugs in the student's internal model . . .

4. The representation of the diagnostic model of the student's behavior can best be done by use of procedural network.

5. It is important to make explicit a goal structure for the computer tutor and also a structure of strategies to be used by the tutor.

6. A theory of causal and teleological analysis is needed for adequate development of models of the student's procedures.

7. There is an essential need for programs that have specialists' knowledge of a given domain . . ." (pp. 299-301).

Suppes' explanation of ICAI features emphasizes psychological and instructional foundations and applications. It also refers to the understanding of both learners and materials, and therefore may be more appropriate for the educational practitioner.

How artificial intelligence will change the instructional format or functions is uncertain. We also know little about the degree that ICAI courseware can "understand" both materials and learners. Since the techniques of artificial intelligence are still developing, it is premature to dogmatically define the functions of ICAI. The term "intelligent" in ICAI should be treated as an adjective which describes the ability of an ICAI program rather than as a condition which separates ICAI from other CAI courseware.

Given the continual improvement of CAI from "dumb" to "intelligent," ICAI is not a concrete, static object. It represents a movement toward excellence in computerized instruction. Therefore, understanding why it is developed and what perspectives it possesses may explain what it will become.

Theoretical Bases

As far as theories are concerned, Tennyson and Merrill, respectively, propose the Two-Stage Cognition Learning Theory (Tennyson et al., 1984) and Component-Display Theory (Merrill, 1980, 1984) to suggest a way to individualize instruction. Based on cognitive psychology, Tennyson divides the learning process into two stages: "prototype formation" and "classification skill development." He explains that learning is "a range of cognitive processes proceeding from the acquisition of concrete (skill) knowledge through a transition phase of acquiring conceptual knowledge and skills to, finally, acquisition of the ability to generate new knowledge (productive thinking)" (p. 3). Because a learner usually begins with no or limited knowledge, expository information is needed to help the learner form a prototype of the concept or the rule. On the other hand, an interrogation method is helpful in developing classification skills. Only after the learner has established a prototype of the concepts is an interrogation of the concepts meaningful. Therefore, CAI courseware must be equipped with an adaptive system to coordinate the sequence, display time, and amount of instruction with the developmental stage of the learner.

Tennyson (Park and Tennyson, 1980) terms the branching technique in traditional CAI as a "response-insensitive" sequencing, since branching is based only on a single response, and the following instructional frame is predetermined. In contrast, "response-sensitive" sequencing is based on a psychological learning need. With the same response, different learners may be branched to different frames according to their individual cognitive stages. Response-sensitive sequencing uses on-task information to dynamically modify instruction. A sophisticated adaptive system which Tennyson calls an "intelligent" system is being developed and tested at the University of Minnesota.

However, whereas Tennyson has developed an intelligent system, Merrill emphasizes an adaptive model based on learner control. His theoretical base, known as Component-Display Theory, identifies four types of cognitive subject matter: "facts," "concepts," "procedures," and "principles" (Merrill, 1980, p. 87). Except for facts, each of these content types can be represented either by "instances" or "generalities." These two representations can be presented to students in two different modes—expository (telling) and inquisitory (asking). Combining the two representations with the two modes defines four different forms of screen display: "telling an instance," "telling a generality," "asking an instance," and "asking a generality" (pp. 87-88).

The four different forms of display information serve different developmental stages of a learner. Individualized instruction is instruction using a learner-controlled system to properly match these forms of information to the cognitive stage of a learner.

While these two theories assert that presenting appropriate instructional materials to a learner may assure the mastery of a lesson, Ackoff (1972) notes that:

> ...teaching is not necessary for learning and hence cannot be its cause. It is equally clear that teaching is not sufficient for learning.... This is not to say that teaching and learning are unrelated; but it does say the essential property of their interaction is missed by designers of instructional systems (p. 128-29).

Ackoff's remark on the interaction between teaching and learning emphasizes the importance of active inquiring in the instructional procedure. The same emphasis can be found in Piaget's instructional theories, holding that a child should actively participate the construction of intelligence.

In educational practice, no matter how detailed the instruction, students still have questions or difficulties during the learning process. If the questions or difficulties remain unsolved, students may be unable or unwilling to engage in the effective learning of new instruction. This may explain the necessity of instructional development going beyond sequenced instruction to adaptive and generative systems.

Two problems of adaptive systems are that: (1) these systems do not allow a learner to ask non-predefined questions; and (2) even knowing what kind of instruction a learner needs, adaptive systems fail to "generate" such kind of materials. The adaptive system in CAI can only "ask" questions and "evaluate" answers (literally compare a student's response with the preset answer); it can neither "understand" nor "answer" students' questions. In other words, the adaptive system "selects" the material built into the instructional sets, but it does not "generate" it.

The development of generative systems, as proposed by Gable and Page (1980), is designed to complement "adaptive" systems. Theoretically, allowing students to interact with an instructional system and generating tailored materials to individuals, generative systems may greatly improve

learning effects and therefore move us closer to the dream of individualized instruction.

Proposed Features of ICAI

ICAI represents an improvement in traditional CAI toward the realization of individualized instruction. The difference between traditional and intelligent CAI is that ICAI is equipped with adaptive and generative functions in order to improve learning effects.

We also need to keep in mind that ICAI is not an assurance of fulfilling individualized instruction. It does move us closer to individualized instruction than any other media-based system. Historically, individualized instruction has only been accomplished by that instruction which involves more or less the intervention of live teachers. No other medium alone has been "intelligent" enough to match and generate the instruction to the needs of learners. The intervention of live teachers is featured with interactions between the instructional system and the learner. It is due to interaction that collecting and evaluating information from learners is possible. It is also due to interaction that a system can provide suggestions or answer questions to students in order to modify their internal processes.

Thanks to the improvements in computer technology, the design of CAI courseware has now advanced to adaptive and generative systems. Information nets based on knowledge rules and natural language inquiry systems are all possible in computer courseware. The recent development of ICAI systems, such as SOPHIE and GUIDON, are just some remarkable examples. While the ability of ICAI is closer to those of highly skilled teachers, the potential of ICAI still remains to be explored in depth.

ICAI programs are not yet practically applied to general instruction settings. However, based on the needs of instructional theories, the perspectives of ICAI programs have been widely discussed. Roberts and Park (1983) point out that there are three main components of any instructional system: "the content to be taught, the inherent teaching or instructional strategy, and a mechanism for understanding what the student does and does not know." Therefore, they believe that an ICAI system should, ideally, have three components or modules: "expertise module, student module, and tutoring module." (pp. 7-8)

1. **Expert module:** The expertise module includes not only the subject content to be taught but also the "procedural knowledge" leading to solve related problems. In other words, this module refers to a knowledge base which consists of the knowledge struc-

ture as well as the static facts. The knowledge base is essential not only because its huge data collection allows a learner to select instructional materials according to his or her interests, abilities, and needs, but also its information structure makes learning, diagnosing, and material generating possible.

2. **Student module:** In nature, this module is a sophisticated management system which not only records the progress of a learner, but also recognizes the knowledge pattern of the student's understanding or misunderstanding. This module is the basis of adaptation or individualization of an ICAI courseware.

3. **Tutoring module:** The tutoring module determines how the instructional materials should be selected, generated, organized, and/or presented. The choice of tutoring method is mainly based on information from the previous two modules. A very important perspective of ICAI systems is that the dialogue of the instructional program and the student is not one-way but rather a two-way communication. The dialogue can be initiated by either side. Ideally, the student can use a natural language to query the instructional system and then receive a proper response from it. This feature is expected to greatly change the learning style and internal processing skills of a learner.

Future Studies and Conclusions

While instructional psychology has shifted to cognitive psychology, traditional CAI courseware cannot satisfy aggressive educators anymore. The successful application of artificial intelligence in the business and industrial world has also encouraged the exploration of Intelligent CAI. To date, instructional technologists as well as instructional designers are eagerly discussing the coming of ICAI. However, most of them only pay attention to technologies which make ICAI a possibility, but ignore questions such as "What is the theoretical base of ICAI?"; "What strategies make ICAI effective?"; and "How will various aptitudes, previous knowledge, and subject topics influence the effects of strategies?"

In the future, we need more theories to explore how ICAI can be designed to carry out individualized instruction. One of the most significant weaknesses of past CAI studies is the lack of theoretical bases. Without a well constructed theory, CAI studies can only be randomly, blindly conducted and their contribution to instruction is therefore

trivial. In fact, while there are thousands of studies comparing CAI effects with those of other instruction, we do not know much about why and how CAI courseware is effective, except the superficial impression of CAI's superiority. A well constructed theory not only provides directions to experimental studies, but also generalizes research findings to other situations.

After the theoretical bases are proposed, we need to examine the effects of proposed strategies on ICAI. Particular emphasis needs to be put on examining the effects of different types of learners as well as various difficulties of subject topics. In promoting individualized instruction, we just cannot ignore the differences between learners and also instructional materials. The existing studies have partially examined the effects of several adaptive strategies of CAI design in general. However, the studies of interactions between treatment and differences of subjects and learners are limited.

Finally, and most important, any study on CAI should be directed to prescriptions of instructional design. That is to say, after conducting the experimental studies, we need to generalize these findings into practical applications. Too many studies have given descriptions of instructional strategies, but, in application, how to determine the appropriate strategy in a situation is unknown or uncertain. Designing ICAI courseware based on individual differences may result in systems that are too complex to be practical. Therefore, the balance between validity and practice needs to be carefully considered and examined.

Clark and Salomon (1985) point out that "no medium enhances learning more than any other medium regardless of learning task, learner traits, symbolic elements, curriculum content, or setting" (p. 474). What makes CAI or any media-based instruction effective is the embedded strategies which may be inefficient or difficult to accomplish in other ways. Until now, only live teachers have had the ability to *understand* learners and materials, and be able to *fully* carry out individualized instruction. Ideally, ICAI may also have the potential to individualize instruction. However, this does not mean that ICAI is superior to a teacher. The consideration of applying ICAI in education is based on economic and efficiency reasons. At the best, in the future, having ICAI courseware may in certain instances be less expensive and more practical than having a good teacher. □

References and Suggested Readings

Ackoff, R.L. Computer and Education. A paper presented at the conference on *Man and Computer*, 1972.

Belland, J.C., Taylor, W.D., Canelos, J., Dwyer, F., and Baker, P. Is the Self-Paced Instructional Program, Via Microcomputer-Based Instruction, the Most Effective Method of Addressing Individual Learning Difference? *Educational Communications and Technology Journal*, 1985, *33*(3), 185-198.

Bergan, J.R., and Dunn, J.A. *Psychology and Education*, New York: John Wiley & Sons, Inc., 1976.

Clark, R.E., and Salomon, G. Media in Teaching. In M.C. Wittrock (Ed.), *Handbook of Research on Teaching*, No. 3. New York: Macmillan, 1985.

Cohen, V.B. A Reexamination of Feedback in Computer-Based Instruction: Implications for Instructional Design. *Educational Technology*, 1985, *25*(1), 33-37.

Gable, A., and Page, C.V. The Use of Artificial Intelligence Techniques in Computer-Assisted Instruction: An Overview. In D.F. Walker and R.D. Hess (Eds.), *Instructional Software*. Belmont, CA: Wadsworth, 1980, 257-268.

Gagne, R.M., and Dick, W. Instructional Psychology. *Annual Review of Psychology*, 1982, *34*, 261-95.

Gay, G. Interaction of Learner Control and Prior Conceptual Understanding in Computer-Assisted Video Instruction. A paper presented at the American Educational Research Association annual meeting, 1985.

Gaynor, P. The Effects of Feedback Delay on Retention of Computer-Based Mathematical Material. *Journal of Computer-Based Instruction*, 1981, *8*(2), 28-34.

Johansen, K.J., and Tennyson, R.D. Effect of Adaptive Advisement on Perception in Learner Controlled, Computer-Based Instruction Using a Rule-Learning Task. *Educational Communications and Technology Journal*, 1983, *31*(4), 226-36.

Jonassen, D.H. Interactive Lesson Designs: A Taxonomy. *Educational Technology*, 1985, *25*(6), 7-17.

Kolers, P.A., Duchnicky, R.L., and Ferguson, D.C. Eye Movement Measurement of Readability of CRT Displays. *Human Factors*, 1981, *23*(5), 517-27.

McEwing, R.A., and Roth, G.L. Individualizing Learning with Computer-Based Instruction. *Educational Technology*, 1985, *25*(5), 30-32.

Merrill, M.D. Learner Control in Computer-Based Learning. *Computers & Education*, 1980, *4*, 77-95.

Merrill, M.D. What Is Learner Control. In R.K. Bass and C.R. Dills (Ed.), *Instructional Development: The State of Art, II*. Dubugue, IA: Kendall/Hunt, 1984.

Page, E.B. Teacher Comments and Student Performance: A Seventy-four Classroom Experiment in School Motivation. *Journal of Educational Psychology*, 1958, *49*, 173-81.

Park, O., and Tennyson, R.D. Adaptive Design Strategies for Selecting Numbers and Presentation Order of Examples in Coordinate Concept Acquisition. *Journal of Educational Psychology*, 1980, *72*, 362-70.

Reiser, R.A. Reducing Student Procrastination in a Personalized System of Instruction Course. *Educational Communications and Technology Journal*, 1984, *32*(1), 41-49.

Resnick, L.B. Instructional Psychology. *Annual Review of Psychology*, 1981, *32*, 659-704.

Roberts, F.C., and Park, O. Intelligent Computer-Assisted Instruction: An Explanation and Overview. *Educational Technology*, 1983, *23*(12), 7-12.

Ross, S.M. Matching the Lesson to the Student: Alternative Adaptive Designs for Individualized Learning Systems. *Journal of Computer-Based Instruction*, 1984, *11*(2), 42-48.

Suppes, P. Observations About the Application of Artificial Intelligence Research to Education. In D.F. Walker and R.D. Hess (Eds.), *Instructional Software*. Belmont, CA: Wadsworth, 1979, 298-308.

Tennyson, R.D. Instructional Control Strategies and Content Structure as Design Variables in Concept Acquisition Using Computer-Based Instruction. *Journal of Educational Psychology*, 1980, *72*(4), 525-32.

Tennyson, R.D. Use of Adaptive Information for Advisement in Learning Concepts and Rules Using Computer-Assisted Instruction. *American Educational Research Journal*, 1981, *18*(4), 425-38.

Tennyson, R.D., and Buttrey, T. Advisement and Management Strategies as Design Variables in Computer-Assisted Instruction. *Educational Communications and Technology Journal*, 1980, *28*, 169-176.

Tennyson, R.D., Christensen, D.L., and Park, S.I. The Minnesota Adaptive Instructional System: An Intelligent CBI System. *Journal of Computer-Based Instruction*, 1984, *11*(1), 2-13.

The author would especially like to thank Richard E. Clark, who gave generously of his time to review early drafts of this paper and gave extremely helpful suggestions.

A Critical Analysis of Research on Intelligent Tutoring Systems

Ronni Rosenberg

Introduction

This article is a critique of intelligent tutoring systems (ITSs), the latest generation of computerized educational systems, which attempt to mimic the capabilities of human tutors. ITS researchers try to do this by incorporating more advanced functions than earlier systems: the ability to meaningfully analyze each student's responses (not just determine whether they are correct by matching pre-defined answers) and the ability to interact with the student—give advice when a mistake is made and answer students' questions.

This is in contrast to other computer-based "educational" systems, in which the computer presents to the student a series of pre-defined problems to be solved, and the sequence of problems may be chosen based on the correctness of the student's previous responses. Such systems have been around for at least two decades. Most have been judged unacceptable by teachers.[1]

Work on ITSs is recent (primarily in the 1980s) and still in the research stage.[2] My review of the work is selective and based on readings in both the computing literature and the education literature. The combination of perspectives is unusual; despite the obvious connection between ITSs and education, most ITS papers I have read reference little work in education.

My readings convinced me that ITS work is characterized by two major methodological flaws. First, ITSs are not well grounded in a model of learning; they seem more motivated by available technology than by educational needs. Many of the systems sidestep altogether the critical problem of modeling the tutoring process, and the ones that do try to shed light on cognitive theories of learning do not provide convincing evidence for their theories. What almost all the systems *do* model, implicitly, is a single learning scheme that is hierarchical, top-down, goal-driven, and sequential. Most of the researchers appear to take for granted

Ronni Rosenberg is with the Laboratory for Computer Science, Massachusetts Institute of Technology, Cambridge, Massachusetts.

that this is the best (if not the only) style of learning, a point that is disputed by educational and social science researchers.

Second, positive claims for ITSs are based on testing that typically is poorly controlled, incompletely reported, inconclusive, and in some cases totally lacking.

Despite inadequate models and questionable test results, the literature is full of highly favorable conclusions about computer-aided instructional systems of all kinds.

Models

A computer-based educational system based on a compelling underlying model of tutoring and learning could be considered a genuine contribution to both education and Artificial Intelligence (AI, the academic home of much ITS work). Such models are hard to come by. ITS implementors are confronted with a paucity of pedagogical theory about tutoring. There is little consensus among educators—the experts—as to the best educational techniques.

This might mean that education is a bad domain for an *expert system*—a computer system that tries to replicate a human expert skill (such as tutoring). Nevertheless, ITSs are being implemented. Specific problem areas are discussed below.

Protocol analysis is a necessary prerequisite to modeling tutoring. Protocol analysis in the context of ITSs means collecting data about actual tutoring situations—with human students and tutors—and analyzing the data for patterns that might form a cohesive model of tutoring. There are well established social-science methods for collecting such data, both quantitative (e.g., tests and surveys) and qualitative (e.g., interviews and ethnographic studies).

ITS implementors use primarily quantitative methods. In an area such as tutoring, this is probably a mistake. Subtle personal relationships play a large role in learning; for instance, we all had a favorite teacher for whom we worked harder and learned "better." Such subtleties are apt to be lost without sensitive qualitative data gathering.

Doing protocol analysis for an ITS should include spending a lot of time with the experts—teachers and students. No compelling model of tutoring high school algebra, for instance, is likely to be developed without spending a lot of time observing high school algebra classes and talking to students and teachers. Such qualitative data collection and analysis is time-consuming and difficult, and few computer scientists have experience doing it.

Some ITS implementors do very little protocol analysis at all. One researcher wrote that his two systems were based on a "rich source of information," but this information turns out to be analyses of only three to four students.[3] Another researcher analyzed 12 students[4]—would a classroom teacher consider this sufficient? Papers about some systems mention no protocol analysis whatsoever; the researchers either did none or did not feel it was important enough to include in a published description of their work.

Two projects did emphasize protocol analysis.[5] In both, the researchers attempted to enumerate conceptual errors in tutoring sessions and develop a unifying underlying model for the subject domain. Unlike the other projects, these two concentrated on protocol analysis to the exclusion of system design and implementation, believing (correctly, I think) that much basic work is needed in data gathering and model formulation before it is appropriate to think about computerization. The models that these researchers worked on are at a very high level of abstraction. Much more work is needed before models are developed at a low enough level of detail to determine whether they can or should be implemented on a computer.

Without adequate protocol analysis, ITS development often proceeds by trial and error: generate a version of the system, test it, modify the system on the basis of the test results, and test it again. The later section on "Testing ITSs" gives some detail about the inadequacy of the testing. One researcher published a paper about a system whose development apparently included only one round of generating and testing, then speculated about the *likely* test results if certain proposed improvements to the system were made.[6]

An exhaustive enumeration of error types is not a model. Without a unifying model of tutoring, several systems instead are based on collections of types of errors made by students learning a particular skill. For instance, a program for tutoring in subtraction enumerates 110 primitive bugs and 58 subskills grouped into a complex skill lattice,[7] and a program for tutoring LISP programming enumerates 325 rules and 475 "buggy" rules.[8]

Analysis of correct and incorrect rules for learning a skill might be a useful component of an ITS project, but lists of error types are only part of the raw data for a model of tutoring. Unanalyzed listings do not illuminate the tutoring process. Moreover, the need to enumerate all error types limits existing ITSs to relatively simple domains (categorized as being "relatively sparse in their importation of extra-domain knowledge.")[9]

A different and, I believe, more promising line of work is exemplified by Matz.[10] Instead of listing all error types for the domain (high school algebra), she examines data from student prob-

lems and proposes a high-level, conceptual system that accounts for or elicits the errors (as well as the correct answers). Her work is singular in its emphasis on protocol analysis and its generation of a cohesive model based on data about student learning. Matz did notable groundwork in data gathering and analysis and in model building, rather than plunging into an implementation.

A data representation is not a model. Representation of domain knowledge is a major emphasis of ITS work. One researcher considers representation to be as important as modeling the student and teacher;[11] i.e., he considers the *technology* of ITSs to be as important as their *content*.

Data representation is an essential aspect of computer technology but not of tutoring. In most cases, a particular representation is chosen to address a technical problem, not a tutoring issue. But if tutoring is of primary importance, data representation ought to follow from models of tutoring. Thus, another system uses a representation that was *ad hoc* by design, to allow the data obtained from tutoring sessions to shape the developing representation, rather than biasing interpretation of the data from the start with a particular representation chosen for reasons unrelated to the domain.[12]

It may be appropriate to impose a particular representation if there is reason to believe it has a theoretical (cognitive) basis. However, most of the researchers do not suggest that their representations have any such basis. In one case where the cognitive basis for a representation is emphasized, the author gives no justification for why that representation (called production rules) is used: "It is an interesting question what the evidence is for production systems. The hypothesis of a production system is too abstract to be put to direct empirical test." Production rules are a good idea, he says, because many other ITSs use them.[13] However, since there is usually little analysis of the limitations of different data representations when applied to actual tutoring situations, problems can be perpetuated easily from one system to another.[14]

An implementation is not a model. Some important design decisions are made entirely on the basis of technical considerations such as machine efficiency, with no regard to how the decisions might affect tutoring. For instance, the DEBUGGY system uses a "full-problem evidence" scheme for determining the subset of known bugs that will become the initial hypothesis set (bugs are selected which explain all wrong answers of at least one student), not because the scheme has a basis in classroom experience or cognitive theory, but because it is efficient to run on a computer.[15]

The LISP tutor uses menus from which the student can select answers to the tutor's questions, not because menus are best for tutoring situations, but because the alternative of allowing natural-language input and requiring the system to parse that input would be too hard to implement.[16] Although the designer of the LISP tutor says that his system is based on a general theory of cognition (his own theory), his decision to use menus of pre-determined answers was not based on any such theory. The same person writes elsewhere that the relative effectiveness of menus is not at all clear.[17]

Such implementation considerations are likely to affect the tutoring process in unanticipated ways, some of which may also be undesirable. Pressure for early implementation is inherent in computing—an experimental field—but it may not best serve educators' interests: "Most [instructional technologists] only pay attention to technologies which make ICAI [Intelligent Computer-Aided Instruction] a possibility, but ignore questions such as 'What is the theoretical base of ICAI?' "[18]

Overall, there is little evidence that the views of learning embodied in ITSs are based on anything but their implementors' intuitions. There is no supporting evidence from classroom teachers or students about how well their own tutoring experiences validate the ITSs. No attempt appears to have been made to verify the systems with the real experts—the teachers and students. There are few references to work on cognitive psychology or education, which might provide some substantive reason for favoring one system's view of learning over another's. (There are noticeably more such references in the two papers about models of learning that have *not* yet been implemented.) The result is a collection of competing intuitions that are impossible to judge substantively.

One survey of computer-based instruction (CBI) concludes: "it should be clear that CBI rests upon a broad foundation of research even though it frequently appears to be almost totally atheoretical . . . ."[19] I believe it "frequently appears to be almost totally atheoretical" because it frequently *is* atheoretical. I am concerned that ITSs are continuing the tradition of poor pedagogy in so-called educational software, most of which has been criticized by educators because it "does not represent sound educational practice"[20] and appears to be designed by people who know little about the classrooms in which the software will be used.

Moreover, the single-minded emphasis on technology in ITS work neglects other factors that every teacher knows are essential to good tutoring. While it is not clear that human tutors formulate exhaustive lists of errors (though they certainly are aware of frequent error types), it *is* clear that they take into account many factors other than errors. Teachers know, for instance, that successful tutoring sometimes has as much to do with human interaction—setting an example as a role model, or fulfilling a child's need for attention and caring—as with correcting errors. Computer systems can address only part of education and its problems. Our own experience teaches us the importance of nontechnical, nonquantitative factors, such as relationships between teachers and students. But are these other factors computable?

Styles of Learning

Although existing ITSs are only beginning to address explicitly the very hard issue of modeling the tutoring process, they are nonetheless modeling implicitly one aspect of tutoring, in one particular way. Almost all the systems I have reviewed enforce one standardized style of learning, described as hierarchical, structured, sequential, top down, and goal oriented. Although one author states that the optimal style of interaction may vary widely across individuals, in his system, the top-down, left-to-right solution is preferred, and students are exhorted to adhere to a hierarchical refinement process.[21] The LISP tutor's "ideal" is hierarchical, structured, and top down, and its goals have a hierarchical representation.[22] Summarizing work on ITSs, a recent article states: "CAI courseware is extolled for providing the function of personal attention. However, the feedback and reinforcement in most CAI courseware is uniform to all learners."[23]

Contrary to the researchers' implicit assumption that there is only one correct or best style of learning, research outside of computer science indicates that there are multiple successful styles. For instance, Sherry Turkle's recent study of children using computers reveals that even in a domain like computer programming, often thought to impose a particular, rigid style, there are multiple styles of learning. She describes two broad *styles of mastery*, hard and soft. Hard mastery emphasizes premeditated control, structure, goals, and control; soft mastery emphasizes interaction, relationships, and accommodation. Turkle's own experience with protocol analysis and other forms of data gathering and analysis (both quantitative and qualitative) is extensive, and her study is much more thorough than any protocol analysis reported for an ITS. She also incorporates related findings from anthropology and psychology.[24]

One system that I reviewed does emphasize multiple perspectives for learning. Two different learning viewpoints are implemented: (1) the *scriptal view* is hierarchical and sequential, and it emphasizes unrelated facts, and (2) the *functional view* is non-linear and interactive, and it emphasizes relationships and underlying causes of things. The scriptal view corresponds to the single view enforced by all the other systems. When the researchers found it insufficient to explain many of the exchanges in their sample tutorial dialogues, they concluded that additional viewpoints would be useful. Indeed, the two viewpoints *together* account for little more than half the exchanges in a sample tutorial dialogue![25]

Explicit recognition of multiple perspectives in tutoring is supported not only by evidence such as that cited above of multiple learning styles, but also by what every teacher knows—different ways of explaining things are needed to reach different students and to teach different types of knowledge. Systems that enforce learning in a single style are sure to leave behind students who naturally have a different style. It is ironic that computer systems, which have been touted as offering almost unlimited flexibility, are being applied to education in ways that force students into a single learning mold:

> Yes, computers have practically infinite branching capabilities, but this matters little when we are unable to foresee more than a very few of the most common possible learner responses. Restricted to narrow ranges of preordained alternatives, the learner is constrained to answer in the program's terms.[26]

"In most AI systems," one reviewer points out, "it is enough to be able to find *one* way to solve a problem."[27] In tutoring, one way is not enough.

Testing ITSs

Another major methodological flaw in ITSs is the testing. In most of the literature that I have read (and all the literature by computer scientists), test results are used to support claims that computerized educational systems reduce learning time, improve student attitudes toward subject matter, and enable students to learn better or at least as well as conventional tutoring techniques. (The most positive claims are made for *adjunct* CAI, in which the computer is used in conjunction with a human teacher.) A closer review of the data—including studies in the education literature—reveals startling flaws in the testing.

Most conclusions about ITS projects are drawn from an *inadequate* amount of test data—too few tests and too few subjects. Papers about a LISP tutor, a geometry tutor, and the LMS system for basic algebra each mention only one evaluation. The test of the geometry tutor involves only three students; the test of the LMS system, only six. A paper about a programming tutor concludes that "it appears to provide a cogent analysis of simple programming, and a coherent framework for extending the analysis to more complex programming," but the author does not report *any* testing.[28]

In some cases, conclusions are drawn from only *informal* testing. In evaluating three students using the geometry tutor, the authors state: "We think they learned faster than with traditional instruction, but we have no way to document this belief."[29]

In still other cases, positive conclusions are drawn from *inconclusive* data. One paper that proposes a theory of tutorial interactions describes only one "representative" tutorial dialogue, in which fully 44% of the exchanges are not accounted for by the theory.[30] The paper about the LMS system describes one test with 6 students, in which 56% of the errors are diagnosed incorrectly by the system. The author proposes additional rules that he claims would enable the system to correctly diagnose a total of 70% of the errors, but this hypothesis is not tested. He suggests that all but one of the remaining errors should be classified as "executive/random" errors and ignored! His conclusion is that his system would diagnose all but one of the errors.[31]

Many of the most positive claims about computer-aided instruction (CAI) are made in the education literature. For instance, I reviewed two "meta-analyses" of studies on the effectiveness of CAI.[32] One paper reviews 59 studies; the other, 51 studies; and both have the same first author. Neither paper considers whether these independent studies can be compared validly. Both conclude that CAI results in better examination scores, lower withdrawal rates, a preference among students for subjects taught with CAI, and faster learning. Typically, results are reported as follows:

> In one paper, 54 of the 59 studies collected statistically significant data on exam performance. Of these 54, 13 favored CAI and one favored conventional instruction. The conclusion is that CAI improves exam performance.

Here is another way to present the same data:

> Of the 59 studies, 22% favored CAI, 2% favored conventional instruction, and 76% favored neither or were not statistically significant. The conclusion is that nothing is demonstrated about the effect of CAI on exam performance.

Here is more data on which the papers' conclusions are based:

- Exam performance: In the second paper, 48% favored CAI, 4% favored conventional instruction, and 76% favored neither.
- Withdrawal rates (reported on in only one paper): 3% favored CAI, 2% favored conventional instruction, and 95% favored neither or were not statistically significant.
- Students' attitudes toward subject matter: In one paper, 3% favored subjects taught with CAI, and 97% favored neither or were not statistically significant. In the other paper, 20% favored CAI, and 80% favored neither.
- Instructional time: In one paper, data in this category was collected in 2 studies out of 51, both of which favored CAI. In the other paper, data was collected in 8 studies out of 59, all of which favored CAI.

One paper notes that the choice of teacher affects the results: When the same teacher is used for both CAI instruction and conventional instruction, test results are more favorable toward CAI. Nevertheless, the authors make strong claims about the positive effects of CAI instruction alone.

Thus, it is an understatement when one survey of computers in education notes a "lack of rigor and specificity of primary research studies."[33] Another survey concludes that testing is categorized by inadequate experimental design, non-random subject assignment, unjustified assumption that different groups get identical instruction, experimenter bias, overly short tests, and questionable analysis techniques; in short, that there are few valid evaluations: "Thus, it has recently been stated that there is no scientifically conclusive evidence that CAI is instructionally effective."[34] (This report goes on to say that the same lack of conclusive evidence is also found in most educational evaluations of non-computer-based methods.)

Both meta-analyses of studies of CAI effectiveness state that other "instructional technologies"—for example, peer tutoring—are *more* effective than CAI.[35] These other methods, which are likely to hold useful clues to successful tutoring, do not appear to be investigated by ITS designers.

Conclusions

The state of the art in ITSs is characterized by two major methodological flaws:

1. The systems are not grounded in a substantiated model of learning. Model formulation should be preceded by protocol analysis, but very little analysis is done, almost none of it qualitative. ITS models should be validated by the teachers and students who will use the systems, but ITS researchers do not appear to consult these experts.
2. Testing is incomplete, inconclusive, and in some cases totally lacking. Data on computerized tutorials is, at best, mixed.[36] The almost universally positive claims for ITSs and other computerized instructional systems—most notably in the education literature—are based on results from severely flawed tests.

It is thus difficult to know how to choose among the different problem-solving schemes proposed for different ITSs. For instance, Matz's and Sleeman's work on tutoring algebra propose different techniques. Sleeman refers to Matz's earlier work but gives no indication of why he proposes a new technique rather than building on hers. Working in another domain, Goldstein and Burton propose two entirely different problem-solving components. All the different schemes claim to have certain intuitive aspects, but none is grounded or tested well enough to be compelling. The reader is left to choose among competing sets of researchers' intuitions.

Despite these problems, many workers in computer-assisted educational systems and many educators are extremely optimistic, predicting imminent revolutionary changes in education because of these systems. A 1980 survey of CAI predicts that cost-effective computer learning is right around the corner.[37] A 1983 survey concludes that "many of the research efforts discussed in this article will undoubtedly influence educational practice in profound ways" (but it states elsewhere that "despite the promise of ICAI, none of these projects have had any real impact on educational practice.")[38] Miller, an ITS researcher, predicts that "the manner in which knowledge is disseminated, in every field from computer programming to English composition, will be radically transformed."[39] Radical transformation is unlikely to occur without acceptance by educators, and such acceptance is not merited: The same year as Miller's paper was published, a study of more than 4,000 CAI systems revealed that 96-97% were judged unacceptable by faculty in the fields concerned.[40]

Whatever is the potential value of ITSs, work done to date does not justify the positive claims that have been made about either its scientific value or the transformation of education that might result from it. A survey of 20 years of computer-based projects concludes that progress has been made in technicalities, not in education:

Twenty years ago, essentially the same set of issues about instructional computing were being discussed. In fact, we have most of the original problems still with us plus many more which have since emerged. However, the level of discussion today is much more technically sophisticated.[41]

ITS work is in its infancy. Based on the papers I have read about ITSs and on both classroom observation and teacher interviews I have conducted about educational software, I suggest that ITSs would benefit from:

- more time spent with teachers and students in actual tutoring situations, before additional systems are implemented;
- better testing and analysis of test results, before more papers are published with unjustified, misleading conclusions; and
- some modesty about the limited role of technology in education, before additional predictions are made of imminent educational "revolutions."

Finally, ITS researchers might keep in mind the following conclusion of the above-mentioned survey of educational technologies: "the potential benefits of CBI . . . all hinge upon the dedication, persistence, and ability of good teachers and courseware developers."[42] Of course, if there were enough dedicated, persistent, able teachers and course developers, and a social commitment to support them, would anyone be interested in ITSs? □

References

Anderson, J.R., and Reiser, B.J. The LISP Tutor. *Byte*, April 1985, 159-175.

Anderson, J.R. *et al.* Cognitive Principles in the Design of Computer Tutors. Carnegie-Mellon University Report, Computer-Aided Tutoring Project.

Atkinson, M.L. Computer-Assisted Instruction: Current State of the Art. *Computers in the Schools*, Spring 1984, *1*(1), 91-99.

Burton, R.R. Diagnosing Bugs in a Simple Procedural Skill. Chapter 8 in Sleeman and Brown.

Chambers, J.A., and Sprecher, J.W. Computer Assisted Instruction: Current Trends and Critical Issues. *Communications of the ACM*, June 1980, *23*(6), 332-342.

Dudley-Marling, C., and Owston, R.D. The State of Educational Software: A Criterion-Based Evaluation. *Educational Technology*, March 1987, *27*(3), 25-29.

Feurzeig, W. *et al.* Microcomputers in Education. Bolt, Beranek and Newman, Inc., October 1981.

Goldstein, L.P. The Genetic Graph: A Representation for the Evolution of Procedural Knowledge. Chapter 3 in Sleeman and Brown.

Keasley, G., Hunter, B., and Seidel, R.J. Two Decades of Computer Based Instruction Projects: What Have We Learned? *T.H.E. Journal*, Part one, January 1983, 90-94 and February 1983, 88-96.

Kulik, J.A., Bangert, R.L., and Williams, G.W. Effects of Computer-Based Teaching on Secondary School Students. *Journal of Educational Psychology*, 1983, *75*(1), 19-26.

Kulik, J.A., Kulik, C.C., and Cohen, P.A. Effectiveness of Computer-based College Training: A Meta-analysis of Findings. *Review of Educational Research*, Winter 1980, *50*(4), 525-544.

Matz, M. Towards a Process Model for High School Algebra Errors. Chapter 2 in Sleeman and Brown.

Miller, M.L. A Structured Planning and Debugging Environment for Elementary Programming. Chapter 6 in Sleeman and Brown.

Niemiec, R., and Walberg, H.J. Comparative Effects of Computer-Assisted Instruction: A Synthesis of Reviews. *Journal of Educational Computing Research*, 1987, *3*(1), 19-35.

Sleeman, D. Assessing Aspects of Competence in Basic Algebra. Chapter 9 in Sleeman and Brown.

Sleeman, D., and Brown, J.S. (Eds.) *Intelligent Tutoring Systems.* Orlando: Academic Press, 1982.

Stefik, M. Review of Sleeman and Brown, *Intelligent Tutoring Systems. Artificial Intelligence*, 1985, 238-245.

Stevens, A., Collins, A., and Goldin, S.E. Misconceptions in Students' Understanding. Chapter 1 in Sleeman and Brown.

Turkle, S. *The Second Self: Computers and the Human Spirit.* New York: Simon & Schuster, 1984.

Yang, J.-S. Individualizing Instruction Through Intelligent Computer-Assisted Instruction: A Perspective. *Educational Technology*, March 1987, *27*(3), 7-15.

Notes

1. J.A. Chambers and J.W. Sprecher. Computer Assisted Instruction: Current Trends and Critical Issues. *Communications of the ACM*, June 1980, *23*(6), p. 338.

2. D. Sleeman and J.S. Brown (Eds.) *Intelligent Tutoring Systems.* Orlando: Academic Press, 1982.

3. J.R. Anderson *et al.* Cognitive Principles in the Design of Computer Tutors. Carnegie-Mellon University Report, Computer-Aided Tutoring Project, p. 4.

4. M.L. Miller. A Structured Planning and Debugging Environment for Elementary Programming. Chapter 6 in Sleeman and Brown, p. 124.

5. A. Stevens, A. Collins, and S.E. Goldin. Misconceptions in Students' Understanding. Chapter 1 in Sleeman and Brown. M. Matz. Towards a Process Model for High School Algebra Errors. Chapter 2 in Sleeman and Brown.

6. D. Sleeman. Assessing Aspects of Competence in Basic Algebra. Chapter 9 in Sleeman and Brown.

7. R.R. Burton. Diagnosing Bugs in a Simple Procedural Skill. Chapter 8 in Sleeman and Brown, p. 162.

8. J. R. Anderson and B.J. Reiser. The LISP Tutor. *Byte*, April 1985, p. 162.

9. Anderson *et al.*, p. 4.

10. Matz, Towards a Process Model for High School Algebra Errors.

11. L.P. Goldstein. The Genetic Graph: A Representation for the Evolution of Procedural Knowledge. Chapter 3 in Sleeman and Brown.

12. Burton, p. 159.

13. Anderson, *et al.*, p. 8.

14. M. Stefik. Review of Sleeman and Brown, *Intelligent Tutoring Systems*, in *Artificial Intelligence*, 1985, (26), p. 241.

15. Burton, p. 167.

16. Anderson and Reiser, p. 162.

17. Anderson, *et al.*, p. 29.

18. J.S. Yang. Individualizing Instruction Through Intelligent Computer-Assisted Instruction: A Perspective. *Educational Technology*, March 1987, *27*(3), p. 14.

19. G. Keasley, B. Hunter, and R.J. Seidel. Two Decades of Computer Based Instruction Projects: What Have We Learned? *T.H.E. Journal*, February 1983, p. 96.

20. C. Dudley-Marling and R.D. Owston. The State of Educational Software: A Criterion-Based Evaluation. *Educational Technology*, March 1987, *27*(3), p. 25, p. 28.

21. Miller, p. 127.

22. Anderson and Reiser, p. 10.

23. Yang, p. 10.

24. S. Turkle. *The Second Self: Computers and the Human Spirit*. New York: Simon & Schuster, 1984.

25. Stevens, Collins, and Goldin.

26. Stefik, p. 244. Quoting A.G. Oettinger, *Run, Computer, Run: The Mythology of Educational Innovation*. Cambridge, MA: Harvard University Press, 1969, p. 180.

27. *Ibid.*, p. 238.

28. Miller, p. 133.

29. Anderson, *et al.*, p. 24.

30. Stevens, Collins, and Goldin, p. 19.

31. Sleeman, pp. 196-197.

32. J.A. Kulik, C.C. Kulik, and P.A. Cohen. Effectiveness of Computer-based College Teaching: A Meta-analysis of Findings. *Review of Educational Research*, Winter 1980, *50*(4), 525-544. J.A. Kulik, R.L. Bangert, and G.W. Williams. Effects of Computer-Based Teaching on Secondary School Students. *Journal of Educational Psychology*, 1983, *75*(1), 19-26.

33. R. Niemiec and H. J. Walberg. Comparative Effects of Computer-Assisted Instruction: A Synthesis of Reviews. *Journal of Educational Computing Research*, 1987, *3*(1), p. 34.

34. W. Feurzeig *et al.*, Microcomputers in Education, Bolt, Beranek and Newman, Inc., October 1981, p. 73.

35. Kulik, Bangert, and Williams, p. 20. Kulik, Kulik, and Cohen, p. 538.

36. M.L. Atkinson. Computer-Assisted Instruction: Current State of the Art. *Computers in the Schools*, Spring, 1984, *1*(1), 91-99.

37. Chambers and Sprecher, p. 339.

38. G. Keasley, B. Hunter, and R.J. Seidel. Two Decades of Computer Based Instruction Projects: What Have We Learned? *T.H.E. Journal*, Part One, January 1983, p. 91 and Part Two, February 1983, p. 96.

39. Miller, 133. I am not aware of any ITS for English composition, which is a much more complicated domain than those used thus far by ITS researchers.

40. Chambers and Sprecher, p. 338; referencing *The ABC's of CAI, Fourth Edition*. Fresno: California State University, 1979.

41. Keasley, Hunter, and Seidel, Part Two, p. 96.

42. Keasley, Hunter, and Seidel, Part One, p. 94.

Intelligent Computer-Assisted Instruction: The Next Generation

Halyna Hajovy and Dean L. Christensen

Conventional intelligent computer-assisted instructional systems (ICAI) have a theoretical foundation which is based in computer science (Dreyfus and Dreyfus, 1986). Current ICAI programs are basically prototype systems whose aim is to enhance instruction through the employment of computer-based software tools. Most of these tools are directly associated with the expert systems methods of the artificial intelligence (AI) field. Given the computer science focus of these conventional ICAI programs, the attention given to learning and instructional theories has been minimal. As such, there is no direct empirical verification to show how the specific software tools may result in improved learning. The assumption of the conventional ICAI proponents is that the tools themselves will improve learning. However, learning and instruction are much more complex processes than are exhibited in the prototype ICAI systems and, when viewed from an educational perspective, these systems have a rather novice approach to both learning and instruction.

The Next Generation

With this perspective in mind, we would like to suggest that the next generation of ICAI will differ from the current software tool-based models, to become instructional systems that have their theoretical foundations in educational and psychological theories of learning and instruction. The aim of the educationally-based ICAI systems will be to improve the acquisition, storage, and retrieval of information by making direct and predictable connections between instructional variables and learning. The next generation ICAI systems will employ the AI/expert systems tools but with variables and conditions directly related to the fields of psychology and education. This article will define the next generation of ICAI

Halyna Hajovy is with Tennyson and Associates, Inc., St. Paul-Minneapolis, Minnesota. Dean L. Christensen is with Control Data Corporation, Minneapolis.

by showing the elaborations and extensions offered by the educational perspective to enhance the ICAI environment.

Conventional ICAI

Conventional ICAI systems, using expert systems methods, have three major modules (or models) (Fletcher, 1984); a knowledge base, a student model, and a tutor model. Each of these modules can be summarized as follows (see Figure 1):

- **Knowledge Base.** This is a data base which represents knowledge of a specific topic that an expert may have in memory. The information in a knowledge base is usually obtained by an interview conducted between an individual labelled as a knowledge engineer and a subject matter expert. The goal of this process is to query the expert so as to obtain both declarative knowledge and procedural knowledge. The idea is to have a knowledge base module that can both generate solutions to previously encountered situations and make inferences from incomplete measures or data.
- **Student Model.** This is a mechanism for assessing the student's current knowledge state of the information in the knowledge base. The student's prior knowledge state is generally represented as either a subset of an expert's knowledge (e.g., overlay model; Goldstein, 1982) or the student's misconceptions of the expert's knowledge base (e.g., buggy model; Brown and Burton, 1978).
- **Tutor Model.** The purpose of this model is to manage the instruction. This is done by a management system (termed an inference engine) that makes decisions such as selecting problems to be solved, critiquing performances, providing assistance upon request, and selecting remedial materials. In conventional form, the tutor model employs basically a single instructional strategy embedded in the system for all students and situations. For example, the most commonly used strategy is a Socratic method of teaching which requires the student to respond to a given stimulus. As such, the strategy borrows heavily from the early programmed instruction (PI) format of intrinsic programming developed by Crowder in the late 1950s.

Educational Perspective

Because of the powerful programming tools offered by the developments in AI software in-

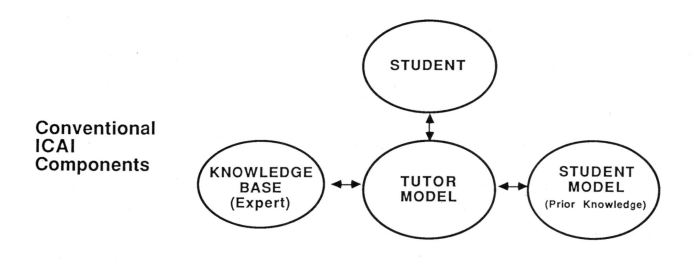

Figure 1

*Elaborations to ICAI from
an Educational Perspective*

**Conventional
ICAI
Components**

STUDENT

**KNOWLEDGE
BASE
(Expert)**

**TUTOR
MODEL**

**STUDENT
MODEL
(Prior Knowledge)**

**Educational
Elaborations**

- Developmental Knowledge
- Different Perspectives
- Creative Search Strategies

- Informal Heuristics
- Meta-Learning Theory
- Meta-Instructional Strategies

- Individual Differences
- Necessary Knowledge
  - Prerequisite
  - Associative
  - Background

telligence methods, we feel that computers can now offer educators a means to more fully utilize the capabilities of the computer to enhance instruction and, thus, improve learning. To fully accomplish this goal, the AI tools need to be employed within the conditions of the educational environment. Proposed for the next generation of ICAI is a system that elaborates and extends the three basic modules of the conventional ICAI systems (see Figure 1). The proposed additions are taken directly from a rich base of cognitive psychological and educational theory and research on learning and instruction.

The educational perspective offers ICAI—in contrast to the contemporary computer science perspective with its limited and narrow understanding of learning and instruction—an integration of AI tools and methods with instructional variables

and conditions empirically tested and shown to improve learning. The basic educational elaborations and extensions can be summarized as follows (see Figure 1):

- Extend the knowledge base to include, in addition to the expert's knowledge, developmental knowledge used by the learner to acquire expert knowledge (i.e., Dreyfus and Dreyfus, 1986).
- Develop knowledge bases in ways that represent different perspectives on problem solving and problem formation.
- Employ inference engines within tutorial models that use informal and fuzzy logic methods in addition to the structured formality offered by the current methods of IF-THEN rule statements. This would allow for much broader applications of

ICAI in less structured domains of information (e.g., the humanities).

- Extend the forms of knowledge representation to include, in addition to the usual tree structures, heuristic systems that create search strategies.
- Design tutor models that more fully exhibit the characteristics of an expert teacher by increasing the potential of the instructional strategy. That is, a tutor model that prescribes, instead of a given single strategy, a meta-instructional strategy formed from a rich pool of instructional variables.
- Expand the student diagnosis to include individual differences. Rather than the simple assessment of prior knowledge to prescribe instruction, additionally evaluate students in reference to cognitive and affective variables.
- Elaborate the student model by assessing in addition to prior knowledge other forms of necessary knowledge. These other forms include: (a) prerequisite knowledge, information directly needed to understand the information to be learned; (b) associative knowledge, information within the domain being learned but not directly connected or linked to the information being learned; and (c) background knowledge, information that provides a context to fully understanding the information to be learned.

In planning a learning environment, it is convenient to consider the division of the educational variables and conditions into curricular and instructional components. The curricular component includes those elements of education not directly linked to student interaction. The instructional component, on the other hand, deals with those elements directly involved with student interaction in learning. Using this paradigm, we will discuss the above defined educational elaborations for ICAI within these two components. Our assumption is that in an ICAI environment, these two components would operate in an iterative fashion such that the conditions of instruction established in the curricular component would adjust according to learner progress and needs while in the instructional component and that learner outcomes from the instructional component would feed back to the curricular component to update the decision making mechanism at that macro level (Seidel and Stolurow, 1980).

Thus, in addition to the above defined elaborations, we propose that ICAI be extended into an educationally-based learning environment that includes both curricular and instructional variables and conditions. Also, that the ICAI system provide for adaptive instruction based on cumulative knowledge and moment-to-moment learning need. Within a curricular component, the system would diagnose the student from initial assessment information and then from continuous information coming back from the instructional component. The curricular component would prescribe the necessary instruction from normative parameters; while, with the instructional component, the system would adapt the prescription according to individual student needs during actual learning. In this sense, assessment and learning would be occurring simultaneously. The next two sections will describe our proposed extension of the current ICAI model to more fully meet the educational situation as contrasted to the tool design paradigm offered by conventional ICAI.

Curricular Component

The primary purpose of the curricular component would be to establish the initial conditions of instruction by considering the interaction of individual difference variables with the specifications of the content domain of a given curriculum. Conventional ICAI has no methodology which can deal with the considerable effect which individual differences have on learning achievement. The curricular component would encompass both the cognitive and affective measures of individual differences.

Cognitive measures would include such constructs as intelligence, aptitude, ability, and cognitive style. For example, a learner may have a high intelligence level but little aptitude or ability for a given curriculum. Thus, to maximize learning, instruction should be adjusted to take the learner's strengths and weaknesses in these areas into account.

Affective measures would deal with constructs such as (a) personality (e.g., introverted and extroverted learners need different optimal learning environments [Eysenck and Eysenck, 1975]; learners with a Type A personality tend to differ in drive from Type B [Friedman and Rosenman, 1974]; (b) motivation (a profile of the learner's initial motivation can be adjusted and have influence as the learner moves through the curriculum [Tennyson and Breuer, 1984]); and (c) anxiety (instructional strategies can be employed to lessen anxiety where it interferes with learning [Tennyson and Boutwell, 1973]).

In conventional ICAI programs the student model is basically represented as a subset of an expert's knowledge base. This error model focuses on the student's prior knowledge and the ability for information recall, while ignoring the acquisition of the information. In this conventional

ICAI model, learners can easily form misconceptions (even though such programs are actually trying to correct misconceptions), particularly in higher order and more complex information structures (Scandura, 1984).

The educational perspective offers to improve on this conventional student model by expanding it to include, in addition to prior knowledge assessment, achievement measures on three other types of necessary knowledge: prerequisite, associative, and background knowledge (Tennyson and Cocchiarella, 1986). Prerequisite knowledge refers to supportive knowledge that is (a) directly related to the information to be learned and (b) the student already has in memory. Associative knowledge refers to information that is in the same domain but is only indirectly connected with the to-be-learned information. Background knowledge refers to information that is generally outside the domain but provides necessary context for fully understanding the information to be learned. Prior knowledge, in contrast, refers to that specific information to be learned that the student already has in memory.

The addition of these other three knowledge achievement measures would influence the conditions of instruction in terms of remediation and the amount of instruction for the to-be-learned information. They would also establish a richer learner diagnostic profile for instructional prescriptions than one based solely on a single variable of prior knowledge as in the case of conventional ICAI.

Each of the above mentioned individual difference variables has differing effects on learning and needs constant adjustment based on the structure of the to-be-learned information. While each of these constructs has implications at the instructional level, because of their trait nature, putting them at the curricular level can definitely expand the capabilities of the conventional knowledge base (expert module) to better deal with the structural conditions of the information to be learned. In other words, curriculum issues can be dealt with in such a way that if learners found that they are either lacking or unsure of specific knowledge, then the system would be able to diagnose the specific knowledge lack and to appropriately adjust the curriculum.

Instructional Component

The tutor module in conventional ICAI is basically limited to one instructional strategy; for example, the Socratic and coaching methods. With only one instructional strategy, the system can run into a number of limitations such as: assuming too much or too little student knowledge, producing instructional material at the wrong level of detail, and not being able to work with the student's own conceptualizations of the information which they are learning.

An educationally-based ICAI system would expand the tutor module by not limiting itself to only one instructional strategy. By assessing individual difference variables and curricular issues during instruction, the system can have the flexibility to prescribe appropriate meta-instructional strategies.

This flexibility would be allowed by the use of informal heuristic methods in the inference engine of the tutor model. The use of these heuristic methods is built around a direct connection to cognitive science theories of learning (Polya, 1945). A heuristic can be defined as a "rule of thumb" search strategy that is composed of variables that can be manipulated to provide increasingly better decisions as more knowledge is acquired. This ability allows the heuristics to adjust to new data and experiences and to add new variables and even heuristics without necessarily influencing the operations of the system.

Frequently, program designers refer to informal heuristics as "fuzzy" logic statements because, unlike the production rule statements needed in conventional ICAI programs (i.e., IF-THEN statements), informal heuristics can be written as abstract flexible statements which acquire assumptions with experience. Therefore, an informal heuristic can start to understand a situation and "think" about possible outcomes that do not exhibit correct or incorrect solutions. Also, informal heuristic methods differ dramatically from the algorithm or tree-structure methodology of AI programming in that they are usually written as conditional probability statement codes. In educational terms, an informal heuristic may be thought of as a higher order rule statement rather than a depository of domain-specific information (Dorner, 1983).

We propose the employment of the informal heuristic approach because the flexibility offered by such programming techniques allows the integration of various theory-based learning variables to a given programmatic method (e.g., few learning variables fit a tree-structure format). These heuristics would be used in the sense of leading to discovery by considering many different learning variables, abstraction levels (shifts from one level to another), and unique combinations which establish the conditions for learning and the conditions of instruction.

Selection of the meta-instructional strategies would be based upon four different sources of information. First, the direct connection to a learning theory which explains learning, memory, and cognition. Typically, from an educational perspective, this would be in the form a meta-learning theory developed because of the educational need to explain both learning and cognition. Second, an understanding of the learning outcomes related to the objectives of the curriculum and instruction. Although, there are many taxonomies by which to specify learning objectives, we favor the well-developed approach offered by Gagne's (1985) conditions of learning (verbal information, intellectual skills, and cognitive strategies). Third, the structure of the information to be learned needs to be analyzed for both learning effectiveness and storage in the data base. Conventional expert system tools and shells provide assistance in the latter development of the knowledge base. However, the presentation structure needs additional manipulation to improve learning.

Much of the recent research findings in human knowledge representation (as contrasted to machine representation as in AI/expert systems programs) clearly indicates that the overt structure of the information directly affects learner acquisition. That is, presenting the information in reference to its schematic structure significantly improves acquisition because the learner is storing both semantic knowledge and schematic knowledge simultaneously. Conventional ICAI knowledge base structures are only focusing on semantic understanding. And, fourth, the instructional variables which can be prescribed into specific and adaptable meta-instructional strategies. Most of these instructional variables are derived directly from educational research findings. For example, some of these variables that can be prescribed based on individual student need and progress are sequence, amount of information, instructional control, time on task, use of text and visuals, cooperative learning, simulations, and others that an expert teacher may employ to facilitate learning.

Summary

In summary, the next generation of ICAI will differ from conventional ICAI on several important variables. First, with foundations in learning and instructional theory, ICAI will use a comprehensive meta-learning model which would take individual differences into account in the assessment and diagnosis processes, and make reference to both the learner's acquisition (i.e., storage) and the retrieval of knowledge. Conventional ICAI programs follow, for the most part (if any), learning models based on the assumptions of a discovery form of learning. Second, ICAI will make no assumption for a given strategy of instruction; rather, the strategies of instruction will be selected from a rich base of instructional variables according to learning objectives and the structure of information to be learned. Third, ICAI will employ the concepts of artificial intelligence in the form of informal heuristics (as well as formal heuristics) that have the capacity to learn and, therefore, to adjust according to given situations.

The proposed educationally-based ICAI systems can be characterized as decision-making systems that are iterative in nature such that with experience, they can continuously improve the learning of each learner. This would be done by an adaptive management system which concurrently diagnoses learning while prescribing instruction. By monitoring learner progress during the actual acquisition of information, the educationally-based system will improve learning in terms of both the effectiveness of amount and quality of knowledge acquired and the efficiency in time required to learn.

At both the curricular and the instructional levels, the variables defined in our article would interact in an almost infinite number of instructional conditions and events. Of special note will be the ability of the entire system to adjust decision-making parameters both with group experience and by individual learner experiences. That is, as experience is gained from both sources, the heuristics which are formed with currently available information and data would adjust accordingly. Because the heuristics would be independent of both hardware and software conditions, they would be easily transferred and generalized to other systems as well as accommodating new development in both hardware and software.

A number of major advantages can be implied by the use of the proposed educational elaborations and extensions of the current generation ICAI systems. For example, the next generation ICAI systems would be designed to improve learning by integrating learning theory with instructional design. Also, the systems would employ a holistic approach of pre-information and continuing information processing about the learner, rather than diagnosing and remediating specific problems as seen in conventional AI programs. Furthermore, the systems would be active rather than passive in nature, and would be able to recognize the totality of the individual and the complexities involved in creating favorable learning environments to improve learning.

In conclusion, we are proposing that the next generation of ICAI be based on educational and psychological theory and research findings. That it employ where appropriate the tools and shells of AI and expert systems methods, but that such tools do not dictate or control the design and implementation of the learning environment. Much like educators have for decades used the research tools from the field of statistics for help in experimentation, we can use the tools offered by computer science in the design of learning environments. In both situations, however, the educator must control the tools as a means to the end, not as the end in themselves, as in the current prototype applications of ICAI. □

References

Brown, J.S., and Burton, R.R. A Paradiagrammatic Example of an Artificially Intelligent Instructional System. *International Journal of Man-Machine Studies*, 1978, *10*, 323.

Dorner, D. Heuristics and Cognition in Complex Systems. In R. Groner, M. Groner, and W.F. Bishof (Eds.), *Methods of Heuristics*. Hillsdale, NJ: Erlbaum, 1983.

Dreyfus, H.L., and Dreyfus, S.E. *Mind Over Machine.* New York: Free Press, 1986.

Eysenck, H.J., and Eysenck, B.G. *Eysenck Personality Questionnaire.* San Diego, CA: Educational and Industrial Testing Service, 1975.

Fletcher, J.D. Intelligent Instructional Systems in Training. In S.A. Andriole (Ed.), *Applications in Artificial Intelligence.* Princeton, NJ: Petrocelli, 1984.

Friedman, M., and Rosenman, R.H. *Type A Behavior and Your Heart.* New York: Knopf, 1974.

Gagne, R.M. *Conditions of Learning* (4th Ed.). New York: Holt, Rinehart, and Winston, 1985.

Goldstein, I.P. The Genetic Graph: A Representation for the Evolution of Procedural Knowledge. In D. Sleeman and J.S. Brown (Eds.), *Intelligent Tutoring Systems.* New York: Academic Press, 1982.

Polya, G. *How to Solve It.* Princeton, NJ: Princeton University Press, 1945.

Scandura, J.M. Cognitive Instructional Psychology: System Requirements and Research Methodology. *Journal of Computer-based Instruction*, 1984, *11*, 14-21.

Seidel, R.J., and Stolurow, L. An Heuristic Meta-Model for Computer-Managed Instruction. *Journal of Research and Development in Education*, 1980, *14*(1), 16-32.

Tennyson, R.D., and Boutwell, R.C. Pretask Versus Within-Task Anxiety Measures in Predicting Performance on a Concept Acquisition Task. *Journal of Educational Psychology*, 1973, *65*, 88-92.

Tennyson, R.D., and Breuer, K. Cognitive-Based Design Guidelines for Using Video and Computer Technology in Higher Education. In O. Zuber-Skeritt (Ed.), *Video in Higher Education.* London, England: Kogan Page, 1984.

Tennyson, R.D., and Cocchiarella, M.J. An Empirically Based Instructional Design Theory for Teaching Concepts. *Review of Educational Research*, 1986, *56*, 40-71.

Article Citations

1. Small Knowledge-Based Systems in Education and Training: Something New Under the Sun. By Brent G. Wilson and Jack R. Welsh. *Educational Technology*, November 1986, pages 7-13.

2. Expert Systems Authoring Tools for the Microcomputer: Two Examples. By Joseph M. Ferrara, James D. Parry, and Margaret M. Lubke. *Educational Technology*, April 1985, pages 39-41.

3. Expert Systems in Education and Training: Automated Job Aids or Sophisticated Instructional Media? By Alexander J. Romiszowski. *Educational Technology*, October 1987, pages 30-38.

4. Applications of Expert Systems in Education: A Technology for Decision-Makers. By Stephen W. Ragan and Thomas D. McFarland. *Educational Technology*, May 1987, pages 33-36.

5. Expert Systems for Educational Decision-Making. By Jacqueline A. Haynes, Virginia H. Pilato, and David B. Malouf. *Educational Technology*, May 1987, pages 37-42.

6. Using an Expert System for Complex Conceptual Training. By Joseph M. Ferrara, Mary Ann Prater, and Richard Baer. *Educational Technology*, May 1987, pages 43-46.

7. A Comparison of Input and Output for a Knowledge-Based System for Educational Diagnosis. By Paul Juell and John Wasson. *Educational Technology*, March 1988, pages 19-23.

8. Expert Systems in the Classroom. By Ronald D. Owston and Herbert Wideman. *Educational Technology*, November 1989, pages 28-31.

9. Developing a Low-Cost Expert System in a Liberal Arts Environment. By Antonio M. Lopez, Jr. *Educational Technology*, July 1988, pages 33-36.

10. An Expert System for On-Site Instructional Advice. By Elizabeth S. Martindale and Alan M. Hofmeister. *Educational Technology*, July 1988, pages 18-20.

11. Training NASA Satellite Operators: An Expert System Consultant Approach. By Jay Liebowitz and Patricia Lightfoot. *Educational Technology*, November 1987, pages 41-47.

12. The Four Generations of Computerized Testing: Toward Increased Use of AI and Expert Systems. By James Olsen. *Educational Technology*, March 1990, paged 36-41.

13. A Knowledge-Based System Allowing Formative Evaluation. By Marie-Michele Boulet, L. Lavoie, P. Labbe, and D. DeMelo. *Educational Technology*, January 1990, pages 19-23.

14. Expert Systems Technology for Training Applications: By Jay Liebowitz. *Educational Technology*, November 1987, pages 43-45.

15. Skilling America: The Potential of Intelligent Job Aids. By Clay Carr. *Educational Technology*, April 1988, pages 22-25.

16. Using Expert System Job Aids: A Primer. By Clay Carr. *Educational Technology*, June 1989, pages 18-22.

17. Artificial Intelligence Techniques: Applications for Courseware Development. By Brian L. Dear. *Educational Technology*, July 1986, pages 7-15.

18. Expert Systems: Instructional Design Potential. By Joellyn Pollock and R. Scott Grabinger. *Educational Technology*, March 1987, pages 35-39.

19. Computer Courseware: Frame-Based or Intelligent? By Jodi Bonner. *Educational Technology*, March 1987, pages 30-32.

20. Using Artificial Intelligence in Education: Computer-Based Tools for Instructional Development. By Ray S. Perez and Robert J. Seidel. *Educational Technology*, March 1990, pages 51-58.

21. The Second Generation Instructional Design Research Program. By M. David Merrill, Zhong-min Li, and Mark K. Jones. *Educational Technology*, March 1990, pages 26-31.
22. Computer-Aided Instruction: Toward a New Direction. By John M. Morris. *Educational Technology*, May 1983, pages 12-15.
23. Intelligent Computer-Assisted Instruction: An Explanation and Overview. By Franklin C. Roberts and Ok-choon Park. *Educational Technology*, December 1983, pages 7-12.
24. Conventional CBI Versus Intelligent CAI: Suggestions for the Development of Future Systems. By Ok-choon Park and Robert J. Seidel. *Educational Technology*, May 1987, pages 15-21.
25. Functional Characteristics of Intelligent Computer-Assisted Instruction: Intelligent Features. By Ok-choon Park. *Educational Technology*, June 1988, pages 7-14.
26. Adaptive Instructional Simulations to Improve Learning of Cognitive Strategies. By Klaus Breuer and Halyna Hajovy. *Educational Technology*, May 1987, pages 29-32.
27. MAIS: An Educational Alternative to ICAI. By Robert D. Tennyson. *Educational Technology*, May 1987, pages 22-28.
28. The Role of Tutorial and Experiential Models in Intelligent Tutoring Systems. By M. David Merrill. *Educational Technology*, July 1988, pages 7-13.
29. Individualizing Instruction Through Intelligent Computer-Assisted Instruction: A Perspective. By Jung-Shing Yang. *Educational Technology*, March 1987, pages 7-15.
30. A Critical Analysis of Research on Intelligent Tutoring Systems. By Ronni Rosenberg. *Educational Technology*, November 1987, pages 7-13.
31. Intelligent Computer-Assisted Instruction: The Next Generation. By Halyna Hajovy and Dean L. Christensen. *Educational Technology*, May 1987, pages 9-14.

Index